"Companies all over the world are recognizing that virtual work is not a fad that will pass with time. People want the freedom to choose where to work depending on context and task. And with the right systems and work practices, companies can reap the benefits too. That's where *The Power of Remote* comes in. Cynthia Watson and Shane Spraggs provide a detailed road map for evolving into a high-performing virtual team so that, as a leader, you can take advantage of this new way of working."

—Lisette Sutherland, director of Collaboration Superpowers
and author of the award-winning Work Together Anywhere

"*The Power of Remote* provides valuable advice and insight on working and succeeding remotely. Maybe more important, it contains context for the changes we're going through, from people who've been there and done that."

—Wayne Turmel, cofounder of the Remote Leadership Institute
and coauthor of the bestseller The Long-Distance Leader

"*The Power of Remote* provides leaders with a much-needed road map to create remote workplaces where organizational objectives are met and employees feel a greater sense of connection to what they do and who they work with. From how to build a healthy organizational culture in remote work environments to changing how and what we communicate to foster greater employee ownership and collaboration, Watson and Spraggs offer tools and insights that will help expand your leadership toolkit to meet the changing needs and demands arising from this new world of work."

—Tanveer Naseer, Inc. 100 leadership speaker,
award-winning author, and coauthor of Leadership Vertigo

"*The Power of Remote* outlines all the problems employers are likely to face with hybrid and remote work and how to address them. The best guide yet for those moving to a more remote operating model."

—Peter Cappelli, George W. Taylor Professor of Management at the Wharton School and best-selling author of The Future of the Office

"*The Power of Remote* is a valuable nuts and bolts review of the remote work revolution that could become essential reading as the remote work trend dominates the future of work."

—Derek Gallimore, best-selling author of Inside Outsourcing

THE POWER OF REMOTE

CYNTHIA WATSON &
SHANE SPRAGGS

THE
POWER
OF
REMOTE

Building High-Performing
ORGANIZATIONS THAT THRIVE
in the Virtual Workplace

Forbes | Books

Published by ForbesBooks, Charleston, South Carolina.
Member of Advantage Media Group.

ForbesBooks is a registered trademark, and the ForbesBooks colophon is a trademark of Forbes Media, LLC.

Printed in the United States of America.

10 9 8 7 6 5 4 3 2 1

ISBN: 978-1-95588-444-0 (Hardcover)
ISBN: 978-1-95588-469-3 (eBook)
LCCN: 2022914071

Cover design by Megan Elger.
Layout design by Matthew Morse.

This custom publication is intended to provide accurate information and the opinions of the author in regard to the subject matter covered. It is sold with the understanding that the publisher, Advantage|ForbesBooks, is not engaged in rendering legal, financial, or professional services of any kind. If legal advice or other expert assistance is required, the reader is advised to seek the services of a competent professional.

Since 1917, Forbes has remained steadfast in its mission to serve as the defining voice of entrepreneurial capitalism. ForbesBooks, launched in 2016 through a partnership with Advantage Media Group, furthers that aim by helping business and thought leaders bring their stories, passion, and knowledge to the forefront in custom books. Opinions expressed by ForbesBooks authors are their own. To be considered for publication, please visit **www.forbesbooks.com**.

Nobody on their deathbed has ever said, "I wish I had spent more time at the office."

—US SENATOR PAUL TSONGAS

To those managers and staffers postpandemic keen to embrace remote work via hybrid or completely offsite, this book was written to help you realize the unprecedented efficiencies that this work style affords.

CONTENTS

PART V: TACKLING REMOTE BUSINESS PROJECTS

Acknowledgments

It just isn't possible in this small space to thank everyone whose influence, innovation, and outlier thinking led to the creation of this book. However, we'll do our best.

To the hundreds of people who have graced our company with their ideas and insight on how to achieve the most time efficient and flexible workstyles on the planet. Whether they've been chasing surf, extreme sports, or an extreme family barbeque, everyone on our team lives their life to the fullest while producing extraordinary results for our clients.

To our clients who have been open minded enough to try our methods and who have provided critical feedback to help us continuously improve our remote framework. Like us, they know that staff don't need to be on site or under constant scrutiny to fast-track revenue or productivity improvements.

To our families who have embraced and support our sometimes-hectic work-life integration, knowing that those times that we catch up on work in a quiet spot is a small price for that extra month staying in a great overseas location.

Finally, thanks to the ForbesBooks team, our amazing editor David Lepeska, and the Virtira team who contributed to the research and production of additional linked materials and kept the project on time and on track.

The New Remote Reality

Work is what we do, not where we are.

— US GENERAL SERVICES ADMINISTRATION, 2012

I n the opening moments of the fifth season of the CBS series *The Good Fight*, which depicts the inner workings of a Chicago law firm, the pandemic has just begun to wash over the Second City, and the world is slowly turning upside down. At one point, two of the firm's top partners explain to a room full of anxious associates how the office will cope with the new stay-at-home order. "We're setting up a teleconferencing infrastructure," says one. "So download a program called Zoom.com. Z-O-O-M."

"Get on your computers," the other chimes in. "Zoom.com."

It sounds ridiculous today, when so many are saddled with "Zoom fatigue," but in early 2020, that was our reality. While some of us had heard of or maybe even used Zoom, only a few could have imagined that within a matter of months, nearly the entire working world would have logged some time in a Zoom meeting, with many doing so multiple times a day.

The sea change began, of course, with the arrival of COVID-19. As the case numbers ticked up, businesses scrambled to adapt to lockdowns and office closures. Long seen as a significant risk, the completely distributed workforce suddenly became a necessity. Yet for the vast majority of firms, this was uncharted territory. Would it lead to disaster?

Even in the "before times," most of us who worked in offices spent much of our workday tapping away at our computers in relative solitude. Occasionally, we'd log in from home to answer a few emails. But very few worked remotely full time or even dared consider such a possibility. Then, in a flash, companies shut their doors and told workers to stay home. Suddenly, poof! The impossible dream fell into our laps: working full time in the comfort of our softest pajamas.

The result has been a seismic shift in the way we view work. In the not-so-distant future, we might have only hazy memories of office life. COVID-19 proved, once and for all, the undeniable value of remote work. With a newly realized opportunity to work from home, as many as twenty-three million Americans planned to move in 2021, according to a survey of twenty thousand workers by the online freelancing platform Upwork.[1] That's more than three times the number of Americans who move in a normal year, and this was just in the first year after the pandemic's arrival. As of the writing of this book in mid-2022, millions more have likely realized that remote work enables them to live in places with a lower cost of living and a higher quality of life, while countless others are enjoying less time in the office thanks to hybrid work arrangements.

---

1   "Economist Report: Remote Workers on the Move," Upwork, accessed June 11, 2022, https://www.upwork.com/press/releases/economist-report-remote-workers-on-the-move.

COVID-19 has remade the workplace, and for the vast majority of firms, some degree of remote work is here to stay. Many companies will likely embrace a hybrid model in which workers spend a few days at home and a few days at the office. In a May 2021 study by Mercer, 70 percent of more than five hundred companies surveyed said that they expected to go hybrid.[2] Two-thirds of the employers polled by Microsoft in March 2021 said that they were redesigning their workplaces to accommodate hybrid work.[3] In *The Nowhere Office*, British analyst Julia Hobsbawm's 2022 book on postpandemic work, she examined a future workplace that's both virtual and physical.[4] For the many workers who feel perfectly comfortable tapping away at their laptop in bed, at their desk, on the beach, or at a local café, a more apt label might be "the everywhere office."

The genie is out of the bottle—expectations about where and how we work have shifted dramatically and irrevocably. A March 2021 survey of three hundred thousand workers in more than thirty countries found that nearly three of four enjoy the flexibility of remote and hybrid work.[5] "The data is clear," the Microsoft study declared. "Extreme flexibility and hybrid work will define the postpandemic workplace."

Meanwhile, companies without flexible work options could face an exodus. A May 2021 survey of one thousand US adults revealed that

2   Ryan Golden, "Most US Employers with Flexible Work Plans Choose Hybrid Work, Mercer Says," HRDive, July 14, 2021, https://www.hrdive.com/news/most-us-employers-with-flexible-work-plans-choose-hybrid-work-mercer-says/603304/.

3   "The Next Great Disruption Is Hybrid Work—Are We Ready?," Microsoft WorkLab, March 22, 2021, https://www.microsoft.com/en-us/worklab/work-trend-index/hybrid-work.

4   Julia Hobsbawm, *The Nowhere Office* (New York: PublicAffairs, 2022), https://www.publicaffairsbooks.com/titles/julia-hobsbawm/the-nowhere-office/9781541701946/.

5   Daniel Howley, "Microsoft Survey: 73% of Workers Want to Be Able to Work from Home after the Pandemic," Yahoo! Finance, March 22, 2021, https://finance.yahoo.com/news/microsoft-survey-73-percent-of-workers-want-to-work-from-home-after-pandemic-130029295.html.

39 percent would consider quitting if their employer offered no remote work options. Nearly half of millennial and Gen Z workers expressed this view, which suggests an even greater shift in the near future.[6] This helps explain why a record 4.3 million workers voluntarily left their jobs in August 2021, according to the US Department of Labor.[7]

We now know that remote work can cut costs and the daily commute while boosting productivity and morale. Still, without strong support from top executives, it has the potential to introduce vast uncertainty and erode the bottom line. Nearly one of five remote workers surveyed by OnePoll and Citrix in April 2020 said that their employers were either not very ready or not ready at all for the shift to remote work.[8]

There's clearly work to be done, and the challenges are already significant. Many companies are just at the starting line when it comes to figuring out how to best incorporate remote workers. They are aware that it will involve establishing new systems, hiring the right people, and keeping communication flowing and goals on track. But few understand the strategies and processes required to accomplish these objectives. In the near future, a wide variety of businesses will need to design and implement the systems, structure, and training that ensure and support results-driven autonomous work.

Crucial questions will include the following:

---

6   Anders Melin and Misyrlena Egkolfopoulou, "Employees Are Quitting Instead of Giving Up Working from Home," Bloomberg, June 1, 2021, https://www.bloomberg.com/news/articles/2021-06-01/ return-to-office-employees-are-quitting-instead-of-giving-up-work-from-home.

7   Ben Casselman, "Workers Quitting Their Jobs Hit a Record in the U.S. in August," New York Times, October 12, 2021, https://www.nytimes.com/2021/10/12/business/economy/workers-quitting-august.html.

8   Katie Clarey, "A Third of Workers Predict Employers Will Allow More Remote Work after Pandemic," HRDive, April 22, 2020, https://www.hrdive.com/news/a-third-of-workers-predict-employers-will-allow-more-remote-work-after-pand/576536/.

How do we hire people well suited to remote work and train them so that they're able to achieve as much outside the office as they did inside?

How can we ensure strong communication and goal-oriented collaboration among remote teams, especially when one team member might be in Alabama and another in Alicante?

How do we ensure that our managers are fully on board and that remote employees engage with their companies and their jobs?

How do we fully execute on projects across a distance?

Imagine an orchestra of musicians who have been rehearsing together in the same space for years. Suddenly, they're practicing separately in different locations, connected only by video link. They may still find a way to make beautiful music—as we learned from the many fine Zoom concerts performed in 2020 by orchestras around the world[9]—but without devising and implementing systems to ensure better long-distance rehearsals, they are unlikely to approach the brilliance of their live concerts.

Businesses today face the same problem. When everyone is working in the office, it's easy to call a quick meeting to keep the team focused. With workers in different locations, however, momentum can easily slow. This is because companies have yet to install the tools and strategies to ensure that remote workers remain as effective as they had been in the office. Despite the impressive productivity we saw from remote workers in the pandemic's early days, a gap remains—one that could threaten productivity as well as employee engagement, well-being, and trust.

---

9   Rotterdam Philharmonic Orchestra, "From Us, for You: Beethoven Symphony no. 9," YouTube, May 20, 2020, https://www.youtube.com/watch?v=3eXT60rbBVk&ab_channel=Rot terdamPhilharmonicOrchestra.

We, the authors of this book, have a profound appreciation for that gap because we've been helping clients achieve better results over distance for decades. Cynthia Watson knew about telecommuting before the term even existed. At ten years old, in the late 1960s, she watched spellbound as her older brother linked his home terminal in Palo Alto via telephone coupler to the legendary CDC 6600 at Stanford, just up the road. In the 1980s, as a systems analyst, she often worked from home by connecting TI's Silent 700 to IBM's 370 mainframe. Cynthia then switched gears to escape the office even more, pursuing a career in enterprise IT sales. In 1993, she wrote her master's thesis on telecommuting and left office work behind for good. Over the past three decades, she's consulted for and led several companies while pursuing a life without boundaries. She's run large global projects and led high-performing teams while on the path to Machu Picchu, at Mount Everest base camp, and in a hut in Patagonia, as well as in countless cafés, conference rooms, and even, on occasion, her home office. Today, as Executive Chair of Virtira, a company dedicated to elevating remote team performance, she oversees the company's training division and contributes to the evolving remote landscape through research and consulting. Long dedicated to never stepping foot in a traditional office, Cynthia endeavors to leverage remote work to expand career opportunities for women in large and small communities and promote sustainable green solutions.

Virtira CEO Shane Spraggs's unparalleled expertise in organizational planning and project management is the perfect complement to Cynthia's experience and vision. For more than a quarter century, Shane has been driving successful projects for some of the world's leading brands, including Disney. An industry leader in shaping innovative project management strategies, he has brought his insights to a variety of top media and software start-ups. Shane's leadership extends beyond the boardroom to postsecondary classrooms, where he continues to teach these methods to aspiring project managers. Often praised by colleagues and clients for his ability to evaluate complex organizational challenges and implement project-based solutions that ensure sustainable success with continuous oversight and improvement, Shane constantly challenges himself and the team to identify remote productivity improvements for Virtira's clients, enlisting the same ambition he uses every morning to hike up Knox Mountain, his favorite trail in his hometown of Kelowna, British Columbia.

Remote work may be new and unfamiliar to countless workers, managers, and executives, but it's our comfort zone, our wheelhouse. For more than a decade, we have been running a completely virtual and highly successful professional services firm. Ensuring the optimal performance of remote workers and teams—which, for many of today's businesses, is suddenly a top priority—is our area of expertise.

The more remote your workforce, the more structure you need to replace office walls with virtual ones.

Our mission is to transform new hires into top-performing members of top-performing remote teams, able to work cross-functionally with other top performers to complete projects, continuing the cycle. Achieving this requires moving away from traditional brick-and-mortar oversight and surveillance and embracing results-driven and flexible work models. Businesses can no longer rely on office-based processes. Managers must implement and support policies, processes, and tools that support flexible, autonomous work while keeping virtual teams aligned and accountable. One refrain you'll find throughout this book is that working on a "remote island" necessitates more attentive management, from ensuring productivity to establishing strong communication and instilling culture and purpose. This is because it bears repeating that the more remote your workforce, the more structure you need to replace office walls with virtual ones.

You'll find that once you install the systems we outline in this book, productivity will be a snap—perhaps even easier than in the office. With our model, workers are no longer forced to guess which task to tackle next. They are instead eminently familiar with their deadlines and their deliverables. This certainty instills a confidence that ensures less stress for all those involved. Eliminating uncertainty makes remote workers and teams more productive and results oriented. And that's just the tip of the iceberg.

If you're part of a company with remote or hybrid staffers or that connects across a number of offices, this book will show you how to optimize remote work to ensure the best results. If you're a newly remote worker looking to up your game, this book will provide a great deal of insight on enhancing your experience and boosting your performance. This book is not about working from home, per se—although it will help you do that better as well. It is, rather, about getting work done—and working better with others—over a distance. Even more, it aims to help business leaders adapt to our new workplace reality and ensure that all employees, whether down the block or Down Under, remain as productive as possible.

How to Get the Most out of This Book

This work has been divided into five parts. Each begins with an overview, followed by chapters on specific aspects of that part's focus that conclude with a "pro tip" of practical advice.

Part I offers a broad overview of the past and present of remote work, with a quick glimpse into the future. The first chapter details the history of telecommuting from its beginnings to its near dominance today, while the second highlights the primary virtues and challenges of working remotely—laying the foundation for what follows.

Part II is your guide to building a team of remote stars, taking you all the way from finding them (chapter 3) and bringing them safely aboard (chapter 4) to ensuring the efficacy of their workplace (chapter 5) and, last but certainly not least, instilling within them a strong sense of company culture (chapter 6).

Part III provides a wealth of insight on achieving optimal remote performance, with chapters 7–10 focused on, respectively, the value of first impressions, strengthening communication and collaboration, making meetings more impactful, and the importance of accountability for your remote staff.

Part IV, the heart of the book, examines the elements of strong virtual leadership. Chapter 11 explains how virtual management diverges from traditional management and provides specific instructions, while chapter 12 examines the crucial nature of purpose and lays out how to align your team with core values. The next three chapters detail how to build ownership to increase engagement and even, in the best of circumstances, instill passion.

Part V lays out the tools we've developed at Virtira to ensure optimal performance and productivity for remote teams tackling remote business projects and to complete that often endless "last mile" in complex sales.

Feel free to read sequentially, from here straight through to the end, or use the book as a reference guide to deliver the insights you need when you need them. Whichever route you choose, we wish you happy reading and virtual success!

Additional Content

 Throughout the book, QR codes and links provide access to additional Virtira content, training manuals, and guidelines that have proved extremely helpful in our work.

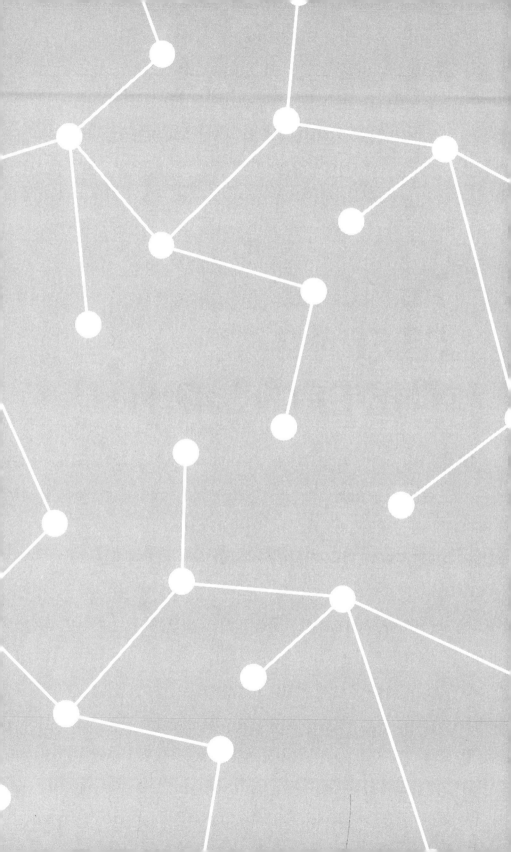

PART I:

REMOTE STEPS INTO THE SPOTLIGHT

Commuting to office work is obsolete.

—PETER DRUCKER, 1993

This is far from the first book promising to boost the productivity of remote and hybrid workers. But it is likely the first one written by two top executives with decades of experience combining remote productivity, project management, and corporate efficiency to solve the problems of virtual work. Unlike many so-called experts, we know how to do it right, and we have the track record to back it up.

Perhaps more importantly, this book arrives amid a seismic shift—perhaps the greatest since the Industrial Revolution drove us indoors—in how and where we work. It's true that remote work had been steadily increasing in the years before the onset of the pandemic: telecommuting increased fourfold in the 2010s. Still, just over a third (36 percent) of more than nine hundred US workers polled in January 2020 said that they did some remote work every week.[10] Today, the script has flipped, as just 40 percent of employees are expected to be on site full time as the pandemic recedes, and a full 90 percent of employers expect employees to work from home.[11]

The megapopular TV series *The Office* has been rendered obsolete because so few workers regularly toil in the same space at the same

10   Macy Bayern, "How Remote Work Rose by 400% in the Past Decade," TechRepublic, January 22, 2020, https://www.techrepublic.com/article/how-remote-work-rose-by-400-in-the-past-decade/.

11   Golden, "Most US Employers"; RealWire, "90% Senior Executives Now Expect to Work from Home, according to Recruitment Research," RealWire, April 6, 2021, https://www.realwire.com/releases/90-senior-executives-now-expect-to-work-from-home-according-to-research.

time. In today's hybrid world, Jim and Pam might be forced to flirt via emoji. Nearly all of the five hundred employers (97 percent) surveyed by Mercer in May 2021 planned to implement increased work flexibility after the pandemic.[12] And in early 2021, JPMorgan chief operating officer Daniel Pinto said that he saw zero chance that all workers would return to the office full time after COVID-19.

The pandemic forced businesses everywhere to hurriedly implement remote protocols. But were they the right ones? Worker morale and even productivity may have ticked up initially, but getting it right in the long term is a much more difficult needle to thread. Employers had no time to prepare for the great remote shift of 2020; thus, it's unlikely that their new protocols incorporated best practices for remote hiring and onboarding, optimal remote project management, or an ability to balance hybrid schedules within teams while ensuring strong bonds between remote members. What's more, this is semi-intentional, as many firms view a full embrace of remote work as a threat to their culture and established management style. Yet our decades of experience have convinced us that, with the right approach, remote work represents an unprecedented opportunity to boost productivity while building a more sustainable culture better suited to today's dynamic working landscape.

---

12   Golden, "Most US Employers."

CHAPTER 1

From Inception to after the Pandemic

We are now at a decision point as a society; we must decide whether the way of life made possible by the automobile since the turn of the century will (or can) continue, or if we should consider alternate or modified modes of working, communicating, and living.

—JACK NILLES, 1973

When the history of office life is written, 2020 is sure to be a swing year after which everything changed. But few know that the seeds of our pandemic-driven shift were planted half a century ago, thanks in part to Los Angeles's legendary traffic.

Physicist Jack Nilles was designing satellites and communications systems for NASA and the US Air Force in the early 1970s when a planning official half-jokingly asked him to find a way to get more people to work at home and stop clogging freeways with their commuting.[13] The question gnawed at Nilles, and when the 1973 oil embargo against the United States led to a surge in gas prices and prompted the University of Southern California to launch a study of the American commute, he signed on. "Given the capability of modern telecommunications and computer technologies to efficiently produce, transmit, and store information, it appears probable that many information industry workers could 'telecommute,'" Nilles wrote in the resulting book. "That is, they could perform their work, using communications and computer technologies, much closer to home."[14]

With this modest assertion, Nilles coined the term "telecommute," conjuring the outlines of our remote future.[15] The concept is elementary today, but nearly fifty years ago, it was revolutionary. In fact, the insurance company that agreed to participate in Nilles's nine-month telecommuting study—which showed higher productivity and potentially millions in annual savings—decided against implementation. "The company said no, we're not going to do that," eighty-seven-year-old Nilles recalled in a 2020 interview. "From every direction, we got resistance. That was my early lesson that this was going to be hard to sell. They're used to business as usual. I've been fighting that ever since."[16]

---

13   Ed Berthiaume, "Jack Nilles Tried to Ignite a Work-from-Home Trend 48 Years Ago. It's Finally Here," Lawrence University, August 17, 2020, https://blogs.lawrence.edu/news/2020/08/jack-nilles-tried-to-ignite-a-work-from-home-trend-48-years-ago-its-finally-here.html.

14   Jack M. Nilles, *The Telecommunications-Transportation Tradeoff: Options for Tomorrow* (New York: Wiley, 1976).

15   Allan Kiron, a scientist in the US Patent Office, beat him to the punch, arguing in the *Washington Post*, in 1969, that new communications tools would soon enable many to work from home. The term he coined, "dominetics," was rather a mouthful and failed to catch on. Still, we tip our cap to Mr. Kiron.

16   Berthiaume, "Jack Nilles Tried to Ignite."

Long before the pandemic forced an attitude adjustment, geopolitics gave the concept an early boost. The oil embargo imposed by the Organization of the Petroleum Exporting Countries (OPEC) not only boosted Nilles's research but also prompted two of the country's most forward-thinking companies, AT&T and IBM, to later install remote terminals in many of their workers' homes in an effort to curb commuting costs. Their programs were so successful that they remained in place decades after OPEC lifted the embargo.

As of 2009, 40 percent of IBM's three hundred eighty-six thousand global employees were working remotely, and the company was saving about $100 million each year. In 2013, nearly all of AT&T's employees (95 percent) and managers (98 percent) said that telecommuting had increased their productivity.

By that time, the idea had understandably begun to catch on. Personal computers had become tiny and cheap, the internet was ubiquitous, and the transition to virtual work seemed a no-brainer. At home we could suddenly do everything we could do at the office except share a coffee with a coworker. In 2000, the Department of Transportation passed a law requiring its agencies to establish telecommuting policies that would allow eligible employees to work remotely as much as possible.[17] In 2005, Best Buy implemented a program that offered flexibility when it came to working location—and soon had four thousand employees working from home.[18] In 2010, then-president Barack Obama signed into law the Telework Enhancement Act, which required every government agency to develop a plan to approve employees for remote work.[19] Several agencies soon proved

---

17 "Telework Legislation," Telework, accessed June 11, 2022, https://www.telework.gov/guidance-legislation/telework-legislation/legislation/.

18 "Smashing the Clock," Bloomberg, December 11, 2006, https://www.bloomberg.com/news/articles/2006-12-10/smashing-the-clock.

19 "Telework Legislation."

that they could manage just fine with more than 75 percent of staff working outside the office.[20] Over the next decade, remote work grew fourfold.[21] Then came the pandemic, which increased remote work another 250 percent.[22]

The road has not been without its potholes. In 2013, Yahoo! CEO Marissa Mayer shocked the tech world by pulling the plug on working from home. "To become the absolute best place to work," Mayer announced in a human resources memo, "communication and collaboration will be important, so we need to be working side-by-side. That is why it is critical that we are all present in our offices."[23] Yahoo!'s remote staff pushed back.

"Why?" one telecommuter responded.[24] "[In the office, we] have to put up with numbskull self-important programmers constantly yakking to each other LOUDLY from the next set of cubicles about non-work-related stuff and being distracted every twenty minutes by some bored soul coming over to my desk to go for coffee or foosball, or just to talk about the spreading ennui of knowing [we are] working for a company whose glory days [are] long over." Ouch.

---

20   Kate Lister and Tom Harnish, Federal Telework: Obstacles and Opportunities (San Diego, CA: Global Workplace Analytics, 2013), https://virtira.app.box.com/s/0aj83jjwq5psf8qa2wio 6jclwpxrx18j.

21   Bayern, "How Remote Work Rose by 400%."

22   "Change in Remote Work Trends Due to COVID-19 in the United States in 2020," Statista, April 2020, https://www.statista.com/statistics/1122987/ change-in-remote-work-trends-after-covid-in-usa/.

23   Kara Swisher, "'Physically Together': Here's the Internal Yahoo No-Work-from-Home Memo for Remote Workers and Maybe More," All Things D, February 22, 2013, https://allthingsd. com/20130222/physically-together-heres-the-internal-yahoo-no-work-from-home-memo-which-extends-beyond-remote-workers.

24   G. Sampath, "Working from Home Sucks: Why Yahoo's Marissa Mayer Is Right," Firstpost, February 27, 2013, https://www.firstpost.com/business/working-from-home-sucks-why-yahoos-marissa-mayer-is-right-641321.html.

Yet Mayer's edict stuck and soon began to alter the perceived wisdom. Tech firms suddenly seemed determined to keep everyone under the same roof. Best Buy ended its work location flexibility program, and in 2017, one of telecommuting's first movers, IBM, insisted that all its workers had to be physically present in the office. The next year, the US Department of Education recalled its teleworkers in an effort to boost collaboration.[25] Google may have had much the same thinking when it built its famed Googleplex compound, which opened in Mountain View, California, in 2004. Spread across two million square feet of office space and extensive grounds, perks and amenities included gourmet cafeterias offering cuisines from around the world, dozens of snack rooms, volleyball courts, massages and ball pits for stress release, gyms with regular yoga classes, and more.[26]

The plan, of course, is that employees find the place so enticing that they never want to leave. Google even operates a fleet of Wi-Fi-enabled biodiesel shuttle buses providing free rides to work for area employees. Once workers arrive at the Googleplex, they can eat pretty much whatever they want, whenever they want, from all of the cafés and snack bars, which are also free. Many new arrivals have gone overboard and put on a few pounds, a development that has come to be known as "the Google 15."[27] Bikes are parked indoors, and workers can toil alongside their pets—one even brought in his boa constrictor.[28] The staff-seducing wonders of the Googleplex likely inspired Apple to build

---

25 Lessons Learned from Remote Working during COVID-19: Can the Government Save Money through Maximizing Efficient Use of Leased Space?, 116th Cong. (2020)(statement of Kate Lister, president of Global Workplace Analytics).

26 Jonathan Strickland, "How the Googleplex Works," HowStuffWorks, accessed June 12, 2022, https://computer.howstuffworks.com/googleplex.htm.

27 Ibid.

28 Bill Kurtis and Peter Sagal, "Google Chairman Eric Schmidt Plays Not My Job," August 16, 2014, in Wait Wait ... Don't Tell Me, podcast, https://www.npr.org/2014/08/16/340647461/google-chairman-eric-schmidt-plays-not-my-job.

its $5 billion Apple Park, which opened in 2017 a few miles south of the Googleplex in Cupertino. The donut-shaped, Norman Foster–designed main building, which is among the world's most energy efficient, was soon dubbed "the Mothership" because of its resemblance to a UFO. The compound one-ups Google with housing for twelve thousand employees, a one-hundred-thousand-square-foot fitness center, an underground one-thousand-seat auditorium, and seven cafés, the largest of which can seat three thousand people.[29]

As with Mayer's edict, Silicon Valley's ostentatious commitment to on-site staffing began to reshape thinking in other sectors. After all, the thinking went, if Big Tech had turned its back on telecommuting, then office-bound staff must be the best way forward. This was not much of a leap, as it largely confirmed many corporate leaders' suspicions about remote work. Top managers and executives have long been of the view that if they could not see staffers at their desks, they should assume the worst—that the vast majority, wherever they may be, are being unproductive. This dovetailed with the business world's tendency to prefer the familiar and resist change in an effort to curb risk. "There's a lot of inertia in the way people work," says Stanford professor Erik Brynjolfsson, who studies productivity in the digital economy.[30] "And it's actually quite hard to change the processes, the culture, the training, the types of work and tasks that people are doing. And so unless there's a shock, most people will tend to continue to do things the old way."

---

29   Sarah Holder and Laura Bliss, "What's Missing from Apple's $2.5 Billion Housing Plan," Bloomberg, November 5, 2019, https://www.bloomberg.com/news/articles/2019-11-05/why-apple-is-investing-2-5-billion-in-housing.

30   Paul McDonald, "Laying the Foundation for a Successful Hybrid Workforce," Forbes, December 16, 2020, https://www.forbes.com/sites/paulmcdonald/2020/12/16/laying-the-foundation-for-a-successful-hybrid-workforce/?sh=6b5c7b801e5c.

That shock came in March 2020 with the pandemic's arrival in the United States. In just a couple of months, the share of the American workforce working remotely leapt from 5 to 60 percent. When, a few months later, jobs site Monster.com asked human resources professionals which policy areas changed most as a result of the pandemic, increased telecommuting accounted for both of the top two responses.[31] Despite its suddenness, the shift seemed largely seamless, as morale spiked and productivity held steady.

This prompted many companies to reevaluate their positions on remote work and relearn the 1970s lessons of IBM and AT&T all over again. For one, a remote workforce would save them a bundle on rent, which is significant in pricey hubs like New York, London, and Silicon Valley. Second, embracing remote work opened up a nearly bottomless labor pool, as potential staffers no longer needed to live near the office. Companies were suddenly able to hire the best people, wherever they might live. This may explain why many top tech firms now plan to allow their staff to work remotely for as long as they'd like. After telling workers that they'd need to be in the office at least three days a week after the pandemic, Amazon shifted its stance and handed the remote decision to team leaders.[32] Twitter has said that its employees can work from home permanently, while Airbnb, Atlassian,

---

31   Bryan Robinson, "New Study: Remote Workers Fudge How Much Time They're on the Clock," *Forbes*, February 2, 2021, https://www.forbes.com/sites/bryanrobinson/2021/02/02/new-study-remote-workers-fudge-how-much-time-theyre-on-the-clock/?sh=3c9fa89742a5. Remote-work flexibility (43 percent of those polled) and adaptable off-site work schedules (40 percent).

32   "Amazon Offering Teams More Flexibility as We Return to Office," Amazon, October 11, 2021, https://www.aboutamazon.com/news/workplace/amazon-offering-teams-more-flexibility-as-we-return-to-office.

and Canva have outlined similar policies.[33] And after spending more than $1 billion on its Frank Gehry–designed campus, Facebook expects more than half of its workforce to be remote by 2025.[34]

Still, some companies are holding fast to in-office work. As summer 2022 arrived, the world's richest man decided to turn the clock back a decade or three. "Anyone who wishes to do remote work must be in the office for a minimum (and I mean *minimum*) of forty hours per week or depart Tesla," Elon Musk told employees in a leaked all-staff email.[35] Rather than a reversal of what's come before, this underscores the extent to which certain segments of the corporate world are still coming to terms with our new virtual reality.

Tellingly, a forward-thinking CEO, Scott Farquhar of Atlassian, saw an opportunity in Musk's diktat. "News from @elonmusk and @ tesla feels like something out of the 1950s," tweeted Farquhar, contrasting Musk's approach with Atlassian's, which told employees in mid-2020 that they never needed to come back to the office.[36] He added that in the past year, 42 percent of Atlassian's new hires lived at least two hours from an office. "This is the future of how we will work.

---

33   Sarah Frier, "Twitter Says Employees Can Work from Home after Virus Recedes," Bloomberg, May 12, 2020, https://www.bloomberg.com/news/articles/2020-05-12/twitter-says-employees-can-work-from-home-after-virus-recedes; Tess Bennett, "Airbnb Employees Join the Work-from-Anywhere Club," *Financial Review*, May 1, 2022, https://www.afr.com/work-and-careers/workplace/airbnb-employees-join-the-work-from-anywhere-club-20220501-p5ahk2.

34   Aakash Gupta, "The History of Remote Work: How It Came to Be What It Is Today," Sorry, I Was on Mute, September 23, 2020, https://www.sorryonmute.com/history-remote-work-industries/.

35   Sam Nissim (@SamNissim), "#Tesla no longer allowing remote work," Twitter, May 31, 2022, 8:30 p.m., https://twitter.com/SamNissim/status/1531810291222192130.

36   Scott Farquhar (@scottfarkas), "News from @elonmusk & @tesla today feels like something out of the 1950s," Twitter, June 1, 2022, 9:31 p.m., https://twitter.com/scottfarkas/status/1532188222511775744.

Highly distributed. Highly flexible," explained Farquhar, offering a link to Atlassian's careers page. "Any Tesla employees interested?"

Despite a few holdouts, the office exit door has been kicked wide open and looks set to stay that way. Yet this happened so fast that few companies had time to do their due diligence and implement remote policies. Remember that in early 2020, many business leaders still viewed the idea of employees working off site as a curb on oversight and a threat to the bottom line.

That's why many companies that were relative newcomers to remote work invested, in the pandemic's early days, in employee-monitoring software. Such programs monitor URLs and keystrokes and might even keep a webcam trained on the worker, putting employees under *more* scrutiny than they faced in the office. This Big Brother–like setup naturally breeds stress, resentment, and distrust in virtual workers, most of whom are already well aware of what they need to get done and when.

More importantly, these monitoring and surveillance tools measure activity, not achievement. An informed approach to supervising virtual teams should begin with the idea that productivity is best gauged by results and output, not hours and activity. Yet consider Hubstaff, a popular monitoring tool for remote workers. Once the employee clocks in, the app starts recording time and worker activity: every second that passes is one in which the worker is either active—moves the mouse, uses the track pad, or types on the keyboard—or inactive. The Hubstaff report sent to the employer highlights the number of hours the employee works and his level of activity.[37] The worker, meanwhile, is congratulated if he's able to maintain an activity level of 50 percent or better. But this is a low bar that in fact says

---

37   Hubstaff does offer an additional monitoring device: screenshots taken every few minutes. But growing privacy concerns have spurred many employers to disable that option.

nothing about productivity. A worker could achieve an activity level of 90 percent while spending 100 percent of his time trolling friends on Twitter. Or he could nap while his five-year-old plays video games. Or even use a remote tool to make the mouse move.[38]

These tools not only are antithetical to healthy and productive self-management but also threaten to turn staffers into mindless droids who become experts at tricking spyware rather than at doing their jobs. Hours and activity levels tell employers very little of value, and requiring that they be recorded is condescending and distrustful. "Monitoring software that takes screenshots of employees' computer screens, reports which apps people are using, or squeals on them if a cursor has not moved for a while," the *Economist* concurred in March 2022, "are tools of mind control, not management."[39]

This might explain why remote workers feel comfortable doing nonwork tasks for nearly a quarter of their reported working hours (nine of forty), according to a 2021 Amazon survey of nearly one thousand telecommuters.[40] This is precisely where the traditional management mindset needs to shift.

Remote workers should no longer be treated like lost sheep in need of herding but as bold fledglings leaving the nest and in need of encouragement to fly.

This will of course be a major shift for companies with little remote worker experience. Countless managers have long been comforted by the sight of a room of associates stiff backed at their desks. These same managers now wonder what their remote workers might be getting up to. But leadership styles need to evolve along with

---

38   "How to Cheat Time Tracking or Employee Monitoring Software," Kickidler, accessed June 12, 2022, https://www.kickidler.com/how-to-cheat-time-tracking.html.

39   "Company or Cult?," *Economist*, March 5, 2022, https://www.economist.com/business/2022/03/05/company-or-cult.

40   Robinson, "New Study: Remote Workers Fudge."

the contemporary business world—a world in which virtual teams occupy a central role.

Are your remote workers caged or free to fly?

Performance metrics that gauge output—projects completed, pages written, candles sold, calls made—not only are more respectful of staff but also actually indicate productivity. Europe seems to appreciate this, as governments there have begun to enforce reduced oversight for virtual workers. In Portugal, bosses can be fined for messaging their employees outside work hours, while French workers have the right to ignore emails sent during nonwork hours.[41] In Canada, the province of Ontario is mulling a law much like Portugal's, but US workers shouldn't expect similar regulations anytime soon.[42] "We have a long history in the United States of not having policies that make it easier to work and have a life, or work and have a family,"

41   Sam Blum, "Employers Who Text Employees after Working Hours Could Now Face Fines in Portugal," HR Brew, November 17, 2021, https://www.morningbrew.com/hr/stories/2021/11/17/employers-who-text-employees-after-working-hours-could-now-face-fines-in-portugal.

42   Sophia Harris, "What If It Were against the Law for Your Boss to Bug You after Hours?," CBC News, October 26, 2021, https://www.cbc.ca/news/business/work-emails-disconnect-ontario-legislation-1.6224826.

says Julie Kashen, director of women's economic justice at the liberal-minded Century Foundation.[43] No surprise, then, that California has taken the opposite tack, with a 2018 law that forces employers to pay workers for all the time they spend working, wherever they may be and whatever the time.[44]

Regardless of the government's take, empowering remote workers is about focusing on results rather than on keystrokes, on what gets done rather than on how long it takes. Managers who watch their workers' every move and spoon-feed them overly detailed instructions while expecting them to develop self-reliance are not only delusional but also bad at their jobs. Remote workers

We have a long history in the United States of not having policies that make it easier to work and have a life, or work and have a family.

thrive when trusted to make their own way, when they have some measure of decision-making control. Too short a leash erodes their ability to get from point A to point B. When employees are no longer harassed with constant monitoring, their spirits and productivity tend to rise. This applies to Zoom calls as well.

"Zoom Fatigue"
Causes

In April 2021, Virtira surveyed more than seventeen hundred managers and employees and found that nearly half (49 percent) experienced "Zoom fatigue," an increasingly common term that refers to a worker's exhaustion with the frequent need to be on camera and to appear

---

43   Adrienne Matel, "Portugal Banned Bosses from Texting Employees after Work. Could It Happen in the US?," *Guardian*, November 15, 2021, https://www.theguardian.com/lifeandstyle/2021/nov/15/portugal-boss-texts-work-us-employment.

44   Barbara Wilber, "In California, All Time Worked Must Be Paid, Even If It's Only Minutes," Alert, January 18, 2019, https://calchamberalert.com/2019/01/18/in-california-all-time-worked-must-be-paid-even-if-its-only-minutes/.

at least moderately enthusiastic during meetings.[45] By now it's quite clear that near-constant surveillance tends to drain rather than boost enthusiasm.

One Step at a Time

Just like remote workers, managers need to be held accountable as well. Setting schedules and targets, establishing efficient and effective processes for team communication and project oversight, and generally keeping remote workers aware of their responsibilities are all musts for sustaining optimal productivity. That's not micromanagement; that's just plain old management. Keeping telecommuters informed about expectations, deadlines, deliverables, and uncertainties is half the battle when it comes to boosting remote performance. Yet many businesses and managers today fail to give remote workers the knowledge and tools they need to succeed. Instead, they weigh their remote workers down with micromanagement. If the worker needs to be micromanaged or has a hard time figuring out how to be productive on his own, he's probably not cut out for remote work. That's why this book emphasizes that remote employees must be given the tools, training, and management oversight that enable them to work independently.

The first objective, therefore, is hiring workers who perform well remotely and are able to align with company culture and values. Employers today likely expect every worker they hire to be perfectly productive inside and outside the office. But that's much easier said than done. For starters, three in four job candidates say that hiring done virtually makes it more difficult to assess the company's values and culture. This suggests that as virtual hiring increases, and it undoubtedly will, so too will the risk of making ill-fitting hires. In addition, most companies' hiring procedures could become more complicated as they become more remote.

It would be fantastic if there were a hiring panacea—one simple step that could ensure that every hire you make will be a star, wherever they end up working. But that's not the reality, which is why a late 2020 Upwork study found that more than 60 percent of firms lacked either the workers or the skills to complete their work.[46] Many firms are struggling with this new reality, so in the coming chapters, we detail hiring practices that can find and retain those most inclined to succeed in remote roles.

In December 2021, as the omicron variant reawakened a pandemic that had seemed set to go into hibernation, the *New York Times* reported a global increase in anxiety and depression. The story bemoaned the continuing uncertainty around COVID-19 and "all that has been lost in a remote world."[47] Much has indeed been lost over these two-plus unfathomable years, over and above the tragedy of millions of people gone and tens of millions of lives eroded. Consider the economic impact: in late 2020, Harvard economists David Cutler and Larry Summers, a former Treasury secretary, estimated the pandemic's hit on the US economy to be $16 trillion, including $7.6 trillion in lost economic output.[48] That represents a greater economic

---

46   "Upwork Study Finds 22% of American Workforce Will Be Remote by 2025," Upwork, December 15, 2020, https://www.upwork.com/press/releases/ upwork-study-finds-22-of-american-workforce-will-be-remote-by-2025.

47   Roger Cohen, "Across the World, Covid Anxiety and Depression Take Hold," *New York Times*, December 13, 2021, https://www.nytimes.com/2021/12/13/world/covid-anxiety-depression-omicron.html.

48   Jonathan Shaw, "The $16-Trillion Virus," *Harvard Magazine*, October 15, 2020, https://www.harvardmagazine.com/2020/10/16-trillion-virus.

catastrophe than the Great Depression, which sounds accurate when you recall the many businesses forced to shut down.

Keep in mind that their estimate emerged when we still expected vaccines to end the threat, long before the delta and omicron variants arrived to upend our thinking. As of mid-2022, the total could be two or three times their figure, but one silver lining—and a potential route to postpandemic economic normality—is that we have gained a greater appreciation of the power of remote work. These days, the working world has largely accepted its telecommuting destiny. There are significant hurdles to overcome—and likely new ones yet to emerge—but the vast majority of today's employers and workers embrace their virtual future. This book is a testament to that.

PRO TIP: DEFINE YOUR TERMS

When it comes to telecommuting, we're sometimes drowning in word soup. The choice of terms includes "remote," "hybrid," "distributed," "mobile," "WFH" (working from home), "virtual," "telecommuting," "telework," "distance working," and more. To get some answers, we surveyed more than one thousand managers and found that "remote" is used mostly as an adjective (as in "a key element of remote work …") and "virtual" as an adverb (as in "while working virtually, it's important to …"). In addition, "hybrid" has replaced "flex" as the most widely used term for those who spend part of the workweek in the office.

This book will use "remote" as a catchall for beyond-office work, whether it is full time or only one day a week in a hybrid model. We will also sometimes use "virtual" and "telecommute" to mean much the same thing while largely setting other terms aside. Whichever terms your firm prefers, it's a good idea to clarify your preferences and stay up to date on the language of relevant laws and regulations.

CHAPTER 2

The Virtues and Challenges of Remote Work

Remote forces you to do the things that you should be doing anyway, earlier and better.

—SID SIJBRANDIJ, COFOUNDER AND CEO, GITLAB

The spring of 2020 showed the working world, once and for all, that remote work, although it has many challenges, also has a good many virtues.

Chief among the virtues of remote work may be that it does not reduce productivity, as long feared, and that it may even increase it.

Productivity

In August 2020, the human resources firm Mercer asked nearly eight hundred employers how the pandemic had affected productivity. More than two-thirds (67 percent) said that productivity had stayed the same, while more than a quarter (27 percent) said that it had actually increased.[49] Of nearly eight hundred businesses, only about 5 percent said that the sharp increase in remote work had eroded productivity.

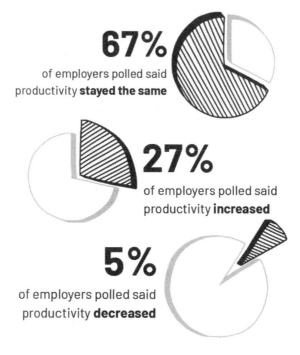

67%
of employers polled said productivity **stayed the same**

27%
of employers polled said productivity **increased**

5%
of employers polled said productivity **decreased**

Remote productivity studies during the pandemic.

And that may be the norm: a FlexJobs survey of more than two thousand employees who worked remotely during the pandemic similarly found that 95 percent felt that their productivity had either increased or stayed the same.[50] Taking a macroview, from mid-2020

---

49   Jeanne Sahadi, "90% of Employers Say Working Remotely Hasn't Hurt Productivity," CNN Business, updated August 27, 2020, https://edition.cnn.com/2020/08/27/success/work-from-home-employer-plans-for-more-flexible-policies/index.html.

50   Rachel Pelta, "FlexJobs Survey: Productivity, Work-Life Balance Improves during Pandemic," FlexJobs, accessed June 12, 2022, https://www.flexjobs.com/blog/post/survey-productivity-balance-improve-during-pandemic-remote-work/.

to mid-2021, a year of unprecedented telecommuting, US labor productivity increased 1.8 percent, which is a more than 25 percent increase from the 1.4 percent average increase seen for the previous fifteen years.[51] An April 2021 study by top economists found that increased remote work boosted worker productivity 5 percent, mainly by cutting out the commute and curbing distractions.[52]

Unsurprisingly, some data do point in the other direction. A University of Chicago study of remote workers during the pandemic, for instance, found that their productivity fell by as much as 19 percent.[53] And in a study by freelancing job site Upwork, 22 percent of managers said that productivity had decreased with greater remote work. Yet in the same study, 32 percent of managers said that it had increased.[54] In those early days, when many firms were still getting their remote work sea legs, the findings were bound to reveal problem areas. We would be wise not to give them too much legitimacy. Some 30 percent of Microsoft workers surveyed in late 2020 reported lower productivity during the pandemic, for example, but overall, Microsoft's Future of Work study found that productivity at the tech firm had generally stayed the same.[55]

---

51   US Bureau of Labor Statistics, "Productivity and Costs, First Quarter 2022, Revised," USDL 22-1081, June 2, 2022, https://www.bls.gov/news.release/prod2.nr0.htm.

52   Enda Curran, "Work from Home to Lift Productivity by 5% in Post-pandemic U.S.," Bloomberg, April 22, 2021, https://www.bloomberg.com/news/articles/2021-04-22/yes-working-from-home-makes-you-more-productive-study-finds.

53   Michael Gibbs, Friederike Mengel, and Christoph Siemroth, "Work from Home & Productivity: Evidence from Personnel & Analytics Data on IT Professionals" (working paper, Becker Friedman Institute, University of Chicago, Chicago, 2021), https://bfi.uchicago.edu/wp-content/uploads/2021/05/BFI_WP_2021-56.pdf.

54   "Statistics on Remote Workers That Will Surprise You (2022)," Apollo Technical, May 11, 2022, https://www.apollotechnical.com/statistics-on-remote-workers/.

55   Jaime Teevan, Brent Hecht, and Sonia Jaffe, eds., The New Future of Work: Research from Microsoft on the Impact of the Pandemic on Work Practices, 2021, https://www.microsoft.com/en-us/research/uploads/prod/2021/01/NewFutureOfWorkReport.pdf.

Broadly speaking, the pandemic revealed that office workers are more adaptable than we thought. According to Donna Venable, executive vice president of human resources for Ricoh North America,

> Our biggest concern for remote work prepandemic was a loss in productivity. However, despite all odds, and competing priorities—from personal health crises, caring for family, and dealing with initial technology challenges of remote work—productivity did not waver. This means that we will not go back to a world where employees are "allowed" to work from home, but rather, they are encouraged to be flexible.[56]

An often-ignored factor in the productivity-telecommuting equation is corporate vulnerability. Security experts warn that corporate networks risk a major breach with the distributed office, but a single-location workforce may be much more vulnerable to disruption.[57] This is the case not only with a viral threat like COVID-19 but also in the face of natural disasters like hurricanes, typhoons, and wildfires, which have become more powerful and more common in recent years. Although cyber risks remain because of increased reliance on the cloud, a mostly remote workforce sharply reduces the risk of high-level disruption and enables a company to keep doing business, even while facing a major threat.

---

56   Joe McKendrick, "Remote Work Evolves into Hybrid Work and Productivity Rises, the Data Shows," *Forbes*, May 30, 2021, https://www.forbes.com/sites/joemckend-rick/2021/05/30/remote-work-evolves-into-hybrid-work-and-productivity-rises-the-data-shows/?sh=95f61de4825e.

57   Kyle Wiggers, "IT Teams Face Employee Resistance to Security Controls," VentureBeat, September 9, 2021, https://venturebeat.com/2021/09/09/it-teams-face-employee-resistance-to-security-controls/.

EMPLOYEE MORALE

It may not be as hard as you think, as remote work tends to boost worker morale, making employees happier, healthier, and less likely to look for another job. This virtue of remote work has been widely known for years. In a 2014 Stanford study of remote call center workers and an in-office control group, the at-home workers reported much higher job satisfaction and less exhaustion and had less than half the attrition rate of office workers.[58] Prepandemic studies on telecommuting by Gallup, Harvard, and other top institutions found a more than 40 percent drop in absenteeism among remote workers.[59]

When people enjoy their jobs more, they tend to show up for work more and stay in their jobs longer. A 2021 study by Accenture found that those working at least partially remotely during the pandemic had better mental health, less burnout, and stronger work relationships and that they were more likely to feel better about their employers.[60] Others reported less stress because of their more comfortable work environments, the lack of a commute, and more time with family.[61]

Remote workers surveyed by FlexJobs pointed to fewer interruptions, a quieter and more comfortable work space, and the absence of office politics as key advantages—and more than half reported improved

---

58   Brian Neese, "Working Remotely Works: How Smart Employers Can Build Morale and Enhance Productivity," AllBusiness, accessed June 12, 2022, https://www.allbusiness.com/working-remotely-employers-build-morale-enhance-productivity-113194-1.html.

59   Laurel Farrer, "5 Proven Benefits of Remote Work for Companies," *Forbes*, February 12, 2020, https://www.forbes.com/sites/laurelfarrer/2020/02/12/top-5-benefits-of-remote-work-for-companies/?sh=b1faa1c16c8e.

60   "The Future of Work: A Hybrid Work Model," Accenture, April 30, 2021, https://www.accenture.com/us-en/insights/consulting/future-work.

61   Pelta, "FlexJobs Survey."

mental health.[62] It's telling that nearly all of the workers surveyed (97 percent) by FlexJobs in summer 2021 expressed interest in remote or hybrid work.[63]

A mostly remote workforce sharply reduces the risk of high-level disruption and enables a company to keep doing business, even while facing a major threat.

The data on this point are vast. Global Workplace Analytics' *State of Remote Work 2021* found that 82 percent of those who worked from home during the pandemic had better mental health, while 84 percent said that they were happier.[64] Supervisors within the federal government concur: more than three of four (77 percent) say that telecommuting boosts morale, while about two-thirds say that it curbs stress (67 percent) and increases employees' desire to stay in their posts (65 percent).[65]

Employees are so keen to work remotely that one study found that more than a third of workers would take a pay cut of up to 5 percent to be able to do so at least some of the time, a quarter would take a 10 percent pay cut, and 20 percent would take an even greater cut.[65] Indeed, 82 percent of US employees want to work from home at least some of the time once the pandemic is over.[66] If not allowed to work from home, 46 percent said that they would look

---

62   Brie Weiler Reynolds, "FlexJobs, Mental Health America Survey: Mental Health in the Workplace," FlexJobs, accessed June 12, 2022, https://www.flexjobs.com/blog/post/flexjobs-mha-mental-health-workplace-pandemic/.

63   Rachel Pelta, "Many Workers Have Quit or Plan to after Employers Revoke Remote Work," FlexJobs, accessed June 12, 2022, https://www.flexjobs.com/blog/post/workers-quit-employers-revoke-remote-work.

64   Owl Labs and Global Workplace Analytics, *State of Remote Work 2021*, 2021, https://owllabs.eu/state-of-remote-work/2021.

65   Ibid.

66   Ibid.

for another job.[67] And these concerns are only going to increase over time: work flexibility is among millennials' most highly ranked job requirements—above student loan help and tuition reimbursement.[68] These voices represent a quiet revolution that today's businesses must respect if they want to attract and retain the best people.

Happier and healthier over a distance.

The New Level Playing Field

This broader desire for remote work could be due in part to the fact that the pandemic-driven uptick in telecommuting has removed its long-standing stigma. Before 2020, it was somewhat rare to have a virtual meeting participant. As a result, the remote attendee might feel less involved and less a part of the group, while all those physically present might even forget about their virtual colleague. Fast-forward to 2022, and nearly all office workers (98 percent) expect meetings

---

67   Ibid.

68   Gallup, State of the American Workplace, 2017, https://www.gallup.com/workplace/238085/state-american-workplace-report-2017.aspx.

to include remote participation.[69] Many calls might have just two or three people in a conference room and a dozen colleagues joining from a distance—a new workplace reality that has left top business outlets like Bloomberg suggesting new shapes for the conference room table (triangle, anyone?).[70]

This new scenario helps even the playing field for the remote worker, widening the recruitment pool to those who are remote by circumstance rather than choice. Some top performers are stuck in dead-end jobs because they were forced to relocate to take care of an ailing family member or deal with some other personal issue. These people should be able to fulfill those obligations while enjoying a top job in their area of expertise, and now they can. Employers, meanwhile, are now more likely than ever to discover and hold on to that impossible-to-find skill set. And let's not forget that higher morale and greater retention also boost productivity and cut costs because fewer positions are left unfilled and fewer resources need to be dedicated to hiring.

Saving Money

Making remote workers and their employers even happier is the money they save. FlexJobs estimates that the average remote worker saves

---

69   "Cisco Launches First Global Hybrid Work Index: Key Findings Reveal Hybrid Work Is Powered by Mobile and AI, Talent Sits Everywhere," Field Technologies Online, accessed June 12, 2022, https://www.fieldtechnologiesonline.com/doc/cisco-launches-first-global-hybrid-work-index-key-findings-reveal-hybrid-work-is-powered-by-mobile-and-ai-talent-sits-everywhere-0001.

70   Ryan Cavataro, "A Trapezoid? Office Conference Tables Take New Shape in the Hybrid-Work Era," Bloomberg, April 23, 2022, https://www.bloomberg.com/news/articles/2022-04-23/trapezoids-the-debate-over-conference-room-tables-in-the-hybrid-work-era.

$4,000 a year in comparison with the full-time office worker.[71] This is due to savings on clothes when most days can be spent in pajamas; a steep decline in eating out, whether that's a coffee and a bagel in the morning or a high-end lunch; and no more pricey commutes.

As for employers, prepandemic studies estimated that companies save $11,000 annually for every hybrid worker thanks to reduced rent and utilities costs, less absenteeism, greater retention, and steadier productivity.[72] Thus, if a midsize company of two thousand employees were to suddenly switch to a fully remote work model, it could save up to $22 million annually. As of 2020, federal agencies had saved nearly $2.5 billion thanks to telecommuting, and Global Workplace Analytics estimates that government-wide adoption of half-time remote work would save $11 billion every year.[73]

ONE PERSON > $11K   2000 PEOPLE > $22M

Employer savings from hybrid work.

Going Green

The disappearing commute drives our most important virtue of remote work: the environmental benefit. You might think that this has little direct

---

71   Rachel Pelta, "6 Ways Working from Home Will Save You $4,000 or More Annually," FlexJobs, accessed June 12, 2022, https://www.flexjobs.com/blog/post/ does-working-remotely-save-you-money.

72   Farrer, "5 Proven Benefits."

73   Lessons Learned from Remote Working during COVID-19.

impact on your bottom line and make it a lesser concern. But these days, being eco-friendly is being socially responsible, and everybody knows that embracing corporate social responsibility (CSR) boosts the brand and, ultimately, profits. As Enrique Dans, professor of innovation at Madrid's Instituto de Empresa, wrote in 2018, "CSR is taking on a deeper hue of green, which is a good thing."[74] Top tech firms such as Microsoft, Facebook, Amazon, and Google, along with established corporations like Starbucks, Unilever, and Maersk, have all committed to being carbon neutral by 2050 or sooner.[75] These days, it's not only activists pushing companies to go green but also venture capitalists and impact investors, who have the funding to gauge green CSR impacts and pressure corporate boards.[76] Climate Action 100+, for instance, represents some $48 trillion in assets committed to pressuring corporations to mitigate climate risk.[77]

The average remote worker saves $4,000 a year in comparison with the full-time office worker.

One significant step toward meeting today's greater green expectations is to go remote first, an approach that makes all workers fully remote, or remote friendly, giving everybody the option to work from home. The main environmental benefit is the reduction in greenhouse gas emissions, the key driver of climate change. Transportation is the

---

74   Enrique Dans, "Corporate Social Responsibility Is Turning Green, and That's a Good Thing," *Forbes*, September 14, 2018, https://www.forbes.com/sites/enriquedans/2018/09/14/corporate-social-responsibility-is-turning-green-and-thats-a-good-thing/?sh=597bc98e4dca.

75   Sarah Holder, "The Environmental Implications of the Return to the Office," Bloomberg, March 29, 2021, .https://www.bloomberg.com/news/articles/2021-03-29/is-telecommuting-really-greener-it-depends.

76   Michael O'Leary and Warren Valdmanis, "How the 137 Million Americans Who Own Stock Can Force Climate Action," Vox, updated October 15, 2020, https://www.vox.com/21509913/climate-change-bp-microsoft-investors-shareholders-accountability.

77   "Climate Action 100+," Climate Action 100+, accessed June 12, 2022, https://www.climate-action100.org/.

largest contributor to US greenhouse gas emissions, with more than half coming from personal vehicles.[78] Before COVID-19, nearly 90 percent of Americans drove to work, most of them alone, accounting for nearly 30 percent of all worker miles driven in the United States.[79] As one might expect, transportation-related CO_2 emissions fell 15 percent in 2020.[80] Keep in mind that the first fifth of that year was before the pandemic, which means that a full year of being fully remote could deliver an even larger reduction.

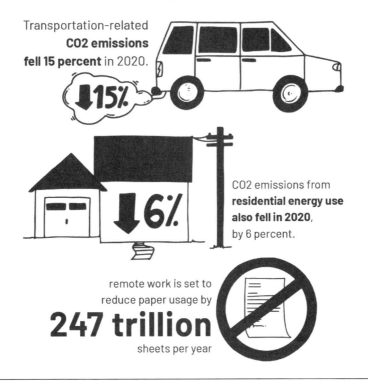

Transportation-related **CO2 emissions fell 15 percent** in 2020.

CO2 emissions from **residential energy use also fell in 2020**, by 6 percent.

remote work is set to reduce paper usage by

247 trillion

sheets per year

---

78 "Fast Facts on Transportation Greenhouse Gas Emissions," US Environmental Protection Agency, accessed June 12, 2022, https://www.epa.gov/greenvehicles/fast-facts-transportation-greenhouse-gas-emissions.

79 US Department of Transportation Federal Highway Administration, Summary of Travel Trends: 2017 National Household Travel Survey, 2017, https://nhts.ornl.gov/assets/2017_nhts_summary_travel_trends.pdf.

80 Kevin Nakolan and Perry Lindstrom, "U.S. Energy-Related CO2 Emissions Declined by 11% in 2020," US Energy Information Administration, April 12, 2021, https://www.eia.gov/todayinenergy/detail.php?id=47496.

Some analysts feared that remote work would merely trade commuter emissions for home-related emissions, such as those from air conditioners, furnaces, dishwashers, and more. But CO_2 emissions from residential energy use also fell in 2020, by 6 percent, according to government figures.[81] The International Energy Agency's view is that working from home or wherever you might find yourself is better for emissions than any personal vehicle–driven commute of more than 3.5 miles, which is less than a quarter of the average US commute.[82] Fewer Ubers, Lyfts, and company shuttles, as well as reduced demand for public transport, will cut CO_2 emissions further still. A year-round, mostly telecommuting workforce has the potential to cut greenhouse gas emissions, curbing climate change and resulting significantly and sustainably in less pollution and cleaner air. This is also a money saver, as every additional cut in CO_2 emissions means that the business will need to spend less on carbon offsets in the looming global carbon market.[83] Another green benefit and money saver is the reduction in paper usage. Remote workers submit reports and make presentations digitally, which has the potential to cut paper use down to nearly zero. One estimate says that remote work is set to reduce paper usage by 247 trillion sheets per year, which would not only conserve a great many forests but also reduce company overhead.[84]

---

81   Ibid.

82   Daniel Crow and Ariane Millot, "Working from Home Can Save Energy and Reduce Emissions. But How Much?," International Energy Agency, June 12, 2020, https://www.iea.org/commentaries/working-from-home-can-save-energy-and-reduce-emissions-but-how-much; David Harris, "How Far Do Americans Drive to Work on Average?," It Still Runs, accessed June 12, 2022, https://itstillruns.com/far-americans-drive-work-average-7446397.html.

83   Isabelle Gerretsen, "How Trading CO2 Could Save the Climate," BBC, October 18, 2021, https://www.bbc.com/future/article/20211018-climate-change-what-is-the-global-carbon-market.

84   Minnesota Office of Environmental Assistance, Reducing Waste in the Workplace, accessed June 12, 2022, https://www.pca.state.mn.us/sites/default/files/w-hhw1-14.pdf.

Global Workplace Analytics estimates that if all US workers capable of working from home started doing so for just half the week, it would "reduce greenhouse gases by fifty-four million tons—the equivalent of taking almost ten million cars (the entire New York State workforce) off the road for a year."[85] That's fifty-four million tons of CO_2 per year.[86] What's more, because of the smaller in-office workforce, nearly three-fourths of Fortune 500 CEOs plan to reduce office space in the wake of the pandemic, which will cut costs and reduce energy use, making for a smaller corporate carbon footprint.[87]

Google and Apple like to talk up the many eco-friendly elements of their vast California compounds. But experts, including a top analyst from the Natural Resources Defense Council, point out that their massive office parks mostly contribute to suburban sprawl, encouraging greater vehicle use.[88] Untethering workers from such places, however eco-conscious they may be, could make us greener. An early 2021 Upwork study found that the possibility of working remotely had tripled the number of Americans looking to relocate.[89] Most have moved from dense, expensive metropolises to smaller cities, towns, suburbs, and rural areas.[90] "Today, with remote work becoming mainstream," Kate Ascher, Milstein professor of urban development at Columbia

---

85   "Telework Savings Potential," Global Workplace Analytics, accessed June 12, 2022, https://globalworkplaceanalytics.com/cut-oil.

86   Denise Mai, "8 Shocking Environmental Impacts of Remote Work," Digital Nomad Soul, updated March 13, 2021, https://www.digitalnomadsoul.com/environmental-impacts-of-remote-work/.

87   Lance Lambert, "74% of Fortune 500 CEOs Expect to Reduce Office Space," Fortune, June 23, 2021, https://fortune.com/2021/06/23/companies-reducing-office-space-fortune-500-ceos/.

88   Kaid Benfield, "If You Care about Cities, Return That New iPad," Switchboard, March 13, 2012, https://web.archive.org/web/20120504000649/http://switchboard.nrdc.org/blogs/kbenfield/if_you_care_about_cities_retur.html.

89   "Economist Report: Remote Workers on the Move."

90   Owl Labs and Global Workplace Analytics, State of Remote Work 2021.

University, wrote in the *New York Times* in September 2021, "opportunities to find home-work balances in even smaller, more affordable places are growing exponentially—underpinning population shifts that work against our largest cities but may lead to happier, healthier, and greener ways of living for the country as a whole."[91]

Diversity

Finally, one rarely mentioned positive change is that women working remotely are now able to decide when or even if they reveal their pregnancy to potential employers or colleagues. This gives women greater control over how they are perceived in the workplace and by their colleagues. "When I logged on to work remotely each morning, all mentions of my ballooning body and imminent life change abruptly stopped," *New York Times* editor Sarah Kessler, author of *Gigged*, a book about the gig economy, wrote in March 2022. "Instead, I focused on, talked about, and was asked about work. I didn't intentionally hide my pregnancy from a majority of my colleagues. It just didn't often come up. Which, I imagine, is how things often work for expectant fathers."[92]

Challenges

Our working future, however, will not be without its challenges. The first, once again, has to do with productivity. In *The Third Wave*, the 1980 sequel to his groundbreaking 1970 book, *Future Shock*, Alvin Toffler predicted that the home would "assume a startling importance"

---

91   Kate Ascher, "Has the Pandemic Changed Cities Forever?," *New York Times*, September 10, 2021, https://www.nytimes.com/2021/09/10/books/review/survival-of-the-city-edward-glaeser-david-cutler.html.

92   Sarah Kessler, "How Moms to Be Get to Act More Like Dads," *New York Times*, March 5, 2022, https://www.nytimes.com/2022/03/05/business/pregnancy-remote-work.html.

in the information age and emerge as a crucial economic mode.[93] He also sounded a note of caution: "It would be a mistake to underestimate the need for direct face-to-face contact in business, and all the subliminal and nonverbal communication that accompanies that contact."

INNOVATION

In the wake of the pandemic, Toffler has a lot of company. A mid-2020 survey of managers found that more than 40 percent expected remote staff to be less productive than their office-bound colleagues and expressed skepticism about the long-term motivation of remote workers, as well as their own ability to manage remote teams.[94] The productivity data presented earlier in this chapter suggest that such fears are largely unfounded, yet they do hint at a subtler, more troubling concern.

Harvard economists Edward Glaeser and David Cutler argue that while remote work can temporarily boost worker productivity, over the longer term, it fails to deliver key benefits—friendships that boost collaboration and learning that leads to innovation—that come from face-to-face interactions.[95] A Microsoft survey of all the messages, emails, calendars, and calls of more than sixty-one thousand of its employees in the first six months of 2020 similarly concluded that "firm-wide remote work caused the collaboration network of workers to become more

---

93   Alvin Toffler, *The Third Wave* (New York: Morrow, 1976).

94   Sharon K. Parker, Caroline Knight, and Anita Keller, "Remote Managers Are Having Trust Issues," *Harvard Business Review*, July 30, 2020, https://hbr.org/2020/07/remote-managers-are-having-trust-issues.

95   Edward Glaeser and David Cutler, "You May Get More Work Done at Home. But You'd Have Better Ideas at the Office," *Washington Post*, September 24, 2021, https://www.washingtonpost.com/outlook/2021/09/24/working-home-productivity-pandemic-remote/.

static and siloed, with fewer bridges between disparate parts."[96] The study found a decrease in real-time conversations—fewer phone calls and video sessions, more emails and texts—which led the researchers to fear that a remote-first approach could make it "harder for employees to acquire and share new information across the network." Another 2021 study by leading consultancy company KPMG found that the pandemic-driven increase in remote work had decreased mobility, which in turn meant fewer in-office interactions between team members from diverse backgrounds and cultures. "Not having that creates an environment where you have less of that spark, that creativity, those new ideas, and that diversity of thinking and interaction," says Marc Burrows, KPMG's head of global mobility services.[97]

The innovations that have driven growth at so many of today's leading companies often emerge from precisely this sort of information sharing and collaboration. Consider Bell Labs, that legendary New Jersey hothouse of mid-twentieth-century innovation. Bell Labs gave the world the transistor, which today powers our phones and laptops, as well as the solar cell, the laser, the first communications satellites, the foundational tool of digital photography, and the programming languages on which much of today's web is based. Journalist and historian Jon Gertner, who wrote a 2012 best seller on Bell Labs, *The Idea Factory*, credits the company's astonishing creativity and productivity to Mervin Kelly, who rose through the ranks to become chairman of its board. "Mr. Kelly was convinced that physical proximity was everything; phone calls alone wouldn't do," writes Gertner.

---

96   Longqi Yang et al., "The Effects of Remote Work on Collaboration among Information Workers," *Nature* 6 (January 2022): 43–54, https://www.nature.com/articles/s41562-021-01196-4.pdf.

97   Matthew Parsons, "KPMG Report Gives Big Thumbs down on Long-Term Remote Working," Skift, November 29, 2021, https://skift.com/2021/11/29/kpmg-report-gives-big-thumbs-down-on-long-term-remote-working/.

Quite intentionally, Bell Labs housed thinkers and doers under one roof. Like an able concert hall conductor, Kelly sought a harmony and sometimes a tension between scientific disciplines, between researchers and developers, and between soloists and groups. He trusted people to create. And he trusted them to help each other create. In an era before cubicles, all employees at Bell Labs were instructed to work with their doors open.[98]

It's hard to doubt the record of Kelly and his colleagues, which inspired the open-plan offices of top tech firms like Google and Apple and has driven some companies to call for a return to an in-office culture.[99] The threat remote work could pose to networking, collaboration, and innovation represents a major challenge—one that will be tackled head on later in this book.

LIMITING CAREER ADVANCEMENT

Connecting to the office from a distance also tends to undermine career advancement, again because of decreased interaction with colleagues and managers. Research has repeatedly confirmed humanity's "proximity bias," the idea that we tend to look more favorably on those we see more often.[100] In business, this means that workers who spend more time with their bosses—who work in the same location—tend to rise more quickly through the ranks than their colleagues working remotely or in another office. The Allen curve is likely as relevant today as it was more than forty years ago, when MIT

---

98   Jon Gertner, "True Innovation," *New York Times*, February 26, 2012, https://www.nytimes.com/2012/02/26/opinion/sunday/innovation-and-the-bell-labs-miracle.html.

99   Joseph Woodbury, "4 Reasons Hybrid Offices Won't Work," *Fast Company*, August 6, 2021, https://www.fastcompany.com/90662837/4-reasons-hybrid-offices-wont-work.

100   Mark Johanson, "Hybrid Work: How 'Proximity Bias' Can Lead to Favouritism," BBC, August 8, 2021, https://www.bbc.com/worklife/article/20210804-hybrid-work-how-proximity-bias-can-lead-to-favouritism.

professor Thomas J. Allen discovered that office communication levels are directly related to proximity and that interactions increase exponentially for those with closer desks.[101] Separate prepandemic studies of a Chinese travel agency and a top US retailer found that call center worker performance improved (by 13 and 7 percent, respectively) when employees worked at home, yet remote workers in both cases were half as likely to get promoted as those working in the office.[102] "Even in the age of Slack, email, and Zoom," behavioral scientist Jon Levy wrote in the *Boston Globe* in May 2021, "the fact remains: out of sight is often out of mind."[103]

This applies even to highly productive telecommuters. Speaking to the BBC, Anat Lechner, a management professor at New York University, envisioned the manager of a remote worker who does great work but is rarely in the office: "Remind me, who's Bryan? Can we not replace Bryan with cheaper labor someplace?"[104] This view has been largely validated by business-focused research that suggests that working together in the office leads to greater communication among teams,[105] deeper connections to colleagues,[106] and reduced feelings

---

101   Brian McElhaney, "The Allen Curve and Why It Matters to Team-Builders," LinkedIn, March 8, 2020, https://www.linkedin.com/pulse/allen-curve-why-matters-team-builders-brian-mcelhaney-edd?articleId=6642563104561594369.

102   Ibid.

103   Jon Levy, "The Hybrid Workplace Probably Won't Last," *Boston Globe*, updated May 9, 2021, https://www.bostonglobe.com/2021/05/09/opinion/hybrid-workplace-probably-wont-last/.

104   Bryan Lufkin, "Why Workers Might Eventually Reject Hybrid Work," BBC, September 21, 2021, https://www.bbc.com/worklife/article/20210920-why-workers-might-eventually-reject-hybrid-work.

105   Yang et al., "The Effects of Remote Work."

106   Johnny Wood, "Why It's Good to Turn Your Colleagues into Friends," World Economic Forum, November 22, 2019, https://www.weforum.org/agenda/2019/11/friends-relationships-work-productivity-career/.

of loneliness and disconnect.[107] This is logical, as fewer face-to-face interactions mean fewer visual confirmations of sincerity and reliability, giving greater breathing room to negative perceptions and assumptions about colleagues.

As with reduced interaction, the consequences of reduced trust and more fragile working relationships may include reduced productivity and innovation. An eight-month pandemic-era study by *Harvard Business Review* (*HBR*) that examined companies involved in consulting, oil and gas, finance, healthcare, telecoms, and manufacturing found that remote work may be undermining trust, particularly between managers and employees.[108] *HBR* cited a sharp increase in employee monitoring. Hubstaff, a digital tool described in chapter 1, has seen a fourfold increase in UK customers since the start of the pandemic, while Sneek, which takes webcam photos of remote workers at regular intervals, has seen business increase fivefold.[109]

Indeed, if your managers hold on to outdated ideas while overseeing remote staffers who see little need for synchronized hours and micromanagement, they're going to face significant distrust and probably attrition.

ISOLATION

One of the main indicators of job longevity has always been strong social ties, but remote work can leave employees feeling marginal-

---

107   Jennifer Moss, "All the Lonely People," Society for Human Resource Management, July 20, 2019, https://www.shrm.org/hr-today/news/all-things-work/pages/all-the-lonely-people. aspx.

108   Mark Mortensen and Heidi K. Gardner, "WFH Is Corroding Our Trust in Each Other," *Harvard Business Review*, February 10, 2021, https://hbr.org/2021/02/ wfh-is-corroding-our-trust-in-each-other.

109   Ibid.

ized, expendable, and isolated. We often forget it because for so long working from home, a café, or the beach was seen as living the dream.

But the reality is that remote workers tend to work more and harder than in-office workers. A late 2020 survey of nearly two thousand full-time office workers found that they spent less than three hours per day on job-related tasks and nearly two-thirds of their time trawling social media and reading the news. Remote workers, on the other hand, are working up to 30 percent more hours than they had in the office and slacking off for less than a quarter of their work time.

2,000 office workers polled reported **slacking off** nearly **two-thirds of their work day.**

Remote workers, on the other hand, **slack off less than a quarter of their work day.**

BURNOUT

The result is a burnout epidemic. Asana, a workflow management tool, surveyed thirteen thousand workers around the globe and found that 87 percent worked late hours in 2020, while 71 percent experienced burnout.[110] Make no mistake, despite the comfort of home or having one's feet in the sand, telecommuting can have its share of agita. A survey of eleven hundred remote workers by digital meeting tool Doodle found that virtual meetings left 38 percent feeling exhausted, while 52 percent

---

110   Asana, Anatomy of Work Global Index, 2022, https://asana.com/resources/
anatomy-of-work.

said that background noise or poor audio often disrupts their focus.[111] Many pandemic-era remote workers have never telecommuted before and neglect to set boundaries between their work and personal life. Suddenly, they find themselves working late at night or on a Sunday afternoon and come to feel frazzled. Some people simply aren't cut out for remote work, while the rest just need a bit of guidance.

Humans are social creatures who like to be around others, yet remote work tends to be solitary and can lead to loneliness for people not suited to this work style. In fact, the coworking movement emerged in direct response to the rise of remote work, as telecommuters sought greater human connection and interaction.[112] This may be even more relevant today. A Yale University study found that during the pandemic personal and professional networks shrunk by 16 percent.[113] Falling out of touch with friends and colleagues tends to enhance feelings of disconnect and solitude. One potential result of a smaller professional network is less creativity and more groupthink.[114] Another is decreased job satisfaction, which can lead to shoddy work, negligence, and looking for greener pastures.[115]

---

111   "The Time Blocking Report," Doodle, accessed June 12, 2022, https://doodle.com/en/resources/research-and-reports/time-blocking-report/.

112   Brad Neuberg, "The Start of Coworking (from the Guy That Started It)," Coding in Paradise (blog), accessed June 12, 2022, http://codinginparadise.org/ebooks/html/blog/start_of_coworking.html.

113   Marissa King and Balázs Kovács, "Research: We're Losing Touch with Our Networks," *Harvard Business Review*, February 12, 2021, https://hbr.org/2021/02/research-were-losing-touch-with-our-networks.

114   Jill E. Perry Smith and Christina E. Shalley, "The Social Side of Creativity: A Static and Dynamic Social Network Perspective," *Academy of Management Review* 28, no. 1 (January 2003): 89–106, https://journals.aom.org/doi/abs/10.5465/AMR.2003.8925236.

115   Albert L. Wang and Qin Sun, "Employee Isolation and Telecommuter Organizational Commitment," *Employee Relations* 42, no. 3 (March 2020): 609–625, https://www.emerald.com/insight/content/doi/10.1108/ER-06-2019-0246/full/html?casa_token=GXyjg7egjp0AAAAA:h-EPjhkbidZSI1604uGqPR8sGzqmkRrpIEQeZ2iM-JDhGSC6CE2V8hAd0f5PmBtgE-LoFW2b7z5C-zl1tLXJjKZWxkgtAhsAQYa7PVS75IFzJ5PhiOt7xiqw.

WORK SPACE FRUSTRATION

Hybrid workers must grapple with the frustration that comes with the near impossibility of setting up two equally productive and comfortable work spaces. One will inevitably be missing an invaluable reference book or photocopier, while the other will be without that perfectly comfortable chair or the window that reliably brightens the mood. "No matter where they are working, they are almost always someplace trying to do something without some necessary tools," says Anita Woolley, associate professor of organizational behavior at Carnegie Mellon University.[116]

Some might dismiss this as "rich man's problems" in light of the assertions of Glaeser and Cutler, coauthors of the 2021 book *Survival of the City: Living and Thriving in an Age of Isolation.* They point out that increased remote work is likely to reinforce the divide between haves and have-nots, creating a less equitable and prosperous society. In May 2020, more than two-thirds of Americans with college degrees were telecommuting, while fewer than 15 percent of those with at most a high school degree were doing so.[117] And that's just part of it. "The remote world may seem heavenly for middle-aged professionals with extensive networks of colleagues and comfortable home offices," Glaeser and Cutler write, "but it is decidedly less appealing for twentysomethings who are trying to find their way in a new company and get work done in dark, cramped apartments. As time passes, those workers may find it harder to land promotions and to thrive more generally."[118]

---

116   Lufkin, "Why Workers Might Eventually Reject Hybrid."

117   "Table 1. Employed Persons Who Teleworked or Worked at Home for Pay at Any Time in the Last 4 Weeks because of the Coronavirus Pandemic by Selected Characteristics," US Bureau of Labor Statistics, May 2020, https://www.bls.gov/cps/covid19/covid19-table1-2020-05.xlsx.

118   Glaeser and Cutler, "You May Get More Work Done at Home."

LOOKING AHEAD

That may have been the case in the prepandemic era, when the working landscape was dominated by in-office teams. Today, the remote worker is seen as an equal, even if employers are still lagging behind. And that's where this book comes in to set out a road map for companies looking to optimize the productivity, efficiency, and enthusiasm of their remote workforces. The first thing to know is that your organization will see the full benefits only if it embraces rather than merely accepts remote work. To do that, your company will need to take clear steps to create high-functioning remote employees capable of delivering peak performance and powerful results.

Today's employers know that remote and hybrid workloads generally do not erode productivity. The next step is ensuring that remote work boosts productivity, which it can indeed do—*if* your company is set up to harness it. This book will help you get there.

PRO TIP: BEWARE FAKE NEWS

Since the pandemic-inspired rush into virtual, remote work has been among the most studied office-related phenomena, and not all the data are as reliable as one might hope. One UK article we included in an early draft of this book had this headline: "Research shows that remote workers who went six months without seeing any colleagues experienced significant dips in motivation, a symptom of burnout."

Close inspection, however, revealed that the workers studied were traffic enforcement agents. Sure, those officers who hand out tickets for parking and traffic violations are technically remote workers since they do not work in an office. And we appreciate the work they do. But the reality is that their experience is in no way representative of office work trends, which renders the data irrelevant.

The bottom line—look beyond the headline to the base data. Many of our sources have a conflict of interest in that they benefit from increasing the number of remote workers or in keeping more of them at the office. This doesn't make these sources unreliable; it just necessitates greater vigilance. As a result, we've fully vetted all of our research and done our best to eliminate all questionable sources and problematic data.

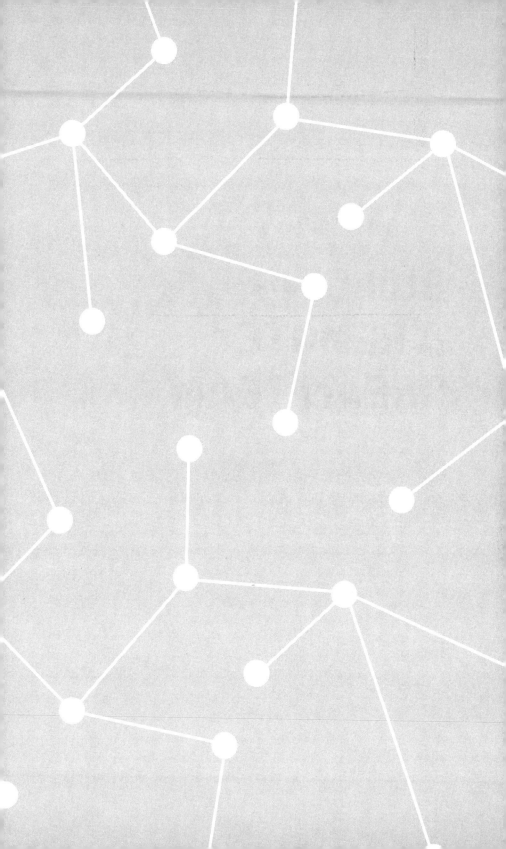

PART II

BUILDING A REMOTE DREAM TEAM

People are not your most important asset. The right people are.

—JIM COLLINS, AUTHOR OF *GOOD TO GREAT*

Ever heard the phrase "Tinkers to Evers to Chance"? It's a reference to three infielders for the Chicago Cubs baseball team in the early twentieth century, Joe Tinker, Johnny Evers, and Frank Chance. Their lightning-fast double play relay—shortstop to second base to first—became so successful that it inspired a poetic lament by a fan of the rival New York Giants who happened to be a columnist for a leading newspaper of the time. Following yet another Giants defeat, Franklin Pierce Adams began a July 1910 column, "That Double Play Again," thus:

These are the saddest of possible words:
"Tinker to Evers to Chance."
Trio of bear cubs, and fleeter than birds.

What, you may be wondering, does this have to do with remote work? Imagine for a moment that the baseball diamond is the United States and that Tinker, Evers, and Chance are not infielders but remote colleagues separated by thousands of miles.[119] The ball they fleetly fire to one another is a business report on a tight deadline. If any of them were to drop or bobble it or to experience a moment's hesitation about what to do next, the whole process would fall apart and the ball—or report—would arrive too late.

---

119   This is not much of a stretch, as Evers hailed from New York, Tinker from Missouri, and Chance from California.

Instead, they succeeded again and again and again, often in the face of great pressure and scrutiny. In the end, their seamless efficiency carried the Cubs to back-to-back World Series victories, while Adams's poem made them legends and helped put all three into the Baseball Hall of Fame. Each had been put in the right position with the right skills and the right motivation at the right moment. Their astonishing success was partially due to innate ability, sure, but it was also the direct result of preparation, of their manager choosing and training the right teammates to begin with.

When everyone is smartly selected, positioned, and trained, high performance is all but guaranteed. Any misstep along the way, on the other hand, can bring the whole operation crashing down: a chain is only as strong as its weakest link.

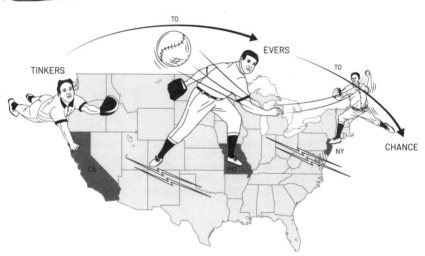

The Chicago Cubs teach us about remote work.

Part II examines how hiring and onboarding have been reshaped by our new, increasingly remote working landscape. We offer detailed guidance on how to attract and select remote superstars and put them into play fully prepared to lead your team to victory.

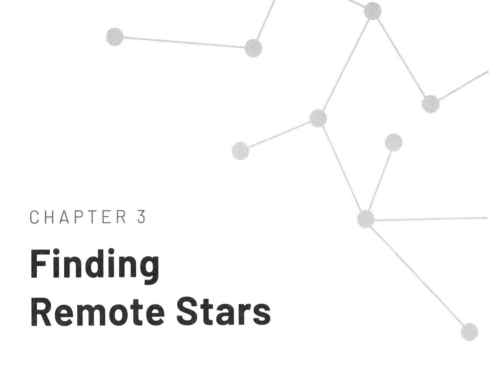

CHAPTER 3

Finding
Remote Stars

Football is a game of inches, and inches make the champion.

—VINCE LOMBARDI

Some years ago, we hired a new staffer who loved to surf. When she wasn't in the office, which was most of the time, she'd often log in from some legendary surf spot along the coast of Portugal, Hawaii, or Australia. We didn't think much of it because regardless of location, she did excellent work. When she recommended a couple of her surfing buddies for available positions, we hired them as well—and found that they too were productive and reliable. Our group of adventure-minded project managers soon expanded to include snowboarders, trekkers, and extreme bikers, and we began to see a correlation.

Because we could offer our employees, even a decade ago, the ability to work from wherever their passions might take them, they stayed with us and consistently overperformed. Being forced to dial in from New Zealand at two in the morning or from India at dawn was well worth it because they were living their dream after years of being stuck in what they saw as soul-sucking office jobs. The lesson that people with a strong nonworking life tend to be excellent remote workers is a key building block to establishing high-performing teams.

Building the Team

Legendary NFL coach Vince Lombardi, quoted at the outset of this chapter, knew all too well that the narrowest of margins often determine the outcome and separate the great from the merely good. The same holds true for building a successful team. Yet a stunning 91 percent of employers struggle to fill their positions, according to Monster's 2022 Future of Work survey.[120] That means that more than nine of ten businesses out there are taking to the field without a complete team. That's not a recipe for success.

Hiring is indeed a tricky proposition, and all the more so when it comes to remote. Candidates who you know in an instant will be great in-office workers can fail badly at remote work for a variety of reasons. When it comes to assessing remote candidates, your top priorities should still be their abilities, experience, and track record, but you also need to look beyond the résumé.

When you start your candidate search, you'll need to know which positions will be done mostly or partially remotely and which will not. A June 2020 University of Chicago study found that 37 percent of US jobs, accounting for nearly half of all wages, could be done from

---

120   Marq Burnett, "Companies Have Big Hiring Plans in 2022. These Challenges Could Derail Them," Business Journals, February 1, 2022, https://www.bizjournals.com/bizjournals/news/2022/02/01/future-work-survey-monster-scott-gutz-2022.html.

home.[121] But a closer look at their research reveals that most of the jobs that cannot be done remotely are lower-paying, nonoffice positions. The leading conditions for these nonremote jobs include "majority of time walking or running," "majority of time wearing protective or safety equipment," and "working directly with the public." Thus, it's highly likely that a much greater share than 37 percent of office jobs are eligible to be remote. Indeed, a Harvard study found that 60 percent of positions within large corporations can be done via telecommuting.[122]

Let's set this as our bar and assume that around six out of ten of your new hires will end up working at least partially remotely, which means that most of your hiring decisions should be incorporating considerations about virtual work. This is precisely why we've written this chapter.

Make Your Company a Talent Magnet

In the 2020s, your firm is far from alone in seeking the best remote candidates. As previously mentioned, 97 percent of workers surveyed by freelancing site FlexJobs in summer 2021 expressed interest in remote work.[123] This means that a degree of remote work is now a primary requirement, even for applicants for office jobs. Like protagonists on the reality TV hit *The Bachelor*, top candidates will have a bevy of attractive suitors and may give each a thorough review.

---

121   Jonathan I. Dingel and Brent Neiman, "How Many Jobs Can Be Done at Home?" (white paper, Becker Friedman Institute, University of Chicago, Chicago, 2020), https://bfi.uchicago.edu/wp-content/uploads/BFI_White-Paper_Dingel_Neiman_3.2020.pdf.

122   Alexander W. Bartik et al., "What Jobs Are Being Done at Home during the COVID-19 Crisis? Evidence from Firm-Level Surveys" (working paper, National Bureau of Economic Research, Cambridge, MA, 2020), https://www.nber.org/system/files/working_papers/w27422/w27422.pdf.

123   Pelta, "Many Workers Have Quit."

The first step is to make sure that you don't lose them before you even find them. It's never been easier to check out a business and examine its history, reputation, and recent news. So be sure to scrub the negative across your company's entire internet presence. To ensure a successful hiring process, it's crucial not only to build a polished and confident website but also to monitor social media and review sites like Glassdoor.com and remove or mitigate criticism and negative portrayals of your business and brand. Also, given the ramped-up competition, your internet presence—company website, LinkedIn, etc.—needs to emphasize the possibilities of remote work. The objective is to have curious potential applicants find only positives on your online profile, which could, if done right, inspire visions of rewarding work done mostly from a Caribbean beach.

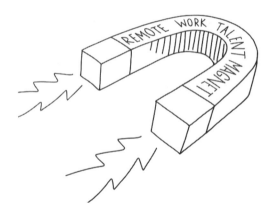

Be a magnet for remote superstars.

The job listing should not only mention remote work but also precisely detail the likely extent of the remote work. Is this a fully remote position, a hybrid job, or a post with merely the possibility of some telecommuting? Being up front and transparent is much better than stretching the truth. Another key element is to detail the specific qualities you look for in a strong remote worker. We tend to favor "independent," "self-motivated," and "proactive"—words that point toward an ability to be productive and efficient with minimal oversight. Well-suited candidates are unlikely to be deterred by such a description, which may, on the other hand, serve to drive away less worthy applicants before they've even applied.

Crucially, as we'll show in the next section, you should advise job applicants to list their volunteer experience and nonwork interests since these point toward how they will perform remotely.

Look for a Life outside the Office

As with our terribly productive surfer, your firm would be wise to keep an eye out for serious hobbies and passions. They could be surfers, trekkers, or snowboarders; they might love to travel or dance, volunteer at their community garden, or spend time with their chickens. The subject of their passion is largely irrelevant; what matters is that it exists and that remote work frees them to live the life they've always wanted. This drives them not only to perform well but also to set clear boundaries between work and life, helping them avoid burnout.

This is not to say that you should keep your eyes peeled for surfers—some are probably a bit like blissed-out surfer/stoner Jeff Spicoli.[124] But in your search for remote workers, you should look for curiosity, passion, and enthusiasm for life beyond the office. You want someone who embraces and enjoys life, as opposed to someone who expects their job to give their life meaning.

It sounds counterintuitive. After all, why hire someone who's more interested in surfing or raising chickens than the work you plan to pay him good money to do? But it is precisely those interests that drive such people to work more efficiently and more productively.

---

124   A character played by Sean Penn in *Fast Times at Ridgemont High*.

They don't want their work to take all day; they want to get it done (so that they can chase their passions with a clear head)—which is precisely what their managers want as well, although for different reasons. Today, most of our best-performing Virtira staffers use their job as a means to a passion project end. They push themselves to excel on the job so that they can earn more money to fund their ideal lifestyle. There's a clear incentive to do the work and do it well.

Contrast this with someone consumed with climbing the corporate ladder or who socializes almost exclusively with colleagues. These individuals tend to perform poorly in remote work because they thrive on the office experience. Their obsession might be career advancement or the need to interact with others at work. Or, if they are new in their careers, the need for in-person mentoring. Someone whose big ambition in life is to land a corner office might work eighty hours a week and be ever present in the office, constantly interjecting in meetings and always smiling in the halls. Her enthusiasm and commitment, however, are largely performative. It's not about being more productive; it's an exercise in apple polishing and catching the teacher's eye in the hope of moving up another rung.

> *The subject of their passion is largely irrelevant; what matters is that it exists and that remote work frees them to live the life they've always wanted.*

This points toward another value of the enthusiastic staffer with a full personal life: because they have spent so much time thinking about how they can live a happy life, they tend to be thoughtful when it comes to others. In our experience, most workers of this sort consider which steps might be best not merely for a certain project but also for their colleagues and the company as a whole. Their personal passion gives them a big-picture sensibility. This echoes the way many of the more impressive professional athletes view their sport as "just a game." It's about performing the right way, respecting colleagues and foes alike, and working together as a team. Not unlike professional athletes, remote workers need to have each other's backs. Appreciating life beyond the office tends to enable workers like those surfers to better appreciate and structure their working life.

The Value of "Broken CVs"

Now you're going through your list of applicants and deciding which to interview. One key question emerges: What exactly are you looking for?

You may not want to be too quick to dismiss résumés with significant gaps, or what we call "broken CVs." Many ambitious workers on the fast track to success can be suddenly derailed by unpredictable circumstances. Maybe their partner accepted a great job in a smaller city, and they tagged along and found limited opportunities. Or perhaps an aging parent or family member requires frequent care, placing demands on their location and their time. We had one employee who left being a bank branch manager to move to a small northern town to take care of her ailing father. She needed schedule flexibility, which meant that the only available jobs were minimum wage jobs. We were able to start her in a part-time position and move her into successively more challenging roles. She was able to care for her father until he passed. She never returned to the daily commute and stayed with us until she retired.

We have hired and supported many workers who for one reason or another, despite strong skills and extensive experience, were forced by circumstance into situations not offering a lot of opportunity. Countless established professionals who've just arrived in a new country are unable to find work because they face a local bias or have no work history in their new home country. We know that these things happen because we've seen them, again and again—and benefited from giving such workers a chance to resurrect their careers through remote work.

This has actually been one of our more pleasant discoveries at Virtira: hiring people with gaps in their work experience usually gives us exceptionally strong performers. Historically, a significant gap in one's work history has been seen as a red flag, a deal breaker. For most recruiters, it suggests one of two things: either the candidate's background and experience were unable to convince a single employer to take her on and give her a chance over this extended period, or she has removed from her CV any reference to a job that she left in disgrace or that might make her seem underqualified for the available position.

For some candidates with work gaps, one of these may be the case, but for many it's not. A few simple questions can identify the cause of the pause. Maybe the candidate took care of an ailing family member, stayed at home with children, struggled with an illness, or dealt with a major life change, such as a divorce or the death of a close loved one. Maybe the candidate decided to travel around the world for a year, was laid off due to budget cuts, or had to take a factory job to pay rent and became stuck in it. In fact, the presumption that people must work continuously from the beginning to the end of their careers should really apply only to the upper and middle classes. These groups have the means to hire caregivers for their families and tend to end up in the types of jobs that would give them a few months off for an illness or birth. The working classes rarely receive such considerations.

Consider that just 14 percent of Price Waterhouse employees are from lower socioeconomic brackets.[125] This is in part because working-

---

125   Daniel Thomas, "PwC Reveals Class Gap among Employees," *Financial Times*, September 15, 2021, https://www.ft.com/content/7ab18305-84cd-4370-b23d-e849c590c00d.

class folks tend to lack a strong safety net and are thus regularly forced to take breaks from the workforce—breaks that have long undermined their attractiveness to employers. But remote work can be a perfect fit for such workers, as it affords them the flexibility to manage their own time, enabling more consistent work. We know this firsthand. At Virtira, we've hired many "broken CVs" and have been almost uniformly happy that we did. Such workers tend to bring a degree of enthusiasm to the position because we've given them, like the surfers, something they've wanted so badly for so long. They have mostly been excellent remote workers and outstanding hires whose engagement and loyalty far exceed expectations.

The Introvert-Extrovert Debate

One commonly used personality gauge for remote work is introvert/extrovert. This tends to be an oversimplification, as most people are a combination of the two. Still, if you're going to lean one way or the other, at Virtira we've found that introverts tend to do better at remote work. Most are observant, thoughtful, and good listeners, which means that they have strong social antennae and are able to see problems developing early. They also tend to think before they speak, which is an excellent quality for workers who log into several group calls each day.

Extroverts can also perform well remotely, as some are able to build a robust social network beyond the office, but they have been hit and miss for us. We have to onboard them carefully to make sure that they have enough people around. We've had extroverts leave us for two-hour commutes and lower pay just to have regular human interaction. We've had others who talked so much that no one would work with them. Extroverts get their energy from other people, and being on camera is absolutely not a substitute for this. Much of the reported employee anguish in the early days of the pandemic was a result of extroverts forced to work alone at home for weeks on end.

After a few days of working alone, most extroverts find themselves in frantic need of social connection. Especially during the pandemic—with the closure of satellite offices and the inability to grab a quick coffee or meet up at a dog park—we found that they needed far more online interaction if they were living by themselves. Most hiring managers are aware that good remote workers tend to be better educated and introverted. While some introverts report struggling with remote work, this may be related more to pandemic lockdowns than to working remotely.[126] Introverts generate their energy internally and can actually be overloaded easily by people.

How can you tell whether your candidate is an introvert or an extrovert? You can't simply ask them because any smart candidate, knowing the preferred answer for a remote position, would just claim to be an introvert. A few straightforward questions about their social behavior, however, can provide you with some real insight.[127] Do they tend to get into deep one-on-one discussions at parties or chat amiably with everyone? Do they do more listening or talking? Does spending time alone energize them or leave them feeling low? Most candidates tip their hand at some point and reveal their nature.

---

126   Meggie Nelson, "Secret Struggles of Introverts in Remote Work Environ-
       ments," Firsthand, March 22, 2021, https://firsthand.co/blogs/workplace-issues/
       secret-struggles-of-introverts-in-remote-work-environments.

127   Sean Ludwig, "How to Tell If You're an Introvert or Extrovert at Work," CO—, June 3, 2021,
       https://www.uschamber.com/co/grow/thrive/introverts-vs-extroverts-at-work.

The Screening Process

Now you've winnowed down your applicants to the top handful of candidates. The next step is to select those with the qualities outlined above—enthusiastic and curious, disciplined, self-motivated, selfless, and maybe just a little outside the box. But how do you ascertain whether they actually possess the skills and mindset to be top-performing remote workers?

Over the years, we have developed a handful of simple methods of assessing whether candidates' skills and mindsets are a fit for remote work. In the early days of the pandemic, we saw countless examples of the wrong fit simply because so many workers who had never telecommuted suddenly found themselves working remotely full time. A lot of them didn't like it. The title of an August 2020 *Forbes* article summed it up: "Working from Home Is Disliked by and Bad for Most Employees."[128] The magazine's survey of more than twelve hundred remote workers revealed "a significant decline in mental health across all industries, seniority levels, and demographics. Job satisfaction, job motivation, and company satisfaction were also negatively affected."

How much of that negativity can be blamed on the realities of the pandemic itself? Probably the lion's share. First off, as detailed in the previous chapter, study after study has shown that increased remote work tends to boost worker morale and satisfaction. The problem is that in mid-2020 many workers were not merely working remotely but had been forced to do so, suddenly and with no training or preparation. That surely led to considerable frustration. What's more, COVID-19 lockdowns meant that for the first time in many of their lives, office

---

128   Benjamin Laker, "Working from Home Is Disliked by and Bad for Most Employees, Say Researchers," *Forbes*, August 24, 2020, https://www.forbes.com/sites/benjaminlaker/2020/08/24/working-from-home-is-disliked-by-and-bad-for-most-employees/?sh=4255d8996734.

workers were forced to stay home all day and night and were deprived of most in-person social interactions. That surely took an added mental and emotional toll. Toss in the stress of a once-in-a-lifetime global pandemic, and dissatisfaction with work is understandable.

Still, the reality is that some people simply do not enjoy working remotely. Whether they are stuck at home during pandemic lockdowns or lounging with their laptop on a Caribbean beach, the solitude of remote work will inevitably trouble some workers and leave them like Tom Hanks's character in *Cast Away*, endlessly jabbering at his best friend, a volleyball. And because most managers had never been trained to supervise remote work in 2020, many either overcompensated by micromanaging or undercompensated by failing to hold workers accountable. They shouldn't, of course, be blamed for not knowing how to handle remote staff, as there was no time to research, choose, and implement best practices. What might be most surprising is that in the end, most of those who worked remotely enjoyed it. A 2021 survey by Global Workplace Analytics found that nearly three of four North American workers (73 percent) felt that their remote experience was a favorable one.[129]

Even so, remote work is not for everyone, and remote work experience on a résumé can be misleading. Just because a candidate worked a full year remotely during the pandemic, for instance, does not guarantee that he is a strong and reliable remote worker. Let's not forget that this period of remote work was rushed from the start. Many managers and employers didn't have time to develop or implement remote worker protocols. Instead, they solved the issue by embracing

---

129   "Work from Home Experience Survey Results," Global Workplace Analytics, accessed June 12, 2022, https://globalworkplaceanalytics.com/global-work-from-home-experience-survey.

surveillance tools that, as detailed in chapter 1, measure activity rather than productivity.

This sort of remote work experience could be a negative rather than a positive because the candidate likely picked up some bad habits. At a firm that understands and embraces remote work, there will be much for this worker to unlearn. The key to assessing candidates' fitness for remote work, therefore, is determining whether they are invested in it as a style of work and possess key attributes that boost their efficacy as remote workers.

Communication Skills

Remote employees don't have the option of knocking on office doors, so they need to know how to communicate succinctly and effectively  in Twitter-size messages.[130] Just as in the story of Goldilocks, you're looking for a candidate who doesn't communicate too much or too little, but just the right amount.

TOO LITTLE   TOO MUCH   JUST RIGHT

Think like Goldilocks when it comes to communications.

If your potential new hires struggle to write clearly and concisely, they are likely to struggle on a remote team. Think of how frustrating

---

130   We cover this issue in detail in chapter 8.

it is to read long blocks of unintelligible text in social media posts. Now imagine having to deal with that degree of incomprehensibility every day, every hour. Overcommunicators can also be a problem: chatty workers who insist on oversharing during online calls limit productive discussion, as do those who send thousand-word emails to make a point that they could have nailed in two sentences.

You also want workers who respond in a timely manner. Keep a close watch on candidates' responsiveness during the interview process. If they fail to get back to you within a reasonable time frame, you may want to think twice about moving forward. This approach has broad applicability. When you begin the standard back-and-forth with qualified candidates, whether via email, text, or a messaging app, pay close attention to how they handle their communications. Are they prompt, concise, and clear? Or do they take days to respond and then ramble on about all variety of extraneous and irrelevant concerns? More broadly, are they focused on highlighting how they would fit in well with your firm and its mission, or do they spend countless paragraphs detailing their own accomplishments? When you're looking for them, the red flags are often easy to see.

This works over the phone as well. Is the candidate verbose or to the point? Do they directly answer questions or go off on tangents? Of course, some tangents are worthwhile—for instance, if the candidate is able to relay anecdotes that shed light on the subject at hand. In some cases, verbal wandering is a sign of nervousness or inexperience rather than a disorganized mind. Some introverts, for example, wander off on tangents because they so rarely speak their minds extemporane-ously. You might further test your candidate's communication skills and personability by requesting a one-minute-long recorded presenta-tion describing why they would make a great addition to your team. In today's working world, in which nearly every team meeting has at least one person logging on remotely, the ability to confidently express thoughts and present proposals on meeting platforms is essential. A brief video often gives great insight into their ability to communicate ideas effectively.

Technology Skills

Accurately assessing candidates' facility with technology is of the utmost importance. Even in 2022, tech still freezes some professionals in their tracks. But remote worker productivity hinges on technology—from Wi-Fi to Google Docs, messaging tools to one's own laptop—so if they don't have at least a minimal comfort level with key apps, platforms, and equipment, their work will suffer. The corporate world still runs on PCs and Macs, not smartphones and tablets. Faced with a tricky upgrade, a computer crash, or a virtual meeting going dark, your remote hires will need to have the know-how to rectify the situation.

Here are some ways to gauge tech savviness during the interview process. Let's say that you find a good candidate and begin the back-and-forth via email. You can switch to a chat app to continue the process and then use different platforms for tests and interviews. For instance, you could use Google Meet for a short initial interview, followed up with a video call on a different platform like Webex to see how the candidate handles logging in and making sure that video and audio are working reliably, all while you gauge the quality of the candidate's home internet. You could also test candidates' facility with a variety of scheduling tools—not just the standard Google Calendar but also OnceHub and Calendly, which are commonly used in remote work. This approach will enable you to assess the candidate's facility and comfort level with a wide variety of communicative tools.

You'll also be able to assess punctuality. Are they logging on at the scheduled start time or a few minutes early, as one might for an important in-person meeting? Are they late to log on, and if so, why? That has happened to us more than once, and it's a clear red flag. It's possible that the candidate had to deal with a sudden emergency on their end, but it's more likely that he managed his time poorly or struggled with the tech. To be sure, you might ask the candidate why he's late.

Their interview location and the quality of the connection are also important. Did they choose a quiet spot with minimal distractions and reliable connectivity? We once had a candidate call in from her local library using the public Wi-Fi. The weak connection and noise level, even in a library, made it impossible to hear the candidate, and the interview had to be canceled. Not a deal breaker but surely strike one. A smart move would have been to use headphones, which reduce surrounding noise.

Are They Ready for Remote?

Another, albeit lesser, concern is space. Some potential hires simply lack the space for a home office, while others are unwilling to invest enough to set up a working space in their home. For example, a candidate living in a big city might share a studio apartment with a partner and a dog—a perfectly reasonable living situation that, however, offers no room to escape distractions. This, of course, does not mean that such a candidate is wrong for the position. The solution could be as simple as finding an affordable coworking space just down the street.

Either way, it's a good idea to make sure that your candidates have a dedicated work space, whether it's at home or nearby, where they are able to focus on work. In addition to details about their home office setup, we ask candidates a variety of questions to test their commitment to remote work:

- Was your remote work experience during the pandemic a good one? What were the advantages and disadvantages?
- What has been your biggest challenge working from home?
- Which apps/tools/platforms did you use regularly while working remotely, and did you face any significant technical issues?
- How do you troubleshoot technical issues when working from home? Are you comfortable tackling computer trouble?

Autonomous Problem Solvers Needed

Remote workers cannot be the type who need hand-holding or wait to be spoon-fed instructions on this or that task. Workers of that sort might do just fine in the office, where there's always a manager on hand to provide guidance. But working remotely, they're capable of frittering away the better part of a day waiting to be told the correct next step rather than being proactive, making an informed decision, and moving forward. Telecommuters must be able to work independently and come up with commonsense, tech-savvy solutions to everyday challenges. If they don't know how to do something, they need to be resourceful and unafraid to reach out to colleagues to find a solution. A good remote worker will send an instant message or even make a phone call to get the necessary info rather than wait for instructions to arrive from on high. A good remote worker knows that she will occasionally come upon roadblocks and must then look for a way around, over, or through them, focusing always on continued progress.

To get a sense of these qualities in a candidate, there are a number of questions you might ask. The first involves a theoretical situation: "Imagine that you're working remotely; your supervisor is unavailable, and you come upon a roadblock that impedes any further progress on a crucial project with a looming deadline. How do you proceed?" You could also offer the candidate a chance to highlight their proven problem-solving ability: "Have you ever overcome a roadblock or other problem while working remotely? If so, how did you solve the issue or figure out a work-around, and what lesson did you learn?" The lesson learned aspect is often crucial and can separate a good worker from one with a steep learning curve.

Part of being autonomous is being a good self-manager. This refers not only to getting enough sleep, eating well, and minimizing life stressors but also to regulating working hours. In the office, work hours are pretty standard, generally a nine-to-five Monday to Friday. When one is working remotely, the hours question is rather more complicated. Some people are able to work only in the evenings. Some candidates might need to care for a child in the morning or live across an ocean and have an imperfectly aligned workday. That sort of thing is fine. What is not fine is a remote worker missing a crucial meeting or deadline to which they had committed. Remote staffers need to be nearly perfect at managing their schedule and communicating their availability to managers. If they are not, there's a good chance that at some point they will hang their colleagues out to dry, leaving them uncertain of the latest steps completed or when they will return and be able to offer insight.

Some simple questions we've directed to potential candidates on these issues include the following:

- What kind of hours do you typically keep while working remotely?
- How do you keep other employees abreast of your schedule?
- Have you ever dealt with any scheduling snafus or missed a key meeting or deadline because of miscommunication? If so, how did you handle it?

Social Smarts

Any manager or business leader worth her salt wants all employees to be as committed to the company as they are to their personal goals and to consider what's best for a project rather than merely what might make that staffer look good. This trait is important in an office worker, but in a remote worker, it's absolutely vital. As we noted earlier in this chapter, people who are thoughtful, considerate, and observant tend to make for strong remote workers, largely because the social safety net for telecommuters is much less reliable than it is for office-bound workers. Not managed carefully, the isolation of remote work can lead to loneliness, burnout, distrust, and dysfunction, throwing a remote team project into disorder.[131] Remote work offers far fewer indicators regarding the current status of a project or the morale of the workers involved. In the office, you can see at a glance that Jim is still at lunch because he's not at his desk

> *People who are thoughtful, considerate, and observant tend to make for strong remote workers, largely because the social safety net for telecommuters is much less reliable than it is for office-bound workers.*

---

131   This book addresses health-related risks and overall wellness in chapter 5.

or that Sally, your supervisor, is chatting by the watercooler and probably not expecting a great deal of progress this afternoon. When you're working on a remote team, your only indicator regarding your colleagues' location, mood, and expectations is their messages, which on some days are all too infrequent.

This is why you want people with strong social antennae—people who are able to look beyond their myopic reality, assess the situation from others' perspective, and empathize. The best remote workers embrace solidarity, are constantly on the lookout for worrying signs, and are confident about when they should step in and offer a helping hand, an encouraging word, or another gesture of support. Some may even be able to recognize fractures as they happen and move to repair them, ensuring continued productivity from remote teams. Finding these qualities is not easy, but we've developed a few interview questions that provide a strong sense of how the applicant might respond in key moments:

- How do you handle work-related conflicts and hurdles while working remotely?
- Tell us about a time when you nipped a work-related conflict in the bud.
- Tell us about a project you managed in which cooperation was crucial.

Now that you know some great ways to sniff out potential remote superstars, it's time to move on to the next phase and bring them aboard with minimal hassle and maximum knowledge.

PRO TIP: LOCATION, LOCATION

One of the most highly touted benefits of the recent increase in remote work is that it has given employers access to a much larger talent pool, as they can now hire people regardless of location. An SEO expert in Timbuktu is suddenly no less appealing than one in Omaha. Broadly speaking, that's true, but there are a few hurdles to keep in mind. The obvious one is time zones. If you're based in New York (EST) and hire a worker in New Delhi (nine hours and thirty minutes ahead of EST), it may be impossible to find a good time for a video call.

Setting that aside, many states, provinces, and foreign countries have complex tax and employment laws that you'll have to grapple with to keep staffers there. At Virtira, we've hired workers in countries with bizarre overtime laws and a variety of different holidays, depending on location and religious affiliation. Other potential hurdles include healthcare and simply paying the new hire, as many countries don't use ADP or PayPal, and setting up a local bank account can mean endless red tape. These elements tend to make foreign hirings more costly and time consuming, so it's wise to be absolutely sure of the candidate's fit before committing.

CHAPTER 4

Long-Distance Socialization

When people are financially invested, they want a return. When people are emotionally invested, they want to contribute.

—SIMON SINEK

magine you're a space traveler, and one day you find yourself on an unfamiliar planet. The air is breathable, the landscape looks pleasant enough, and the locals generally seem friendly. The problem is that you know nothing about their society, cultural norms, or overarching mission. There are, in essence, two ways in which you could learn about the planet's society: either you could begin to move about their world, observing and recording their practices and teaching yourself their language and traditions, or they could take you under their wing; show you their ways through books, lessons, and *Star Wars*–like holographic presentations; and make you a productive member of their society.

In management terms, the first method would be called individual socialization, as it's led by the new arrival, while the latter would be institutional socialization, as the established organization takes the initiative to indoctrinate the outsider. Both are means of organizational socialization, better known in today's working world as "onboarding." New hires are not unlike strangers in a strange land, in need of guidance and understanding if they are to begin making a positive impact within a reasonable time frame. With remote work, new hires lack the sizable advantage of physically being in that new land. Instead, they will probably only catch glimpses of it from a distance. That's why it's absolutely crucial that today's businesses have robust and comprehensive institutional onboarding programs.

If you don't already have your onboarding process mapped out before new hires log in on day one, you could be in for a disaster. Talent optimization website the Predictive Index provides countless real-life onboarding horror stories.[132] Here are two of them, followed by one of our own:

Next to the desk lay a chair. I say "lay" because it was in parts. Apparently, I was supposed to assemble it myself before getting down to work.

On his first day, I received a call from him saying, "I'm standing outside the office, and nobody is opening the door. I rang the bell a number of times without any luck." When I talked to the client, he said they usually open a bit late—a fact that wasn't communicated to my recruit. Later, I found out they didn't even allocate a workstation for him or provide him with a

---

132   "Predictive Index," Predictive Index, accessed June 12, 2022, https://www.predictiveindex. com/.

laptop and other office equipment. After spending a week in the conference room, he submitted his resignation and left.

My worst onboarding was for a company in Missouri. I arrived at the office, and no one seemed to have remembered I was due to start that day. It turned out the person I'd been dealing with beforehand was away on vacation. Since no one else had the time to onboard me, they simply had me go through a folder of company policies—most of which bore no relation to my role. It was unstimulating and, in my opinion, an unproductive waste of time.

To continue the hit parade, a friend recently told us her onboarding disaster tale after getting a long-desired government job. In her first few days, she had zero contact with anyone and soon felt deeply isolated. No supervisor dropped by her desk to say hello or introduce colleagues, so she just sat at her computer all day doing onboarding tasks and checking her email. She attended a few video meetings, but she didn't know anyone, and none of the other participants ever acknowledged the new face on the call.

Remote hires start off blind, which puts a great deal more responsibility on the employer to establish structure. Without a clear, rigorous, and effective onboarding program, new hires could soon be lost, without a road map or compass. And that friend of ours with the government job? She lasted two weeks.

Failed onboarding often leads to attrition, cutting into productivity and the bottom line. The average cost of a new hire is nearly $4,500 and twenty-four days of work.[133] In addition, decreased productivity as a result of new hire learning curves can mean a revenue loss of as much as 2.5 percent.[134] This is likely because you have a better than one in four chance of losing new hires fairly quickly—28 percent leave within six months.[135]

The good news is that a strong onboarding and training process gives you the best chance of your new professional relationship being an unmitigated success. Organizations with a strong onboarding process improve new hire retention by 82 percent and productivity by more than 70 percent.[136] And when they experience great onboarding, nearly seven of ten employees are more likely to stay with a company for at least three years, and at least half of them are more productive.[137]

Yet despite such findings, the vast majority of companies still fall short when it comes to institutional socialization. Nearly nine of ten employees (88 percent) say that their employer did a poor job with onboarding, according to a Gallup poll.[138] Do your firm a favor and place it among the upper echelon that provides an empowering onboarding process. Some of our guidance below dovetails with traditional onboarding, and many of its benefits remain the same;

133   Talya N. Bauer, Onboarding New Employees: Maximizing Success (Alexandria, VA: Society for Human Resource Management Foundation, 2010), https://www.shrm.org/foundation/ourwork/initiatives/resources-from-past-initiatives/Documents/Onboarding%20New%20Employees.pdf; Glassdoor Team, "How to Calculate Cost-per-Hire," Glassdoor, July 5, 2019, https://www.glassdoor.com/employers/blog/calculate-cost-per-hire/.

134   "Candidate Recruiting, Employee Relocation, Internships: Resources to Move Your Greatest Assets," UrbanBound, accessed June 12, 2022, https://www.urbanbound.com/resources.

135   Arlene S. Hirsch, "Don't Underestimate the Importance of Good Onboarding," Society for Human Resource Management, August 10, 2017, https://www.shrm.org/resourcesandtools/hr-topics/talent-acquisition/pages/dont-underestimate-the-importance-of-effective-onboarding.aspx.

136   Madeline Laurano, The True Cost of a Bad Hire (Delray Beach, FL: Brandon Hall Group, 2015), https://b2b-assets.glassdoor.com/the-true-cost-of-a-bad-hire.pdf.

137   Hirsch, "Don't Underestimate the Importance."

138   Gallup, State of the American Workplace.

however, the remote version of integrating new employees also has its own distinct challenges.

Hitting the Ground Running

It's time to transform the new hires into remote superstars. We suggest a ninety-day onboarding plan that ensures that new employees master remote skills and technical functions, that they embrace their job and place within the team, and that expectations are set and met.

Setting specific expectations helps new hires come to the table knowing how best to fit in, how work is measured, and how they can progress in their role. New hires who have been given a clear career development plan within their new organization are significantly more likely to express satisfaction with their onboarding process.[139]

One-on-one meetings, along with reviews, should be scheduled after the first week, the first month, the second month, and the first quarter. Inform the new hire of these planned meetings at the outset so that they're aware of them and so that you, the manager, can be held accountable. At each meeting, help the new hire set goals to be achieved by the next meeting. Asking new employees what they would like to achieve helps you gauge their outlook and approach and makes them mindful of their productivity and growth.

At the end of the ninety-day probationary period, detail the new hire's strengths and gaps and set new goals and expectations for the next quarter. Throughout this process, regularly emphasize the company's guiding principles. The first step might be a day one briefing that describes the firm's vision and mission before outlining the new hire's position and broader role. This way, the new hire is

---

139   Jen Dewar, "10 Employee Onboarding Statistics You Must Know in 2022," Sapling, March 3, 2022, https://www.saplinghr. com/10-employee-onboarding-statistics-you-must-know-in-2022.

better able to see how her work fits into the bigger picture. Generally, the best approach to induction is to start macro and progress to the micro: explanations and lessons should begin with a broader view that, like a Google Map on your phone, eventually zooms into focus on the work of the relevant staffer. For instance, the manager of a solar panel firm might begin to onboard a new hire this way:

> We believe in being green. And that's not just a slogan here but a guiding principle. We're a business, so of course we aim to make money. But equally important is our mission to be environmentally friendly and achieve carbon neutrality. This should also be a guiding principle in your work as project manager. When in doubt, choose the option that most curbs emissions or energy use.

The new employee now has a better understanding of company culture and a clear guidepost should she arrive at a point of uncertainty. Again, this sort of structure is valuable for in-office work but crucial for remote work, in which such situations are not only more common but also potentially more damaging. Establishing clear guiding principles from the outset empowers your remote workers to make decisions that align with your business and enable continued productivity. In fact, the imprinting of company culture and values should begin before the new hire starts on the job, with the sending out of a welcome package and company handbook prior to their start date.

The next guiding principle could underscore that your firm measures work not by activity but by productivity. The solar firm manager might, for instance, tell the new hire that her employers are largely unconcerned about how many hours she works per day. Instead, her work will be measured by the number of solar panels her team sells or the number of useful research findings her team provides within a given period. As these points are made clear, the new hire is also shown the tools and documentation used to log results and given instructions on how to use them. In the end, the new employee understands how her remote work will be assessed and what's expected of her. Onboarding for remote work is in part about replacing office walls with virtual structure. All remote workers should be firmly grounded in culture, policies, tools, and templates so that nobody is forced to reinvent the wheel.

It should go without saying, but this all begins at the top. As detailed in part IV, top executives and other managers need to put in the time to ensure that the firm's hiring and onboarding are robust and uniform. They need to establish strong guiding principles that set a foundation for key policies and procedures. This is the corporate culture into which the new hire will be socialized. If it's not firmly established—if, for instance, one manager embraces unpredictability and another is all about discipline—your productivity could suffer because staffers are left uncertain. Leadership creates the conditions for alignment, especially when a new hire joins a team. Businesses need to demonstrate consistency in their approach to remote work, even if that consistency is all about flexibility.

It's a good idea to build tools and guidelines that are accessible to all workers and provide a detailed overview of the company and their place within it. You might start with a simple online document with links to relevant material and build it out to a full learning management system that's integrated with your human resources system. It's the structure of that discipline and commitment that enables remote workers to relax in the knowledge that they are on the right path and focus on the tasks at hand. Once your firm has established its key guiding principles, ingrain them early and often at all levels.

Developing an Onboarding Process

The key to robust and effective onboarding is a consistent series of steps laid out in a detailed timetable. We've learned that it's best to map out, in bullet point form, every item new hires need to learn. If you don't have this list, start with a brainstorming session with a couple of staffers in similar or related positions.

For all new employees, Virtira uses a one-hundred-point checklist that includes every step that needs to be done, from obtaining banking information to inviting the new hire to the next "all-hands" meeting.[140] The crucial elements are ensuring that new staffers have access to everything they need, have been invited to all relevant meetings, and are officially introduced as new members of the team.

Once you have your list or lists in hand, determine how the new hire will learn each step. Might this point be better explained via written guidelines, in-person instruction, or a video walk-through? No onboarding process is perfect from the start, and you'll likely discover what works best through trial and error. Ultimately, the bullet point lists should be paired with teaching tools such as videos, slide presentations, and executive speeches.

New hires should be encouraged to contribute to this effort by reviewing various stages of the onboarding process once they're complete. New hire feedback—such as "I'd never used this platform, and nobody explained it to me"—often provides invaluable insight that can further improve your onboarding. Perhaps more importantly, new employees appreciate being heard: more than nine of ten (91 percent) say that being asked for feedback improves their relationship with their new employer, while about eight of ten (79 percent) say that it increases their willingness to recommend their new employer to

---

140   See our website for an example.

others.[141] Despite this, only about one in four companies (26 percent) ask new hires for feedback, according to a survey of some two hundred thousand workers—which suggests that this is an easy way to stand out and generate good vibes early on.[142]

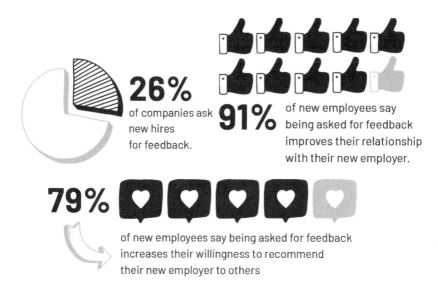

26%
of companies ask new hires for feedback.

91%
of new employees say being asked for feedback improves their relationship with their new employer.

79%
of new employees say being asked for feedback increases their willingness to recommend their new employer to others

Why feedback starts things off on the right foot.

Without a system in place, it's difficult for employees who have never met their fellow team members to succeed, whether those employees are at home or in the office. So those initial introductions to coworkers are crucial and should be done as soon as is reasonable. In those first hours and initial introductions, your firm has an opportunity to imprint itself positively on the new hire, establishing an understanding of company culture, forging strong connections, and laying the groundwork for a long and fruitful professional relationship. This is particularly true for remote employees, who will mostly work in solitude,

141   Dewar, "10 Employee Onboarding Statistics."

142   Talent Board, 2021 Candidate Experience Global Research Reports, 2021, https://www.thetalentboard.org/benchmark-research/cande-research-reports/.

far from any colleague or manager who, in an office setting, might have made her feel more welcome. Take advantage of that opportunity by telling stories that lay out the company's history and values, winning the hearts and minds of new hires, and making sure that they decide to engage with rather than disengage from their new working home.

On day one, for example, the new hire could watch a video on the company's vision and mission, learn about her job and place within the organization, and be introduced to the team. On day two, her manager might detail the duties and responsibilities of her position, as well as the expected outcomes, before beginning to instruct her on the use of the firm's main tech tools.

Beyond that point, it's important to schedule regular reviews to give the new hire opportunities to demonstrate knowledge and abilities. We also have a series of quizzes throughout the process to boost comprehension and find areas that need improvement. As detailed in the ninety-day plan, progress reviews are crucial. In the first couple of weeks, daily check-ins should be part of your onboarding process to make sure that the new hire is comfortable and facing no significant roadblocks.

Providing as much information as possible is often the best way to get a new working relationship off on the right foot. We subscribe to the uncertainty reduction theory, which asserts that greater initial understanding makes for a smoother road ahead. The alternative is that after a few days of initial onboarding, the new remote hire sits in front of her laptop with nothing to do and no one checking in. Remember, it's far easier for new hires to start work in an office setting, where they experience company culture firsthand. It's ironic that, at least initially, remote workers require a bit more hand-holding.

Give New Hires a Buddy

A great way to accelerate new hire induction and build a stronger connection is to pair them with an onboarding buddy, preferably one with a similar or related role. This buddy should be someone with enough time to work with the new hire throughout the ninety-day onboarding and to sit in on the periodic review meetings. Befitting the name, buddies must be peers rather than authority figures who might one day evaluate their charges. New kids on the block need someone with whom they feel comfortable enough to confide in about their role or their problematic boss. Choosing the wrong buddy, one lacking in enthusiasm, understanding, or patience, for instance, could lead to poor performance or even attrition and repeating the process all over again. New hires should never refrain from asking their buddy a question out of fear that it might make them look mediocre. Assigning new hires a friendly, reliable buddy sharply reduces the risk of feelings of isolation in those critical first few weeks.

Buddies should also be trained in helping new employees. For instance, they might be taught that all questions are good questions and that no issue is too small and shown how to explain company culture and help the new hire navigate their new place of work. Buddies must be deeply familiar with the company's guiding principles because they will serve as the new hire's mentor in terms of company culture. Think of how

> *Assigning new hires a friendly, reliable buddy sharply reduces the risk of feelings of isolation in those critical first few weeks.*

much more quickly our space traveler would be integrated into that alien society if he had a local mentor/buddy alongside him every step of the way.

Buddies should make a point of giving the new hire an office tour. If the new employee is unable to do this in person, the buddy can walk around the office during a video call, introducing the new hire to colleagues and providing considerable insight into how the physical office operates. A virtual tour of this sort often leads to the sort of casual introductions that encourage more friendly relations rather than the strictly professional interactions that tend to occur in meetings. The buddy can provide detail about when team members should act more professionally and when interactions can be more casual.

The Tech Bible

A buddy is also the perfect guide for the company's network, as well as for the communications platforms and tech tools the new hire will be expected to use. Your firm should have a tech master plan, or "bible," mapping your network architecture and identifying the platforms used for email, file storage, internal and external messaging, scheduling, workflow, project management, and more.

Of course, your firm will have an internal or external IT department available to offer expertise, but in those first weeks, the buddy is perfectly placed to walk new hires through that bible and get them acquainted with your company's tech norms. A new remote worker going rogue on email or chat, bringing in old habits from past jobs, could imperil his future with the firm and undermine team productivity and cohesion. So the bible should clearly communicate the company's tech architecture, including where to find and store key documents and bits of information and even how to name files for safekeeping.[143] And the buddy, aided by your IT team as needed, should ensure that the new hire accepts this information as dogma. The buddy can lay out the team's and the company's favored communication platforms, outline how the new hire will receive key updates, and highlight which tools are most often used for various kinds of messages and where to find help when they need it.

PRO TIP: MOVE HUMAN RESOURCES TO THE CLOUD

Make things easier on yourself and your company by taking advantage of cloud-based human resources services to manage remote team recruitment, onboarding, off-boarding, and employment records.

Factor the cost of these tools into your overhead in the same way you would if you had to provide an office for your team. Using these kinds of virtual tools just makes sense if you have a lot of remote workers.

Starting a new remote job can be overwhelming, and embracing these platforms significantly reduces stress and the likelihood of a new hire drowning in information overload.

---

143   It amazes us to learn how many organizations don't have naming conventions—a standard file and folder naming process followed by all. We provide new hires with links on our dashboards by department to everything anyone needs to find, and we have a quarterly process to make sure that each department updates them. This prevents those new to the team from needing to search through our cloud storage to find what they need. The emphasis is less on how you create conventions than on making sure that you standardize them and train everyone on your process.

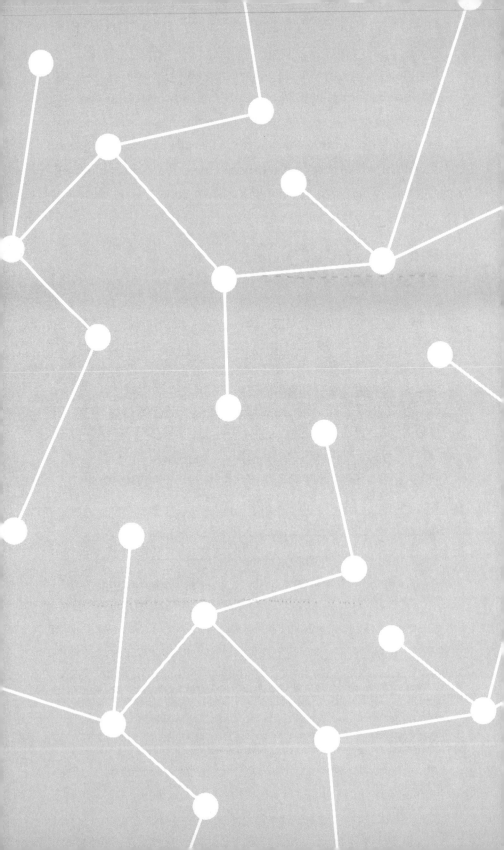

CHAPTER 5

The Remote Workplace

We like to give people the freedom to work where they want, safe in the knowledge that they have the drive and expertise to perform excellently, whether they are at their desk or in their kitchen. Yours truly has never worked out of an office, and never will.[144]

—RICHARD BRANSON

What good is a firefighter without a hose, a baker without an oven, a painter without a brush? Now picture your new remote hire with an ancient computer that makes angry whirring noises every time they click open an app, a two-dollar headset that crackles with static, a folding chair that makes their body ache after an hour, or a severe case of burnout. In an office, it's easy to

---

144   Aimee Groth, "Richard Branson Says That Marissa Mayer Got It Wrong about Remote Employees," Business Insider, February 25, 2013, https://www.businessinsider.com/richard-branson-says-that-marissa-mayer-got-it-wrong-about-remote-employees-2013-2.

make sure that employees have everything they need—desks; chairs; computers; printers; a supply closet stocked with pens, staplers, and paper clips—and that they are mentally and emotionally OK. But that's not the case for remote workers.

Home office setup and remote working wellness have historically been viewed as the employee's responsibility, but new legislation indicates that this may soon be a thing of the past. With that in mind, your company could begin by establishing policies that ensure that every remote worker has the proper setup to do their job, starting with the home office. Because when people lack the proper tools to do their job, they either struggle mightily or fail altogether.

Home Office Setup

The first step is determining your firm's approach. Will you provide a laptop and other equipment for new remote hires, or will they be expected to take care of their tech needs? We might recommend an approach between these two extremes, in which your company would fill in any shortcomings in the new hire's arsenal. For instance, the new hire might have a reliable laptop and excellent headphones, and your firm would provide graphic design software and a comfortable chair.[145] Google and Shopify take a similar approach by providing all remote hires $1,000 to upgrade their home office.

---

145   As for what happens to any equipment you provide to remote hires who later leave the company, you will have to determine whether you let them keep it or whether you want it shipped back. At Virtira, we feel that, if the person has been working for us for a year and a half or more, it's more of a hassle to deal with the computer being returned to us. This is because we then have to store it somewhere and send it on to someone else when needed. It's easier and more cost efficient to just let them keep it, unless of course there's some reason not to. For example, if the person leaves on bad terms, human resources may want them to return the PC.

Your policy should also provide enough flexibility for workers to customize as necessary, which is why providing a stipend is often the best approach. For example, if a new hire already has an ergonomically correct chair, there's no point in providing one, so you might instead ship out a new PC and establish a strong home workplace from the outset.

With the policy established, it's time to assess your new hire's home office setup to make sure that it's comfortable and includes all the necessary tools. It should also be a place where they can shut the door and keep out external noise and distractions, such as a guest bedroom, basement, attic, or private area in a coworking space. Speaking of which, if their home offers no possibility for a private work space, your firm might want to provide them with a membership to a local coworking outfit. Whatever the case, you want to encourage them to make their remote office as comfortable, healthy, and productive as possible.

Health and Wellness

When you're managing a virtual team, burnout can easily escape your notice. But it's an incredibly common problem for remote workers, who face a variety of unique challenges. The biggest one may be that working from home makes some employees feel like they're *always* at work. While the five-second commute is great, the lack of any physical distance between work and home often leads to increased stress.

Then there's the isolation inherent in remote work, especially if the worker has no family or strong social network. Even if a remote employee lives with other people, there is still a good chance that they can feel cut off from their team and their employer simply because they rarely see their colleagues in person. Released in 2020, Buffer and AngelList's study on the state of remote work found that loneliness ranked among the top complaints of remote workers.[146] Research has repeatedly shown that working together in the office leads to deeper connections with colleagues and reduced feelings of loneliness and disconnect. Thus, a good manager must be vigilant for signs of isolation and burnout and act quickly when they appear.

Before we detail the warning signs, it's important to clarify what we mean by burnout. The World Health Organization (WHO) defines burnout as an occupational phenomenon characterized by fatigue or exhaustion, negativity toward or mental distance from one's job, and reduced efficiency and productivity. While it's not an official medical condition, it has been known to lead to chronic anxiety, high blood pressure, and even depression. Even setting aside the considerable health concerns, companies also have a bottom-line reason to ensure their employees' mental and physical well-being: burnout significantly undermines productivity. Employees who experience high levels of burnout are 63 percent more likely to take a sick day and 23 percent more likely to visit the emergency room.

As the frequency of remote work increases, so too will days and hours lost to burnout. Companies need to be aware of the considerable risk, respond to early warning signs, and have a process in place to quickly identify burnout and help employees progress beyond it.

Coping with Burnout

As previously detailed, the COVID-19 pandemic forced many people who weren't suited for remote work to work remotely. Management, too, was largely unprepared, and the resulting spike in burnout in

---

146   Buffer and AngelList, State of Remote Work 2020, 2020, https://buffer.com/state-of-remote-work/2020.

2020—in more than seven of ten remote workers, according to workflow tool Asana—likely surpassed the level we should expect in the future.[147] But that's not to say that burnout and related mental health issues are not of serious concern for remote workers and managers. The WHO issued a warning about burnout-related health risks in early 2022, pointing to excessive stress, fatigue, exhaustion, insomnia, sadness, anger, irritability, alcohol and substance abuse, heart disease, diabetes, and weakened immune systems.[148]

As a manager, you will of course not be expected to detect all the signs and symptoms of burnout during a regular video call, but you can keep your eyes peeled for warning signs. Here are some questions you might ask yourself during and after calls with remote workers:

- Do they seem disengaged, irritable, or unusually negative?
- Are they slow to respond to queries? Do they have heavy eyelids or raccoon eyes?
- Do they seem disorganized, disheveled, or less presentable than usual?
- Do they lash out, fall silent, or otherwise act abnormally?
- Has their quality of work declined? Any recent late projects or missed deadlines?

One or two affirmative responses to the above list are not enough to call in the cavalry and organize an intervention. But it would call for greater vigilance, and if the worrying behaviors repeat themselves over a period of several weeks, you might request a one-on-one call

---

147   Moshe Beauford, "Asana: 7-in-10 Workers Experienced Burnout in 2020," UC Today, January 18, 2021, https://www.uctoday.com/collaboration/asana-7-in-10-workers-experienced-burnout-in-2020/.

148   "Burn-out an 'Occupational Phenomenon': International Classification of Diseases," World Health Organization, May 28, 2019, https://www.who.int/news/item/28-05-2019-burn-out-an-occupational-phenomenon-international-classification-of-diseases.

and ask the employee how they're feeling about work. You may have to press, as nobody likes to talk about their own doubts or shortcomings. At the same time, it's important to stop short of applying any real pressure, which could lead to greater discomfort.

If the staffer is quite certain that they are not feeling burnout and nothing is troubling them at home, the best move is simply to let them know of your concern. If the employee does acknowledge a sense of fatigue or burnout, it's best to offer them some time off or a period of leave. Regardless of whether that offer is accepted, ask how you might help them reengage in their job. More work? Less work? More challenging work? A shift in responsibilities? There are several adjustments a manager might make to accommodate a troubled employee without requiring added budget or approval from a superior.

If your work queries fail to make much headway, don't be afraid to ask personal questions, such as whether they live alone, what sort of social outings they've recently taken part in, or whether their family—children, spouse, aging parents—might be causing anxiety. These are all valid questions for an employee potentially dealing with debilitating burnout. And a manager has every right to ask them, as long as it's in the spirit of seeking out the root of the problem rather than attempting to assign blame. After all, if any single person is to blame for your employee's burnout, it would probably be you, their manager.

Burnout is usually the result of a confluence of factors, from the company, the manager, the team, the workplace, the culture, and the job itself to the isolated nature of remote work and the complications of home and personal issues. In most cases, however, one or two of these stand above the rest, and it's crucial that a manager do everything possible to get at the heart of the problem and work to resolve it, including referring the employee to human resources for additional questions and care.

The leading causes of worker burnout, according to the Mayo Clinic, include the following:

- **Lack of control:** Workers can feel left out of decision-making or as if they lack the resources to do their jobs.
- **Unclear job expectations:** Vague job descriptions and duties leave workers feeling helpless and flailing in an effort to figure out what they should be doing.
- **Dysfunctional dynamics:** A toxic workplace, an overbearing boss, or bullying by colleagues to the point that the worker dreads video calls can create added stress.
- **Extremes of activity:** Workers may be either constantly overloaded with assignments or too often left with nothing to do. Both can lead to considerable anxiety.
- **Lack of social support:** Workers who lack a strong support system of friends and family can easily slip into feelings of isolation and loneliness.
- **Work-life imbalance:** With their office now part of their home, some workers spend too much time at their desks and miss out on more relaxing and pleasurable activities.

Long before burnout emerges, managers should do their best to avoid or minimize key work-related risk factors. It's always good to delegate some authority, be clear about job expectations, enable transparent communications and relaying of complaints, keep your team busy but not too busy, and do your best to make sure that your employees are finding ways to enjoy their off-hours. On that last point, managers should proactively relieve the pressure of any staffers who might feel that they're on the clock twenty-four seven. Their happiness and productivity will inevitably begin to diminish as a result of the stress. People need nights and weekends, or whichever hours they choose, to relax, unwind, and let go of work anxieties. Be sure to reinforce that they don't need to be a hero. Encourage them to hand off as much as possible and to enjoy their downtime.

If you are the type of manager who sends after-hours messages, be sure to let recipients know that they are not expected to respond until their next workday. Advising team members to maintain a reasonable work-life balance is also a good idea. One way to do this is to set boundaries at the beginning and end of each workday. For instance, they could refrain from doing any work in the morning—answering calls, checking emails—until they've sat down to their desk and logged into the office messaging tool. In the evening, they could make a clear break from work by taking the dog for a walk or starting to cook dinner—any task that takes up enough time to sever the connection to work.

work/life Boundaries

Burnout can also be triggered by problems within the virtual team. Workers might feel underappreciated or in conflict with the team's direction or be unaware of internal team politics. This could lead a team member to suddenly stop responding to other team members' emails and messages. Suddenly, a key project is left adrift. When this happens, reach out to the employee, set up a one-on-one call, and tactfully ask questions until they explain the problem. Deal with it as soon as possible, or the situation is likely to spiral. Your company should choose a reliable staffer, preferably a top human resources employee, to be responsible for the health of the remote staff. This burnout czar could put in place reliable systems for regularly checking in on remote staff, red-flagging and sharing potential early warning signs, and dealing with burnout and other mental or emotional issues when they arise.

Managing a virtual team is like trying to raise a child who's in a different building—it's not easy being hands on over the internet. That's why wellness is a more urgent matter for remote workers. On that point, here's a bold idea you might want to embrace: remote workers need not always be working. Even when supposedly logged in and on the clock, they should be free to take a five- to ten-minute walk around the block, do laundry, or help their fourth grader with math homework. To maintain their sanity and avoid burnout, most remote workers require a bit of "me time" every now and then. They may need to occasionally do things that their boss would in normal circumstances find unacceptable during the workday. Of course, managers and execs would prefer that they always seek to maximize productivity. And in a way, by maximizing morale, mental health, and well-being, they will be. Think of these little breaks like the time in-office workers spend chatting in the break room or by the watercooler. You might also encourage other steps remote workers can take to boost self-care, such as regularly getting up to move, meditating, eating better, and maintaining a regular work and sleep schedule, as detailed on our website.

> *To maintain their sanity and avoid burnout, most remote workers require a bit of "me time" every now and then.*

Ergonomics and Safety

A year into the pandemic, the number of US lawsuits involving the phrase "work from home" had doubled from the previous year.[149] There's little doubt that the business world will soon see a rise in the number of lawsuits initiated by workers who have injured themselves while working at home or who struggle with mental and emotional issues or with health problems because of poorly designed mice,

---

149   "The Rise of Working from Home," *Economist*, April 8, 2021, https://www.economist.com/special-report/2021/04/08/the-rise-of-working-from-home.

keyboards, and chairs. Most governments have yet to enact laws that make employers liable for workplace injuries that occur outside the office, but it's likely only a matter of time. Many states already have regulations under which, as in Ontario, Canada, "an injury sustained while working at home will be treated like any other injury—all the circumstances will be considered to determine if the injury is work related."[150]

This explains why a German court ruled in December 2021 that a telecommuting man who fell and broke his back while walking down a staircase from his bed to his home office had suffered a workplace injury.[151] Not two weeks later, a Quebec court ruled that a customer service staffer who fell and hurt herself on the stairs while working at home was eligible for worker compensation from her employer.[152] Few remote workers are likely to sustain injuries this severe, but already, some 45 percent work from a couch, while 38 percent regularly work out of their beds.[153]

We enjoy the comfort of our couches and beds as much as anybody, but we also understand the punishment they are likely to inflict on our spines over a forty- to fifty-hour workweek. Forget major accidents or injuries; the last thing you want is lost productivity, not

---

150   "Can I Get Workers' Compensation for an Injury while Working from Home?," RavenLaw, June 25, 2020, https://ravenlaw.com/news/can-i-get-workers-compensation-for-an-injury-while-working-from-home/.

151   Oliver Holmes, "Fall on Walk from Bed to Desk Is Workplace Accident, German Court Rules," *Guardian*, December 9, 2021, https://www.theguardian.com/world/2021/dec/09/fall-on-walk-from-bed-to-desk-is-workplace-accident-german-court-rules.

152   Christopher Nardi, "Air Canada Employee Who Fell on Stairs in Her Home Eligible for Worker's Compensation: Judge," *National Post*, December 21, 2021, https://nationalpost.com/news/canada/air-canada-employee-who-fell-on-stairs-while-headed-to-kitchen-from-her-home-office-eligible-for-compensation-judge.

153   Jaclyn Crawford, "Study Reveals the State of Home Offices in 2021," CraftJack, October 6, 2021, https://craftjack.com/toolbox/remote-work-from-home-statistics-2021/.

to mention possible lawsuits, resulting from half of your employees struggling with carpal tunnel syndrome or back pain.

How can you ensure that your new remote workers' working environments are ergonomically safe when they're off site? You could invite an ergonomics specialist to join an onboarding call and offer recommendations, record that meeting, and put it in your onboarding training. Later, follow up with an on-camera meeting to make sure that new hires have a healthy setup in place. We also suggest implementing a program that not only guides all employees, whether on or off site, through how to set up their offices ergonomically but also allows them to check their setup virtually.

Remote Work Agreements

Moving beyond safety, court rulings and legislation designed to protect the remote workforce represent a dual-edged sword. On the one hand, they hold out the promise of keeping remote workers safe and productive; on the other, they could strike a blow against the flexibility and freedom that are inherent to remote work. Portugal's ban on after-hours messaging, for instance, flies in the face of the idea of a collaborative and flexible global work space.[154]

At the time of this writing, some fifteen countries have passed permanent teleworking legislation or addressed the so-called right to disconnect.[155] Many US states appear reluctant to introduce non-pandemic-related remote work legislation, perhaps waiting to see which way the wind will blow. Countries tend to prefer to conserve

---

154   Laetitia Bitaud, "Remote Working: Four Cutting-Edge Ideas Straight from Portugal," Welcome to the Jungle, December 6, 2021, https://www.welcometothejungle.com/en/articles/remote-work-portugal.

155   "New Remote Working Legislation around the World," Lockton Global Compliance, updated June 1, 2022, https://globalnews.lockton.com/new-remote-working-legislation-around-the-world.

the status quo because in-office work is much simpler in terms of tax collection. There are also jurisdictional issues, such as how to tax an

employee who works in two different districts or both domestically and abroad. Imagine that you're a remote employee based in Dubai who's working for a manager and team based in Brussels and a company headquar-

Remote Work
Agreement Example

tered in London. Which country's laws and regulations should you follow? Will you need to incorporate bits of all three?

This also raises the issue of working hours, which are of course not universal. At some point we'll see a major European firm that maintains flexible working hours embark on a project with a company that restricts work-related communications to the US West Coast workday. How will they collaborate? Will the entire European team work the graveyard shift? German law ensures that all workers have at least eleven hours off between stints of work, so future collaborations will need to align with an agreed set of hours. This will also lead to issues of overwork, overtime, and the amount of remote work allowed because countries have different laws on the books. Another potential sticking point is that one firm in a joint project may embrace the use of surveillance tools to keep an eye on remote workers while its partner may ban them completely, as Portugal has done.

Yet belief in the right to disconnect is increasingly widespread. A March 2022 survey by the invoicing firm SkyNova found that nearly two of three workers (66 percent of salaried workers and 63.3 percent overall) demand a Portugal-like law banning after-hours messaging.[156] One of five employees said that they were contacted outside work hours every day, with 84 percent adding that it led to more work.

---

156   Bhavna Sarin, "More Employees Call for 'Right to Disconnect' Law," People
Matters, March 30, 2022, https://www.peoplematters.in/news/culture/
more-employees-call-for-right-to-disconnect-law-33381.

Finally, nearly two-thirds (63 percent) agreed that after-hours communication should be acceptable only when there is a work emergency.

US labor laws have yet to embrace a right to work from home or lay out explicit guidelines. Yet as mentioned in chapter 1, California passed a law in 2018 requiring employers to pay their staffers regardless of where or when they work, which suggests that the United States might embrace a no-holds-barred approach. At Virtira, our policy is to allow after-hours messaging, mainly because it's unrealistic to expect someone in New Zealand to keep the same working hours as a colleague in California. We have also found that curbing after-hours messages limits the insights that can drive collaboration and innovation. We do give everyone the right not to respond, which enables those who are fully integrating life and work to be flexible while allowing those on a nine-to-five schedule to remain free during their nonworking hours.

Remote work is international almost by default, and in the near future, we will likely see a domino effect as one country after another nails down and adopts the optimal approach. Until then, we could continue to see businesses take advantage of legal loopholes, as a handful of Russian firms did early in the pandemic, exploiting a law that allowed them to cut pay for those working from home.[157] Countries and companies have tended toward maintaining the status quo in terms of taxes and jurisdictional concerns, and as long as COVID-19 lingers, they are unlikely to budge. But at some point, their death grip on the old way of doing things will weaken, these loose ends will be tied up, and we will move into the postpandemic era of remote work. According to an Upwork study, nearly two of three (64 percent) hiring managers feel that their company has the resources

---

157   "The Rise of Working from Home," *Economist*, April 8, 2021, https://www.economist.com/special-report/2021/04/08/the-rise-of-working-from-home.

and processes in place to support a remote workforce, yet most of their employers (57 percent) lack a remote work policy.[158] For now, businesses would be wise to put in place a remote work agreement with all of their virtual and hybrid staffers that details when they are expected to work, what their pay plans and benefits are, and which issues the company will be liable for.

Getting Tech Right—Especially Audio

Having the right technology in place is of course critical to the success of remote work. Be sure to set high standards that ensure that all your remote and hybrid workers at least have fast, reliable Wi-Fi, a quality laptop, a working headset, and a quiet work space. You probably want to set a minimum bandwidth speed since their internet connection will be the lifeblood of their productivity. They'll do all their communicating and research via that Wi-Fi, so the connection should be as fast and furious as possible. You want them to be able to interact with coworkers without interruption. Keep in mind that for some remote workers, any potential connectivity problem may not be with their internet service provider but with the people who live with them. If their roommates or children are clogging up the connection with constant TikToking, downloading, or gaming, for instance, those are issues that could be addressed with a conversation and a simple internet usage schedule.

We rarely think about it, but high-quality audio is an absolute must for today's telecommuter. Consider this scenario: you've just begun welcoming attendees to a virtual meeting at which your

---

158   "New Report Finds Majority of Companies Are Embracing Remote Teams, yet More Than Half Lack a Remote Work Policy," Upwork, February 28, 2018, https://www.upwork.com/press/releases/future-workforce-report-2018.

business development lead, Jim, is expected to make a presentation in the hope of landing a massive new client.

Which would be worse, if Jim accidentally turned on a cartoon cat filter and can't figure out how to turn it off, or if his audio is poor and he can't be heard? The former is undoubtedly the more comical scenario, but it's the latter that's more problematic for your business. With a cat filter, Jim can still make his presentation—and perhaps gain legendary status as "Catman"—but with no sound, he's finished, along with your firm's chances of landing that client.

So don't underestimate the impact of furnishing new hires with a durable, reliable, and comfortable headset. Good communication is the very foundation of productivity, within and beyond the office environ-

> **Good communication is the very foundation of productivity, within and beyond the office environment.**

ment. And if you're reading this book, you likely have enough experience with video calls to know that audio problems can be among the most vexing of workplace issues. Be sure to address them before they drive your remote workers and their bosses to tears.

PRO TIP: REMOTE SECURITY

Security is a persistent tech risk for all companies and an even greater concern as telecommuting increases. In 2020, hackers accessed more than thirty-seven billion government and private sector records, a 140 percent increase from 2019. Meanwhile, ransomware attacks in which hackers demanded payment doubled.[159] This is likely to get worse as remote work continues to increase in the years ahead. Meetings previously held behind closed doors now occur on minimally secured online platforms. Most companies store at least some bits of crucial data and information in the cloud, while the rest is supposedly secure on their in-house network.

All of your remote workers should install a topflight password management system. We suggest LastPass, Keeper, or Dashlane. Relying on browser-based password storage or autocomplete is a hacker's dream—and your company's potential nightmare. We urge companies to be safe or risk being sorry.

---

159   Dan Lohrmann, "2020 Data Breaches Point to Cybersecurity Trends for 2021," Government Technology, January 22, 2021, https://www.govtech.com/blogs/lohrmann-on-cybersecurity/2020-data-breaches-point-to-cybersecurity-trends-for-2021.html.

CHAPTER 6

Building, Sustaining, and Instilling Culture

*We reinforce our culture every chance we get ...
from the hiring, onboarding, and training of new
recruits to town halls and management meetings
to how we reward and incentivize our people.*

—JAMES DIMON, CHAIRMAN AND CEO, JPMORGAN CHASE

Whether it's a government agency, business, nonprofit, or social group, an organization is defined by its culture, the set of shared principles and assumptions that guides its behavior. Any new arrivals who expect to stick around for a while—like our aforementioned space traveler—must be socialized, be introduced to this organizational culture, and understand the group's values, norms, and goals. Of course, when an organization's principles and assumptions are positive, new arrivals tend to be more willing to identify with and bond themselves to the organization.

In an office setting, communicating culture is fairly straight-forward—in fact it's all but inevitable, assuming that management actually lives up to the company's purported values. Office workers are exposed to the corporate culture every day and, with any luck, soak it in. But remote workers, toiling on their virtual islands, are cut off from that in-person experience. As a result, when the pandemic began in March 2020, many companies took significant steps to reinforce their culture for new hires working from home. Slack, for example, changed its onboarding process dramatically, converting on-paper content and in-person learning sessions to online and video while presenting cultural values and norms in interactive sessions with leadership and teammates. Slack also transformed formal monthly all-hands-on-deck meetings into more casual biweekly twenty-min-ute virtual get-togethers during which executives hosted town hall sessions. IBM also sensed the opportunity that the spike in remote work presented to make stronger connections with new remote hires. Nickle LaMoreaux, IBM's human resources lead, noticed that meeting with remote colleagues made her feel as though she had been invited into their homes. She learned of family members and pets she had not been aware of before and began to feel as if she knew them on a more personal level. For many firms, this emerged as an unforeseen bonus of remote work and accelerated bonding.

A Cultural Cautionary Tale

Other companies, meanwhile, have found maintaining company culture much tougher sledding than expected. As this new age of remote work dawned, few business leaders seemed as well placed to provide insight and guidance as Jason Fried and David Heinemeier Hansson. Back in 1999, Chicago-based Fried founded the tech firm 37Signals, named after the number of radio signals a leading astronomer identified as possible messages from extraterrestrial beings. From its very inception, Fried's company was focused on remote connection, on reaching out and collaborating from great distances. In late 2003, Fried hired Hansson, a Danish programmer, to build a web-based project management tool. Hansson first devised Ruby on Rails, a development framework that today serves as the basis for the likes of Airbnb, GitHub, and Bloomberg, and from that he developed Basecamp, an online project management and messaging platform.

By 2006, investors in 37Signals included Jeff Bezos, and MIT named Fried one of the best young innovators under thirty-five.[160] In 2010, Fried and Hansson coauthored a book titled *Rework*, a combination of entrepreneurial guidebook and internet-era manifesto, laying out their working philosophies and business wisdom. The work emerged as a *New York Times* bestseller and pushed Fried and Hansson further into the spotlight. The duo seemed to foresee our telecommuting future with their 2013 book, *Remote: Office Not Required*, which detailed how 37Signals had achieved success with a mostly remote workforce. It too became a bestseller. The next year, the firm changed its name to Basecamp, in recognition of its primary product, and in 2017, Fried and Hansson launched the *Rework* podcast to highlight "a better way to work and run your business."[161]

By the time the pandemic arrived, they were poised to be gurus of twenty-first-century work. That all changed in April 2021, after Fried announced in a public blog post that Basecamp was banning discus-

---

160   Werner Vogels, "The 2006 Young Innovators," All Things Distributed, September 8, 2006, https://archive.ph/20210313203507/https://www.allthingsdistributed. com/2006/09/the_2006_young_innovators.html; Rob Hof, "37Signals, 1 Big New Investor: Jeff Bezos," Bloomberg, July 19, 2006, https://www.bloomberg.com/news/ articles/2006-07-19/37signals-1-big-new-investor-jeff-bezos.

161   Jason Fried and David Heinemeier Hansson, *Rework*, 37Signals, accessed June 12, 2022, https://www.rework.fm/.

sions about society and politics on its internal messaging platforms.[162] "Today's social and political waters are especially choppy," Fried wrote. "Sensitivities are at 11, and every discussion … quickly spins away from pleasant." Basecamp staffers expressed outrage, which spurred Hansson to write his own post further explaining the decision.[163] The news got out and sparked widespread discussion on platforms favored by Silicon Valley. To be clear, Basecamp was not the first firm to enact such a ban. Leading cryptocurrency exchange Coinbase put in place a similar policy about seven months prior, with CEO Brian Armstrong saying that he wanted "the workplace to be a refuge from the division that is increasingly present in the world."[164] The tech world mostly shrugged in response, and Paul Graham, the founder of leading tech accelerator Y Combinator, saw Armstrong as a trailblazer. "I predict most successful companies will follow Coinbase's lead," he told his 1.4 million Twitter followers.[165]

But Coinbase is not known for its wisdom on company culture or for understanding how to keep remote teams connected and productive. Basecamp is, and the internal anger and pointed public questions had the potential to erode its productivity, as well as its brand. Three days after the ban, Fried hosted an all-hands Zoom call to allow staffers to air their grievances. The discussion turned

---

162   Jason Fried, "Changes at Basecamp," Jason Fried (blog), April 26, 2021, https://world.hey.com/jason/changes-at-basecamp-7f32afc5.

163   David Heinemeier Hansson, "Basecamp's New Social Etiquette regarding Societal Politics at Work," David Heinemeier Hansson (blog), April 26, 2021, https://world.hey.com/dhh/basecamp-s-new-etiquette-regarding-societal-politics-at-work-b44bef69.

164   Casey Newton, "Why Coinbase Will Struggle to Ban Politics from the Workplace," Verge, September 30, 2020, https://www.theverge.com/interface/2020/9/30/21493906/brian-armstrong-coinbase-blog-post-politics-workplace-activism.

165   Paul Graham (@paulg), "Yet again, @brian_armstrong leads the way. I predict most successful companies will follow Coinbase's lead. If only because those who don't are less likely to succeed," Twitter, September 28, 2020, 9:13 a.m., https://twitter.com/paulg/status/1310583298666696705.

intense—at one point Fried and Hansson, as well as head of strategy Ryan Singer, appeared to refuse to denounce white supremacism— and several employees ended up in tears.[166] By the next day, more than a third of the firm—twenty of fifty-seven staffers, including the heads of marketing, design, and customer support—had accepted a buyout.[167] Singer, one of the few who had been around longer than Hansson, also left.

Basecamp was suddenly a cautionary tale. So how did Fried and Hansson so misjudge the flexibility of the company culture they had painstakingly built and for which they'd received great praise? They lost sight of what had brought them success. According to numerous reports, the ban was not an effort to avoid problematic political discussions, such as Trump versus Biden or whether to get vaccinated. Rather, it was about diversity and internal dissent. Back in 2017, Fried explained how he had come to realize that his staff was mostly white and mostly male, and he moved to change it. "We've come a long way," he wrote in *Inc.* magazine, pointing to 35 percent female employees and more minorities. "However, we're still not where we want to be."[168] In December 2020, a new hire volunteered to lead an effort to push Basecamp forward on diversity, equity, and inclusion and received considerable support from coworkers.

The group soon found an old internal list of purportedly funny customer names. Titled "Best Names Ever," the list made fun of

166   Casey Newton, "Inside the All-Hands Meeting That Led to a Third of Basecamp Employees Quitting," Verge, May 3, 2021, https://www.theverge.com/2021/5/3/22418208/basecamp-all-hands-meeting-employee-resignations-buyouts-implosion.

167   Kim Lyons, "Basecamp Implodes as Employees Flee Company, including Senior Staff," Verge, April 30, 2021, https://www.theverge.com/2021/4/30/22412714/basecamp-employees-memo-policy-hansson-fried-controversy.

168   Jason Fried, "Diversity Is Not an Accident. Here's How One Founder Is Trying to Make Change," *Inc.*, September 2017, https://www.inc.com/magazine/201709/jason-fried/2017-inc5000-diversity-in-the-workforce.html.

many Asian, African, and Middle Eastern names and made some in the group uncomfortable. They thought that it was racist and that it reinforced outdated power dynamics, an urgent concern in the wake of the Black Lives Matter protests.[169] The creator of the list had left Basecamp, but in early April 2021, as the diversity discussions continued, two employees apologized internally for having contributed to the list in the past. Members of the diversity group pointed out how mocking names could lead to hate crimes and acts of violence, noting that there had never been an internal reckoning over the list.

Hansson chimed in, acknowledging that he and Fried had failed in allowing the list. But he added that he thought the diversity group had gone too far in suggesting that such a list could lead to extremes like violence and genocide. This reescalated the discussion and precipitated Fried's announcement of the ban, which in turn led to the call and finally the departures. Yet neither Fried's announcement nor Hansson's follow-up mentioned any of these internal discussions. So the company leaders not only barred employees from discussing the urgent issues of the day but also stymied their efforts to expose past failings and clear the way for a more open, diverse, and equitable future. "It was actually a positive thing we were doing," one employee said of the list discussion. "We had identified the problem, how it happened, and vowed not to do it again. It was a company doing exactly what it should do. The founders refused to lead, and so the company was doing it itself."[170]

The two leaders' memos seemed to hint at fiery and problematic internal discussions of partisan politics, when in reality, the political discussions on its messaging platforms were about Basecamp and

---

169   Newton, "Inside the All-Hands Meeting."

170   Casey Newton, "Breaking Camp," Verge, April 27, 2021, https://www.theverge.com/2021/4/27/22406673/basecamp-political-speech-policy-controversy.

improving company culture. The firm's leaders turned authoritarian and upended that culture. In a flash, Basecamp went from a place where all voices were embraced, where bold thinking and strong opinions were encouraged and prized, to a place where stepping out of line was verboten. The company paid a steep price. "Everybody is leaving because they're tired of Jason and David's behavior—the suppression of voices, of any dissent," one employee said.[171] "We've hired opinionated people, we've created opinionated software, and now basically the company has said, 'Well, your opinions don't really matter,'" said another.[172]

It's hard to imagine a better example of the power (and potential pitfalls) of strong company culture. Basecamp had staked its internal reputation and built a strong brand on the idea that its leaders embraced progressive management practices based on openness, equity, and other principles fit for the twenty-first-century workplace. Yet when its leaders became annoyed by an internal discussion that dragged skeletons out of the closet, they moved away from all this, and the house of cards came crashing down. Interestingly, Fried seemed to foresee this outcome in his blog post announcing the ban:

Some changes are immediately appreciated. Some changes take time to steep, settle in, and get acquainted with. And to some, some changes never feel quite right—they may even be deal breakers.[173]

Just a few paragraphs later, he laid out what would become a deal breaker for more than a third of his staff. The first lesson of the fall of Basecamp is that leaders and managers would be wise to act in moderation rather than take extreme positions. It's of course reasonable to be wary of potentially explosive political discussions among

---

171   Newton, "Inside the All-Hands Meeting."

172   Newton, "Breaking Camp."

173   Fried, "Changes at Basecamp."

employees. But taking the draconian step of banning any such talk is only likely to compound the problem—just as forbidding one's teenage daughter from seeing a certain boy tends to drive her straight into his arms.

As with Basecamp, such a ban is also likely to move your firm away from its company culture—a step that is almost impossible to undo. Imagine, for example, that you walk in on two colleagues kissing passionately in the break room. Their roles are equal, so there's no fear of power dynamics at play. At the same time, you don't want the office to turn into a hothouse and thus hope to discourage such behavior. Enacting a ban on all physical contact within the workplace risks turning management into Big Brother, constantly watching for signs of intimacy or affection and suspicious of even innocent, friendly contact. A much better response would be to issue a memo to the effect of "We like all of our employees to get along and appreciate when some become friends or even more. But we ask you to please refrain from publicly expressing your affections in the workplace." This way, they know where you stand, but they also feel more accepted than restricted. One of the employees who left Basecamp said that the problem there was "as simple as creating a space where people do not feel welcome."[174]

The next lesson is about accountability. Company culture means nothing if it's not backed up with integrity. Everybody makes mistakes; we're human, after all. The goal is not achieving perfection—nobody's capable of that. The real test is acknowledging errors, making amends to those who might have been hurt, figuring out how the mistakes occurred, and taking steps to avoid them in the future. And keep in mind that sycophants are a dime a dozen: that's why the

---

174   Newton, "Inside the All-Hands Meeting."

emperor ended up marching the streets in his birthday suit.[175] The truly valuable employees, the ones with more interest in company success than internal politics, are those with the courage to tell their boss when they're wrong. Those are the employees who might one day take your job and lead the company to bigger and better things. Rather than silenced, they should be applauded and given a platform to express their views.

Of course, leadership errors should be pointed out in the right channels, respectfully and with tact, not shouted out gleefully or angrily on social media. In such cases, the onus is then on the managers, the leaders, to reassert established culture by acknowledging the error and taking steps to make the company as strong as it can be. At one point during the Basecamp brouhaha, after Hansson chimed in on the group discussion about the problematic list of names, a staffer pointed out that the way people view and talk about names is deeply connected to racial and social hierarchies. Rather than acknowledge the problem, Hansson took the time to dig through old chat logs, found an example of when that staffer had participated in an earlier discussion about "funny-sounding" names, and posted it for all the company to see.[176] This is the opposite of accountability.

Particularly in smaller firms, there's often nobody there to hold the founders' feet to the fire and make sure that they follow company principles. For leaders with unchecked power, the line between what's good for that leader and what's good for the company can blur. Leaders and managers should instead be about keeping the peace, calming the waters of internal criticism. Staffers will occasionally bring forward ideas that challenge leadership and force them to rethink their views.

---

175   Hans Christian Andersen, *The Emperor's New Clothes* (Cambridge, MA: Candlewick Press, 1997).

176   Newton, "Breaking Camp."

These should generally be seen as opportunities to evolve and earn employee trust by embracing company values.

Every firm should have slightly different introductions into company culture, as no two companies embrace the same exact culture and principles. As with any indoctrination, there's going to be some trial and error before you hit on what works best for your company. But there's no question that culture becomes diluted when the office is remote, and thus culture needs to be stressed all the more. Even so, as IBM's human resources chief learned, sometimes telecommuting can enhance the human connection.

CEO's Welcome

Socialization begins long before the first day on the job. Once the hiring is official, the first thing new remote employees should see, even before their company-purchased laptop lands on their doorstep, is a "Welcome from the CEO" message that lays out the company's purpose and core values. Why does the company exist? What do we stand for? What is our mission and vision? The medium and method of delivery are largely immaterial, although of course it should be attention grabbing and visually appealing. What truly matters is that it captures and conveys the essence of the firm.

Everything the new hire will learn as part of her job—from policies and procedures to office setup, meeting protocols, and other common practices—is anchored by this first impression of the company culture. It is an absolute necessity that this message arrives quickly, underscoring the company's enthusiasm for the new hire, and strongly communicates the firm's vision, mission, and core values. These messages must then be reinforced throughout the onboarding process, including by the new hire's in-house buddy, to deepen their understanding.

Understanding key principles should be uniform and company-wide. This way, managers, whether they are in the office or remote, new arrivals or established veterans, need not shoulder the entire burden of teaching new team members the company's foundational values.

Don't Overwhelm with Details

Once you've covered your company's "why," it's time to move on to the "whats" and "hows"—the nuts and bolts of operations. As with the CEO's welcome, this information should also be anchored in well-presented visuals. Such visuals should illustrate the following:

1. Policies on vacation, holidays, sick days, and time off; guidelines on the flexibility of remote working hours; and recommendations for blocking off time for work.

2. Diversity and respect in the workplace. As we've learned from the Basecamp turmoil, staffers need to feel heard, respected, and understood. It's a good idea to lay out what is acceptable, what is not, how remote work more easily leads to misunderstanding and tension, and how to minimize the potential for such.

3. Expectations on after-hours e-communications. At Virtira, our stance is that it's fine to send messages at any time, but the sender should not expect a response until working hours. As detailed in chapter 5, some countries already have laws in place restricting after-hours messaging, so you might want to make sure that your approach aligns with local regulations and establish a remote work charter.

> *Understanding key principles should be uniform and company-wide.*

4. Guidelines on social media use, personal and in house, including the use of company logos, slogans, and other elements of branding.

5. Security protocols. These should not be a simple list of rules. Make them understand the motivation behind them, the "why."

6. Tech tools they are expected to use and best practices on how and when to use each.

Don't expect new hires to memorize all this on their first day; it's important to avoid overloading them with text-heavy manuals and instructions. It's also important to make this information engaging and blend the "why" with the "what" and the "how" to provide context and link everything back to company culture.

PRO TIP: LEARN FROM EVERY NEW HIRE

Your onboarding process should always be a work in progress. With each new hire, note what worked and what could have been done better. New hires can play a key role in this process by writing down which elements of the onboarding were the most useful and informative and which gave them trouble. Then, at each scheduled review meeting, go over their feedback and use it to improve your firm's onboarding process. This will improve your ability to hire candidates who stay with your company, make new hires feel more comfortable more quickly, and give new hires a sense that their experience is beneficial to the firm—thus increasing collaboration and encouraging them to trust that you value their input.

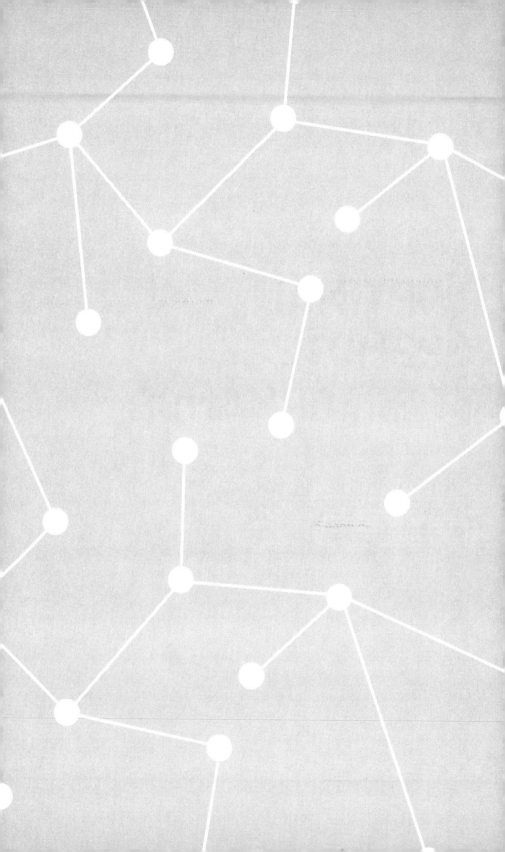

PART III

OPTIMAL REMOTE PERFORMANCE

Tell me and I forget. Teach me and I may remember. Involve me and I learn.

—BENJAMIN FRANKLIN

New remote hires should hit the ground running, ready to embrace their role and start performing, ready to learn and adapt to their new coworkers and workplace culture. One key element that should not be left to managers to explain is creating a great first impression with colleagues and clients. New hires need to be made aware of the crucial nature of strong communications, know how to optimize their time spent in virtual calls and online meetings, and remain reliably accountable and productive while working remotely.

We've said it before, but it bears repeating that the more remote your workforce, the more structure and consistency you'll need to keep them aligned. In the workplace, distractions tend to be momentary—bumping into someone in the hall or chatting while getting a coffee, for instance—because of the general aura of productivity, the hum of office momentum. Remote work has no such hum; staffers are on their own islands. As a result, you'll need to cut through the chaos and hold their attention.

Training might officially end when the employee is fully embedded in their job, but learning must not. Principles and protocols should be constantly reinforced with annual refresher courses, internal messaging, and a consistent, company-wide focus on effective communication and real accountability.

These are the practices that separate remote success from mediocrity. We've covered how to find promising remote workers and bring them on board. The next step is training new hires and your entire remote and hybrid workforce in the elements of optimal remote performance.

CHAPTER 7

A Great
First Impression

Two things remain irretrievable: time and a first impression.

—CYNTHIA OZICK

In February 2021, Texas judge Roy Ferguson welcomed three lawyers to an online hearing in a civil forfeiture case and soon noticed something curious in the video of county attorney Rod Ponton. "Mr. Ponton, I believe you have a filter turned on in the video settings," the judge said, referring to the concerned kitty face appearing in Ponton's on-screen video box.[177] Another lawyer on the call put on his glasses and leaned forward to examine the appearance of a feline at what he had expected to be a sober affair.

"I don't know how to remove it," explained Ponton, after an exasperated sigh. "I've got my assistant here and she's trying to." Ever

---

177   Daniel Victor, "'I'm Not a Cat,' Says Lawyer Having Zoom Difficulties," *New York Times*, February 9, 2021, https://www.nytimes.com/2021/02/09/style/cat-lawyer-zoom.html.

the professional, Ponton moved to begin the hearing. "I'm prepared to go forward with it," he vowed. "I'm here live. I'm not a cat."

What image are you projecting?

This courageous Texas lawyer quickly went viral, and he's far from alone. Visual surprises have upended countless pandemic-era video calls, from the appearance of a scene-stealing toddler to the pantsless spouse strolling through the frame, not to mention the prominent writer caught in a moment of indiscretion and subsequently fired.[178] We've seen it all, and it's no longer shocking. Still, without a certain level of facility with the most commonly used tech tools and platforms, you risk making a poor first impression and eroding trust in your abilities.

That's why it's crucial that remote workers not only master the tech tools of their trade but also pay considerable attention to presentation and appearance. At Virtira, we make sure that all our workers

---

178   Oliver Darcy, "Jeffrey Toobin Fired from the New Yorker after Exposing Himself on a Zoom Call," CNN Business, November 11, 2020, https://edition.cnn.com/2020/11/11/media/jeffrey-toobin-fired-new-yorker/index.html.

understand the importance of presenting themselves well across all platforms, which means that their email signatures and profile and photo on messaging and video platforms should present them in the best light.

The goal should be to maintain a high standard in formal calls with customers and partners and ease off in more casual calls with coworkers. Since remote workers may never be in the same physical space with some of their colleagues and clients, their online presence may be the sole point of contact.

A consistent, professional look goes a long way toward offsetting the absence of the office, where nonverbal clues and gestures and the general workplace aura help establish professionalism and productivity. This doesn't mean spending hours in hair and makeup and wearing the latest business attire. It simply means maximizing the opportunities across social, meeting, and messaging channels to present oneself confidently and professionally, whether that's in Prada or a hoodie. It also means understanding the context of online interactions and upping one's game if the situation requires it.

People who look professional online tend to be taken more seriously and seen more positively by others. Social science has shown again and again that personal appearance is a crucial factor in being perceived positively, whether in the workplace or social settings.[179] Consider the psychological concept known as "the halo effect": upon first impressions, attractive people are perceived as having strongly positive traits, such as altruism, stability, intelligence, and competence.[180] Your remote workers don't need to be beautiful to get the

---

179   Batjar Halili, "Impact of External Appearance on Positive Social Perception," *Academic Journal of Interdisciplinary Studies* 2, no. 1 (March 2013): 131-134, https://www.mcser.org/journal/index.php/ajis/article/view/70.

180   Kjerstin Gruys, "How Does Appearance Affect Our Success?," University of Nevada, Reno, May 1, 2019, https://www.unr.edu/nevada-today/news/2019/atp-appearance-success.

halo effect to work for them—they just need to have a consistent and professional online presence.

Is Video Really Necessary?

In late 2020, Virtira conducted a survey to examine the impact of frequent video calls, polling more than seventeen hundred remote managers and staffers. The survey addressed company policies regarding the use of video during online meetings, why meeting frequency seemed to be increasing, and the impact on employee well-being. We also considered several additional parameters, including introversion/extroversion, age, and income.

Nearly half of the respondents (49 percent) reported feeling anxious and exhausted. The majority were introverts, and the younger the respondent, the greater their troubles. The number of daily online meetings skyrocketed during the pandemic, and more than six of ten (61 percent) reported that all of their meetings were on camera.

Camera or
No Camera? Crucially, they felt that being on camera wasn't a choice—they were either compelled by corporate mandates or felt peer pressure to be on video.

Managers unaccustomed to the new distance of their employees often equate being on camera with being present and connected. In conversations with business leaders throughout the pandemic, most said that they mandated camera use to increase engagement and productivity. Others used it as an inspection tool, with some even requiring employees to leave their cameras on all day. Invasion of privacy, much? These approaches underestimate or completely ignore potential negative impacts, and indeed, staffers in these situations often report feeling self-conscious and uncomfortable, undermining their work and self-esteem.

Virtira's study found that 63 percent of remote workers participated in more meetings online than they would have in the office, with 30 percent spending a minimum of two hours on Zoom every day. The increased time in front of webcams was compounded by well-meaning managers seeking to raise morale via online happy hours and pizza parties. "These platforms give us more opportunities to feel dissatisfied with our appearance," says Lisa MacLean, a psychiatrist with Detroit-based Henry Ford Health System. "There is a strong correlation between how a person rates their outer appearance and how high they rate their self-esteem. If you don't feel good about your body image, it can negatively impact you and prevent you from socializing or taking on challenges."[181] Some people enjoy seeing themselves on the screen, but many dislike it intensely. Why make someone who hates green beans eat them? That's what mandating camera use feels like for the camera shy, and forcing the issue tends to do more harm than good.

The decision about whether to make webcams optional or mandatory for virtual meetings is a crucial and complicated one. Why do managers feel that everyone needs to be able to look into each other's eyes, to see each other working in their own space? Does this open up the possibility for deeper personal connections, or does it intrude on privacy? What if half the workforce doesn't welcome this connection?

Even educators increasingly feel that making all students appear on camera for online classes is a bad idea. According to Roxanne

---

181   Henry Ford Health Staff, "How Staring at Our Own Faces on Video Calls Can Impact Body Image," Henry Ford Health, April 13, 2021, https://er.educause.edu/blogs/2020/9/dear-professors-dont-let-student-webcams-trick-you.

Russell, director of online education at Columbia University, professors teaching online see greater levels of distraction, as students become preoccupied with their appearance and that of others.[182] Instructors have also found it impossible to monitor all their students' little video boxes at once, leading to cognitive overload.[183] Some virtual meeting hosts know just how they feel.

Our view is that the best option is to make video optional. To start with, comfort level and level of control are directly related. When people feel that they have a measure of control in how they present themselves, whether walking in the park or logging into a Zoom call, they feel more confident and comfortable. Except in certain cases, such as client meetings and hiring interviews, the decision should be up to the individual. The simple fact is that appearing in live online video does cause anxiety in many workers, deterring engagement and sapping productivity. The worker's personal preference should be respected because it's good for the worker as well as the company. In addition, for those who do choose to use video, we show them how to hide their video stream on their own screen while on virtual calls, which can be very easily done and reduces the chance of appearance-related stress.[184] Even if the host wants to start the meeting with everybody on camera, attendees should be given the option to decline. We also instruct meeting schedulers to indicate in the meeting invitation the degree to which video use will be expected.

Mandating video means more preparation time—which can cut into work time. This may be even more of an issue for female staffers,

---

182   Ibid.

183   Matthea Marquart and Roxanne Russell, "Dear Professors: Don't Let Student Webcams Trick You," *EDUCAUSE Review*, September 10, 2020, https://er.educause.edu/blogs/2020/9/dear-professors-dont-let-student-webcams-trick-you.

184   "See or Hide My Video," Zoom Support, updated February 28, 2022, https://support.zoom.us/hc/en-us/articles/115001077226-Hiding-or-showing-my-video-on-my-display.

as women spend, on average, nearly a third more time than men getting ready in the morning.[185] Thus, mandating video may represent an additional hurdle for female remote workers, who, according to a 2020 study, are already significantly less likely to receive raises and promotions than their male telecommuter counterparts.[186]

Some situations, such as important client meetings, introductions, and presentations, do require camera use. But companies would be wise to limit webcam mandates to calls that fall into those baskets and leave it up to the individual in all other cases—and make sure that staffers know it's optional. As of mid-2022, we've started to see some of our larger clients back off their camera mandates, a trend we welcome. In the near future, we may well see legislation that bans or limits video mandates.

Optimize All Contact Points

Businesses should ensure that their remote and hybrid workers do all they can to look professional across all online business platforms. Absent the interpersonal environment of the workplace, remote workers need to compensate by presenting themselves in their best light. And they should be driven to do so by the understanding that doing so doesn't just benefit the company but also enhances their career prospects.

Much like the company itself takes steps to scrub negativity from its online presence prior to interviewing job candidates (see chapter 3), remote workers should make sure that their personal online

---

185 Devon Kelley, "This Is How Much Time the Average Person Spends Getting Ready in a Year," Yahoo! Life, January 26, 2016, https://www.yahoo.com/lifestyle/this-is-how-much-time-the-average-person-spends-214856853.html.

186 Megan Cerullo, "Working from Home Is a Better Deal for Men Than Women, Survey Indicates," CBS News, August 28, 2020, https://www.cbsnews.com/news/work-from-home-men-more-productive-women/.

presence maintains a certain level of professionalism. Start with personal photos and avatars on workplace messaging platforms like Slack and Microsoft Teams, and continue through email signatures, covering any virtual contact points between remote workers and colleagues, bosses, and clients. In many cases this extends across social media.

> **Absent the interpersonal environment of the workplace, remote workers need to compensate by presenting themselves in their best light.**

A high-end professional photo and impressive CV on LinkedIn mean little if your new remote manager is wearing a white supremacist T-shirt in his Facebook profile photo or your new human resources manager advertises her OnlyFans page on her Instagram account. This is not to say that your company should dictate your employees' personal lives or online presence, but staffers should be aware of the potential negative impact on their future work prospects and be encouraged to keep problematic and unprofessional, not to mention illegal, content out of public view. Your remote employees work online all day; thus, to some extent their online presence also represents the organization with which they are most closely affiliated.

The Power of Headshots

Creating a strong and confident online presence is not just about one's appearance on video calls. A 2012 study on facial features found that people decide to trust someone within a tenth of a second of seeing their face.[187] First impressions, then, happen literally in the blink of an eye, which is why the foundation of a positive online presence is

---

187   Timothy R. Campellone and Ann M. Kring, "Who Do You Trust? The Impact of Facial Emotion and Behaviour on Decision Making," *Cognition and Emotion* 27, no. 4 (2013): 603–620, https://www.tandfonline.com/doi/abs/10.1080/02699931.2012.726608.

an excellent headshot. Long dismissed in many parts of the corporate world, a strong headshot not only casts the worker in a good light but also casts the company in a good light, suggesting a commitment to professionalism. We encourage managers to budget for all employees to sit for professional headshots and put their best face forward across all platforms, from the company website to LinkedIn, messaging apps, and email. A strong headshot can ace that first impression and quickly earn a client's trust, while the lack of one suggests a certain unprofessionalism and may sow seeds of doubt.

The most important place for headshots is on meeting and chat platforms. All staffers should be encouraged to post a professional headshot, along with the company name, on any platforms they use for work. This enhances their credibility and makes it much easier to introduce all attendees, especially when it comes to cross-functional multicompany calls.

Over time, many of us have come to expect people to express themselves in their profile photos on platforms like WhatsApp and Gmail. But your company website should be free of party and vacation photos. Adam Jacobs, head of a major casting and talent management firm, explains it this way:

> You could have the most clean-cut, polished website, but it won't matter. Clients now associate your business with a selfie of Amanda and Bobby together at Taco Bell. While these kinds of "casual" photos are relatable, you don't want to confuse the client. Yes, it's important to highlight the human side of your company. But you can do that and maintain an aura of professionalism. Casual corporate headshots are

acceptable and may even be the better option, depending on your line of work.[188]

That last point is a good one because corporate headshots need not be one size fits all. A major law firm, for instance, is unlikely to present the same style as a tech firm. It's perfectly fine to be casual in presentation, as long as it's company-wide and professionally done.

At Virtira, which not only is fully remote but also advises companies on achieving optimal remote performance, it's crucial that we have a positive and professional online presence. We've even taken extra measures such as establishing lighting and background guidelines with a major headshot firm. Today, any one of our employees, wherever she may be, can sit for her portrait and come out looking, professionally speaking, much like the rest of us.[189]

On-Camera Presentation

Although we promote camera-optional video calls, we understand that webcams are a must for certain types of virtual meetings and that some remote workers may simply prefer being on camera. Particularly in a business environment rife with Zoom fatigue, a simple set of guidelines can help all of your employees, whether remote or not, make a strongly positive and professional impression in video calls, even when not at their best.

The below recommendations may seem elementary, but you'd be surprised how many workers forget them:

---

188 Adam Jacobs, "The Importance of a Good Corporate Headshot," *Forbes*, May 11, 2021, https://www.forbes.com/sites/forbesbusinesscouncil/2021/05/11/the-importance-of-a-good-corporate-headshot/?sh=31939b9c1108.

189 "Captivating Branding Headshots," Art of Headshots, accessed June 12, 2022, https://artofheadshots.com/branding-headshots/.

Smile: Nothing lays the groundwork for positive and productive interactions better than giving off joyful and friendly vibes from the get-go. Smile at "hello" and throughout the meeting to ensure a stronger positive energy.

Simple dress: The objective is not to draw too much attention. Loud, brightly colored outfits and T-shirts with political slogans should be avoided, as should clothing that aims to titillate. Dark, solid colors project confidence and professionalism.

Sit up straight: Posture says a great deal about level of interest. Slouching in one's chair or moving about the room to take care of a dog or toddler highlights a lack of commitment to the call. Sit up straight, listen, and stay engaged.

Curb negative signaling: Many movements give off a negative vibe. Crossing your arms signals superiority, touching your neck or face suggests boredom, and too much blinking means that you're anxious. You're not always going to avoid them, but just being aware of them and conscious of on-camera movements makes a big difference.

When your remote employees set up their work space, they should be advised to consider how they will appear on camera, particularly in terms of lighting and background. It's crucial that their faces are lit well enough that fellow attendees can see their eyes, which helps build trust. We are still amazed by the number of people who join a business call with only a giant forehead or their face in complete shadow. Nobody wants to make a deal with an extra from *The Blair Witch Project*. You might consider sending portable ring lights to any remote and hybrid staffers having lighting issues. These can also serve double duty as stands for mobile devices.

In terms of background, everybody wants to appear as if they spend their out-of-office work hours in a space with the warmth and gravitas of an Oxford library, but most of us work out of homes with neither a library nor a dedicated office space. The key is finding a background that's simple and neat. A clean, brightly colored wall works fine. A stocked bookshelf, a few vacation photos, a stylish poster, or a classy work of art will also do. There's nothing wrong with displaying some personality, as long as it's positive. Cynthia, for instance, often uses a wall of stringed instruments she's collected in her travels for her background, hoping that people asking about them might drive her to try playing one. Such personal touches can stimulate nonwork conversations and build stronger connections. But anything that might suggest a warehouse, junkyard, or raw space—think bare concrete, piles of junk, or stacks of boxes—should be kept out of frame. And you might want to consider whether you really want your kids, spouse, or roommates highlighted on platforms that are just a screen share away from social media.

Keep in mind that background is also dictated by the webcam's field of view: the smaller the field of view, the less background is visible. A webcam with a 62- or 78-degree field of view is preferable to a 120-degree cam since it's easier to control what people see. Portable green screens that attach to chairs or larger pop-up ones can hide a problematic background. You might also consider customizable background templates for your organization. Most platforms now allow you to upload your own graphic, so you can curate a look with your logo and have several options for staffers to choose from. These can be particularly beneficial for employees who interact with clients, vendors, and investors.

PRO TIP: LEAD BY EXAMPLE

Those in a position of authority should lead by example when it comes to virtual presentation. Make sure that your own online presence is as professional as you expect your remote workers' to be in terms of your online persona, your appearance in meetings, and your on-camera office space. Follow the guidelines in this chapter during on-camera meetings, and when sending meeting invites, indicate whether you expect cameras to be on or off and be willing to respect people's preferences.

CHAPTER 8:

Communication and Collaboration

Any problem, big or small, always seems to start with bad communication. Someone isn't listening.

—EMMA THOMPSON

Back in 2011, when remote work was in its infancy, David Grossman, founder and CEO of a Chicago-based communications advisory, examined four hundred large US and UK firms with a total of one hundred thousand employees and put their cumulative cost of poor communications at $37 billion, or an annual $62.4 million per company.[190] It's hard to imagine what these totals might be today, considering how much more difficult effective communications have become with the explosion of messaging apps and collaborative platforms and the rise of remote work. But the fact that a recent Salesforce survey found that 86 percent of employees

---

190   David Grossman, "The Cost of Poor Communications," PRovoke Media, July 16, 2011, https://www.provokemedia.com/latest/article/the-cost-of-poor-communications.

and executives cite ineffective communication as the primary cause of workplace failures hints at the depth—and cost—of the problem.[191]

The effectiveness of remote collaboration is inextricably linked to your team's ability to communicate. Being an expert in the most potent online tools is useless if you're unable to understand your colleagues' input or share your views with others. Communication is one of the primary challenges of remote work, which is why it's mentioned again and again throughout this book. In this chapter, we focus on the two main facets of remote communications—the words and messages sent and the tools and platforms used to convey them—and highlight how both must be done correctly to achieve optimal results.

Remote work requires more skillful and precise communication than in-office work, where managers can largely expect subordinates to pick up information by osmosis. Succinct, clear, and accurate communications are paramount in remote work, as miscommunications cannot be easily corrected by an impromptu in-person chat in the break room. It doesn't matter whether it is office to office, office to home, or office to field—today's working world runs on bite-size chunks of information that quickly get the message across.

Let's set aside the issue of having too many e-communications tools—Slack, Facebook Messenger, phone calls, emails, WhatsApp, Telegram, Zoom, Signal, and Google Meet—and assume that your company has been able to follow the guidance laid out in chapter 4 and has instilled in your workers an understanding of when to use each. The fact remains that remote work necessitates more skillful communication.

Businesses can no longer make assumptions about their managers' ability to guide staff on how to communicate effectively. Firms need to

---

191 "Workplace Communication Statistics (2021)," Pumble, accessed June 12, 2022, https:// pumble.com/learn/communication/communication-statistics/.

ensure that their managers devise and implement consistent communication protocols and practices. The more you standardize communication, the more focused and targeted it will be—substantially reducing the chance of missing or misconstruing messages. With that goal in mind, let's talk about how to create a viable communications strategy that enables remote workers to collaborate as efficiently as possible.

Even if your new hires have remote work experience, there's a good chance that it involves bad habits picked up as a result of problematic oversight.[192] As a result, it's crucial to lay the foundation for strong and effective online communication. In face-to-face conversations, it's difficult to ignore what the other person is telling you, although of course it does happen. Remote communications, on the other hand, can be exceedingly easy to ignore. This is why one of our most repeated bits of remote communications advice is don't assume that anyone is paying attention to anything you write or say. It's a motto you might want to post in the margins of your primary online communications tool.

The realization that there's a decent chance their messages will be ignored should help spur remote workers to craft more intelligible and effective messages that aim to appeal to the recipient rather than highlight their own concerns. After all, if the main risk is nobody paying attention, shouldn't engaging the recipient be the primary objective?

Message writers should seek to imagine the mindset of their recipients and practice the concept of WIIFM (What's in It for Me), focusing their communications on their audience's concerns and interests. Let's say that recently hired telecommuter Jane is messaging her remote colleague Thomas because she wants to know how she should process the latest data files. She might frame it by reminding

---

192   See chapter 3 for more detail.

Thomas that the quicker she's able to process the data, the sooner she'll be able to get started on the report he needs her to do. Suddenly, Thomas has more reason to respond quickly and helpfully. This is good WIIFM.

Regardless of the topic, the focus should be on engaging ideas and stories, not merely disseminating or requesting information. People tend to be turned off by data and lengthy reports and engage with easy-to-understand messages that are relevant to them.

Say More with Less

Shorter attention spans are part of the nature of any work performed over a distance, so it's crucial to help employees block out distractions. From the moment they wake up in the morning, workers are bombarded by social media pings, coworkers' messages, emailed offers, news notices, and texts from friends, dating apps, and their mobile service provider. This doesn't even include, if they're working at home, pleas for attention from their spouse, children, and pets or noise from neighbors and nearby construction work. Diversions are all but inevitable because of the steady bombardment. Yet in-office staffers and remote workers alike are left to run the daily gauntlet on their own.

To minimize the potential for distraction, your remote workers might set their phones aside and listen to calming background music, such as classical or atmospheric music or whatever their personal preference is. Much more important, however, is that all work-related communications grab the reader's attention and remain simple and succinct, with an eye toward the visual. The best staffers can catch a manager's attention in just a handful of words and convey their message in a few sentences. We are a bite-size society, and at Virtira, we encourage everyone to think in Twitter-size messages with everything they send out. We constantly reinforce this. When Cynthia gives an internal presentation, she'll often show a series of slides full of crossed-out text, revealing the editing process that delivers a stronger final message. During our updates, we highlight not only targets met and results achieved but also particularly effective and impactful messages between colleagues. We urge managers to regularly hone their skills and pass them on to subordinates. Like wearing a mask during the pandemic, taking the time to write clear, concise messages is a kindness to others that reflects well on you.

Employees should always assume that messages will be shared with the world. If someone curses or insults others over email or instant message, it's very easy to take a screenshot and send it company-wide. Operate under the assumption that all your messages will at some point be read by coworkers and superiors who are not among their intended recipients. From there, write all communications with the same level of care and attention to detail as those written for the boss. This

> **Employees should always assume that messages will be shared with the world.**

way, employees are always aware of the importance of language regardless of intended recipients or message content. Even an invite to a virtual happy hour event should be succinct, professional, and inoffensive. References that might elicit an appreciative chuckle from coworkers in person might go over less well with other coworkers in writing. The goal in content and tone should be to ensure that one's grandmother would be neither offended nor confused.

Messaging Style

To put it simply, employees need to focus on writing less to communicate more. They should avoid pointless comments and asides and be strategic and concise with their messaging. In addition, they and their managers should be aware that writing strong, effective, and shorter messages tends to take more time than writing longer, rambling missives. That's to be expected. One of the more insightful statements on writing comes from seventeenth-century French philosopher Blaise Pascal, who informed a friend: "I've written you a long letter because I didn't have time to write a short one."[193] The implication, of course, is that dense, concise writing takes a great deal of time because of edits and rewrites. The vast majority of writing, in fact, is editing. Putting words on the page is not even half the battle. Your employees should understand this. Your remote hires may have their struggles and slipups in their early days, but eventually, if these concepts are drilled into them, their messages will be free of pointless jabber and filled with clear, succinct sentences.

To speed up their learning curve, you might want to give all of your employees the best guide on succinct communications ever written, *The Elements of Style*, by William Strunk Jr. and E. B. White.[194] Countless writers and journalists keep a well-worn, dog-eared copy of Strunk & White, as it's known, within arm's reach. It's barely one hundred pages, but few books hold more insight—particularly today, as the careers of millions of workers rely on their ability to put one word after the other. Here's an almost randomly chosen sample:

---

193   "If I Had More Time, I Would Have Written a Shorter Letter," Quote Investigator, April 28, 2012, https://quoteinvestigator.com/2012/04/28/shorter-letter/.

194   William Strunk Jr. and E. B. White, *The Elements of Style* (London: Pearson, 1999).

Choose a suitable design and hold to it.

A basic structural design underlines every kind of writing. Writers will in part follow this design, in part deviate from it, according to their skills, their needs, and the unexpected events that accompany the act of composition. Writing, to be effective, must follow closely the thoughts of the writer, but not necessarily in the order in which those thoughts occur. This calls for a scheme of procedure. In some cases, the best design is no design, as with a love letter. But in most cases, planning must be a deliberate prelude to writing. The first principle of composition, therefore, is to foresee or determine the shape of what is to come and pursue that shape.[195] ☐

Message style and design are crucial elements of clear communication. It's not always *what* is said, as much as *how* it's said, that determines success. Staffers should be trained to be brief and direct, organize their thoughts in a structured manner, avoid flowery and inappropriate language, and cut out the bits that are unnecessary or irrelevant. The objective is to take advantage of short attention spans, not challenge them.

How many times have you received an email that takes a good eight to ten minutes to wade through only to realize when you finally reach the end that it has nothing to do with you? You'll never get that time back. This should rank among the writer's top objectives: don't waste people's time. Messages should flow logically from one point to the next and minimize adjectives and adverbs as well as overwriting, or what's often called "purple prose." Nobody needs to struggle to understand your point or be distracted by excessive descriptions and

---

195   Ibid., 15.

overblown language. "Just the facts, ma'am" could be your motto. Stick to the point because people are busy and want to know what's being communicated as quickly as possible.

The goal is to make your entire company gobbledygook-free. The problem is that a lot of people, even established professionals, are unable to tell gobbledygook from insight, especially when it's about an issue that's close to their heart. A good way to determine whether this or that bit of text within an e-communication is worthy of inclusion is to ask two questions: "How important is this to the broader thrust or main goal of my message?" and "How important is this to the message's primary audience?" If the answer to either of these questions is "not very," bid adieu to the section in question.

Cynthia's childhood on the farm brings to mind a good example. If a storm was coming and a cow got stuck in the mud in the back forty—the section of farmland farthest from the house—her father wouldn't stroll into the house and start talking about how lovely the cow was, which of its parents it looked like, and what it had eaten for lunch. He'd shout, "Cow down!" and everybody would pile into the truck to make the rescue. Of course, there's no need to shout, and more than two words can be used, but generally speaking, your remote workers should emulate Cynthia's farmer father: get to the point already.

Another useful exercise is to use the billboard messaging approach to help visualize communications. The idea is that the time you have to make your point is equal to the amount of time it takes to drive past a billboard—about three seconds, give or take. With that in mind, communications should convey only the absolute essentials. They should be both front and center and visually engaging. Whatever the content, this makes it much easier for recipients to quickly grasp the bottom line.

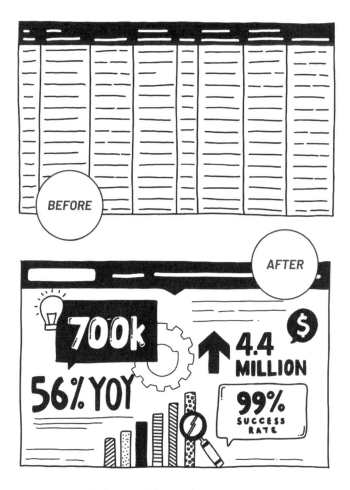

Make your information engaging.

These two images perfectly illustrate the point. Would you rather receive an unfathomable list of microscopic numbers or an appealing and lively infographic highlighting key data points? For most, the choice is clear. Again, the focus should always be on engaging ideas and compelling stories rather than on the numbers themselves. Data visualization works well in the office, but it's much more valuable and impactful when working remotely—the equivalent of a meeting room presentation from hundreds of miles away.

Collaboration

We now have at our fingertips about a billion tools (only a slight exaggeration) that aim to boost productivity, even for colleagues separated by thousands of miles. Forget phone calls, texts, and email; today, it's all about video calls, chat, collaborative platforms, and more. One area in which remote work shines is in real-time cloud collaboration.

We recently took part in an online meeting in which all seven participants—none of whom were in the same location—had the same shared Google document open on their screens and reviewed the report together. To be clear, the meeting's host did not lead attendees through the document on a screen he was sharing. Each attendee had separately used their browser to open this same document just as the meeting began and then proceeded to go through it, making corrections and comments and suggestions while on the Zoom video call. Within the document on their screen, every participant could see the cursors of the others. Thus, when anybody made a comment or expressed a thought, everybody knew which part of the document the speaker was referring to and could quickly grasp the point.

In less than fifteen minutes, the group made its way through a three-page document, and all the relevant tasks—who would do additional research, who would reach out to the client, who would do the final edit and review, and when all of this would be completed—had been decided and assigned. Would they have gotten all of this done as quickly had they been in the same room together? Probably not.

There are countless other examples of valuable collaborations through cloud-based tools. Centralized collaboration platforms can also help boost your company's structural integrity. We favor Kajabi, Smartsheet, and Confluence, but many platforms offer invaluable organizational tools. By putting as much as possible under the same virtual roof, you simplify company-wide communications and the learning process for new hires. At any given time, our team is often spread to the four corners of the earth.

These tools make it much easier to ensure that everyone is optimally productive wherever they might be. All employees are able to scan all the latest data, assignment statuses, reports, and so on at any time, from anywhere. Everybody is thus expected to be aware of the latest policy decisions and meeting discussions shortly after they happen. Nowadays, we rarely send files—they've been replaced by links to shared docs, databases, and spreadsheets. These speed up communications and reduce the storage burden on our servers and staff computers. Every file is simultaneously available everywhere, on every device.

This brave new collaborative world comes with a few hurdles. The first is the tool licensing and platform subscription fees, which for any sizable business can add up fast. Suddenly, you're paying thousands of dollars each month for services few employees use. At Virtira, we regularly review all of our subscriptions and licensed tech tools and cancel any that are no longer worthwhile. We urge you to do the same.

The next challenge is security. The more you put on the cloud, the greater the chance that the inner workings of your business could be exposed or compromised. It's important to consult with a cybersecurity professional about your firm's potential exposure and take widely recommended steps to increase security, such as ensuring two-factor authentication and only single sign-on for each username. Your firm would also be wise to create a password management system under which all user passwords, particularly remote user passwords, are periodically changed.

Email versus Messaging

Email has been in wide use in the business world for eons, and you'd think that we would have gotten the hang of it by now. But it's often misused when it comes to remote work. One issue is that work emails can easily be lost in a sea of spam, newsletters, social media updates, and messages from friends and family. Even with dedicated work email addresses, important information can be impossible to find in a thread that runs for weeks on end. Not to mention the cc messages that everyone responds to ad infinitum.

Most emails cannot be unsent, even when you've realized a millisecond after hitting the send button that you've written the wrong thing to the wrong person.[196] There's no way to guarantee that you can retract and rewrite. This can of course be a huge problem, especially if the email includes private information. One of our managers at Virtira once composed an email for other managers about firing a problematic staffer, and when he sent it, he must have had that staffer in mind because he had included him among the recipients. Let's just say that the situation would have had a much better outcome had that manager been able to unsend the message.

You know what does allow message retraction? Messaging platforms like Microsoft Teams, Webex, and Slack. These tools also enable easy, flowing conversations among groups of colleagues and help us find key bits of information more efficiently. We learned this the hard way after hiring someone who had never worked remotely before. Our new hire was unfamiliar with messaging platforms and sent informal discussion communications almost entirely via email.

---

196   Nithya P. Nair, "Gmail's Undo Send Feature Now Allows You to Set Time for Recalling Emails: How to Enable It," Gadgets 360, December 8, 2021, https://gadgets360.com/apps/news/gmail-undo-send-email-feature-web-ios-update-recall-message-time-frame-rollout-google-2641956. As of 2021, Gmails can be unsent up to thirty seconds after "send" is hit.

As a result, Cynthia, who checks email only periodically, kept missing key bits of information about a crucial ongoing project. The entire process was solved by setting up a dedicated channel on a messaging platform where the back-and-forth could happen more easily.

Of course, email can still have a role, and sometimes it's the best option—for instance, when you need to time-stamp when a message is sent or when you need to send external communications to suppliers and customers. Email is also often best for lengthy, complex messages that lay out a problem or situation in detail (we still tend to use online tools like Confluence for these types of situations).

When they do write emails, staffers should be aware that the subject and first three lines are like Park Place and Boardwalk in Monopoly—and should similarly be ridden to success. The vast majority of the crucial information should go there. Recipients will allot maybe three seconds to your subject line and opening, so grab their attention by being direct and concise. Attention-grabbing subject lines work well when emails are urgent or when a response or action is required. Use asterisks if necessary. Last, encourage everyone to use the "delay send" feature, providing a chance to reflect on the tone and content of the message before possibly ruining a relationship or their own career in a fit of pique.

This is not to say that messaging and chat are panaceas. One issue we've recently discovered with chat and instant messages is that some of our staffers use them to store information, files, notes, or links to documents. One problem with this is that if their employer is not fully subscribed to that tool, older messages are likely to be deleted, leaving that staffer out of luck. But this also points to the broader point that chat and instant messaging should be used primarily for real-time discussions happening now, today—not for long-term record keeping and document storage. That's a recipe for trouble.

In addition, as companies grow and add teams, clients, and vendors, many are willing to keep adding one new online platform after another. The end result is that your company finds itself wrestling with a dozen different chat platforms, none of which allow everybody to communicate in one place. Your work may not be as important to national security as counterterrorism, but this echoes the siloing of roles within the FBI and CIA that led directly to the attacks of 9/11. Once your teams and staffers start separating into smaller groups, embracing this or that tool or platform, communications and connections are likely to erode, undermining productivity and engagement. At Virtira, we recently undertook a comprehensive assessment of our chat tools and platforms and reorganized around those that best serve our staff and our goals. Within days of its completion, we felt a stronger sense of connection.

PRO TIP: STANDARDIZE AND TEMPLATE EVERYTHING

How should your staff best take advantage of today's communication and collaboration tools? Creating organization-wide templates for operational practices sharply reduces uncertainties, keeping everyone moving in the same direction and helping new hires speak the same "office language" as everyone else.

So establish standards for everything: meeting agendas, minutes, action items, project plans, dashboard use, status updates, escalation, and risk callouts. Allow customized alterations and iterations of the template, and conduct annual reviews to update employee innovations, as the goal is striking a balance between ensuring uniformity and creating opportunities for employees to contribute. Be sure to make all templates readily available in an easy-to-find dashboard or online drive.

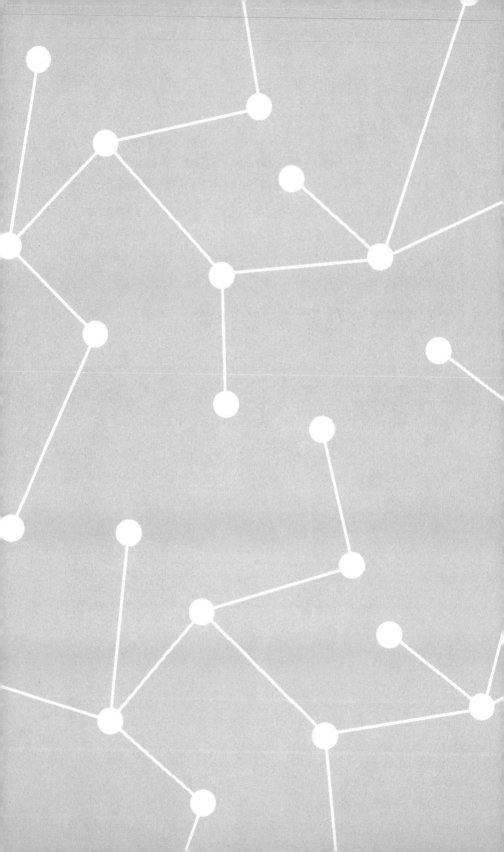

CHAPTER 9

Making Meetings Work

People who enjoy meetings should not be in charge of anything.

—THOMAS SOWELL[197]

When everybody works in the same office, meetings are a simple affair: just send a message to all relevant staff, and everybody heads into the conference room. Somebody might be out getting coffee or busy making copies, and there's always the possibility that the meeting itself is a complete waste of time. But generally, the process of getting together is relatively seamless.

Virtual meetings are a whole different animal. So much can go wrong, starting with gathering the troops. Some may be in a far-off land and miscalculate the time difference. How many meeting requests for four in the morning have you received? We've had our fair share,

---

197 "Thomas Sowell Quotes," BrainyQuote, accessed June 12, 2022, https://www.brainyquote.com/authors/thomas-sowell-quotes.

which is somewhat understandable considering the global distribution of our staff. Others might have trouble figuring out how to launch the meeting platform, while some are able to log on but can't hear or be heard. Presentations don't share properly, or they freeze. The wrong camera is broadcasting, or the recording feature malfunctions. In professional settings, such incidents can destroy credibility, so you want to make sure that they don't happen on your watch.

For starters, it's important to make clear the differences between in-office and remote meetings. In the office, for example, conversations often begin with a casual back-and-forth, the kind of friendly, personal chat that builds rapport. Such chitchat often includes inside jokes and personal exchanges. In remote meetings, on the other hand, small talk is difficult because one-on-one exchanges are all but impossible, and nobody wants to tell all the attendees about their neighbor's barking dog or troublesome hair. Furthermore, familiarities that are commonplace in the office can be inappropriate in a virtual meeting. For these reasons we advise managers to keep the pleasantries professional and no longer than three minutes at the start of a call. That's more than enough time to say hellos and make sure that everybody's present before getting down to business. If they go longer, say, even ten minutes, there's the risk that some attendees might start showing up late in the expectation that the preliminary chatter will mean that they don't miss anything. If that happens, you've suddenly lost crucial meeting time.

Another key difference between in-office and remote meetings is that the latter are often recorded. In an office meeting, somebody might be taking notes, but that off-color comment your colleague made about your new client will quickly disappear into the ether. Things said on virtual calls, meanwhile, could one day end up as evidence in court. It's important that staff and management are aware of this and speak with care. You don't want to end up in a Perry Mason moment. Advise remote workers that if they're not sure about the language they're about to use, they should always lean toward safety. As we said in chapter 8, all communications should be grandma approved. Even in terms of joking, others might see the humor differently. And since body language can be impossible to read when all you can see is a person's head, any physical signals are likely to be lost in transmission.

We've Got to Stop Meeting Like This

Few workplace tropes are as apt as the useless meeting. And those of us who have left our twenties far behind are all too aware of how much of a problem this was even in the pre-COVID-19 era. In 2013, software firm Atlassian estimated that unnecessary meetings cost US businesses $37 billion in lost salary hours each year.[198] Around that time, executives were spending nearly twenty-three hours per week in meetings, up from less than ten hours in the 1960s.[199] Even a decade ago, nearly half of all workers (47 percent) felt that their biggest time waster was too many meetings, while more than seven of ten said that they brought other work to meetings, underscoring just how little they expected to get done.[200]

The more things change, the more they stay the same. How popular did videoconferencing become when the pandemic hit? In

---

198 Sebastian Bailey, "Just Say No: How Your Meeting Habit Is Harming You," *Forbes*, August 8, 2013, https://www.forbes.com/sites/sebastianbailey/2013/08/08/just-say-no-how-your-meeting-habit-is-harming-you/.

199 Leslie A. Perlow, Constance Noonan Hadley, and Eunice Eun, "Stop the Meeting Madness," *Harvard Business Review*, July–August 2017, https://hbr.org/2017/07/stop-the-meeting-madness.

200 "$37 Billion per Year in Unnecessary Meetings, What Is Your Share?," Meeting King, October 21, 2013, https://meetingking.com/37-billion-per-year-unnecessary-meetings-share/.

April 2020, Cisco's Webex logged twenty-five billion meeting minutes, more than a threefold increase from the total reported that January.[201] But the better question, one much more difficult to calculate, is how many of these meetings were necessary or effective.[202] At the start of the pandemic, many managers likely went a bit overboard in their efforts to make their newly isolated workforce feel more comfortable, mandating online happy hours and pizza parties in an attempt to keep everyone connected. Unsurprisingly, this yielded mixed results. Many workers found little joy in the obligatory get-togethers, mainly because, in one of the most nerve-racking periods of their lives, potential chill time became work time.

An absolutely crucial managerial skill today is the ability to determine when a meeting is necessary and when a group chat will suffice. By now we're all aware of the very real problem of Zoom fatigue. It's not a myth: endless hours spent being attentive and relatively chipper on camera make for exhausted and less productive workers. This is why managers and team leaders need to decide wisely. Before scheduling a meeting, they should ask themselves whether it's *really* necessary. All meetings, but particularly virtual meetings, should have a clear purpose beyond the simple sharing of information.

Unless you're making a presentation to many people, all of whom will be muted, off camera, and limited to Q&As, you should also consider pruning your guest list. Just because your software can handle

---

201 "Reported Meeting Minutes of Cisco Webex Worldwide in 2020," Statista, accessed June 12, 2022, https://www.statista.com/statistics/1106500/cisco-webest-meeting-minutes/.

202 We see these as the two best indicators of meeting utility. In large part, the level of necessity is about premeeting—the understanding and determination, beforehand, that the meeting needs to happen. Effectiveness is a measure of the host's organizational ability and attendees' willingness to engage. A necessary meeting could end up being ineffective, while an unnecessary meeting could deliver some information that ends up driving greater productivity. The best of both worlds, of course, is a necessary meeting that ends up being terribly effective.

fifty people at once doesn't mean that you have to invite everyone involved in a project. When preparing the invitation, think like legendary organizer Marie Kondo, and leave off anyone who doesn't "spark joy."

Consider no-meeting days across the organization. Instead of a four-day workweek, consider a four-day meeting week. We implemented this a couple of years ago, and the response has been overwhelmingly positive. Your staffers will love you for it, and meeting-free Fridays mean more time to get work done before the weekend.

Meeting Excellence as Core Competence

Encouraging everyone in the organization to be familiar—and up to date—with all the bells and whistles of multiple meeting platforms is critical. Following the recent company-wide platform switch, for instance, that button used two weeks ago to share a screen might now be the "Leave Call" button. Oops. At Virtira we've been using some of these platforms for more than a decade, but we still face occasional challenges. We rotate meeting leads so that everyone is constantly honing their skills and familiarity with different platforms. It should be a continual learning system that emphasizes doing rather than knowing, if only because today's virtual collaborative environment is a fast-changing landscape. You don't want your employees to spend fifteen minutes at the start of a meeting figuring out how to hear someone they've accidentally muted. (Full disclosure—one of us did this while testing a new platform. Never mind *who*!) And you *definitely* don't want remote hires shouting, "Hello? Hello? *Hello?*" into their mics for what feels like an eternity.

Speaking of which, your new remote stars should know how to recover from muting mishaps, screen freezes, and bandwidth crashes, both for their own sake and to help fellow team members. Make sure that a backup presenter has access to the presentation and can click through slides while the presenter talks. And as highlighted in chapter 5, sound quality is paramount. Testing audio before meetings should be routine, not an occasional precaution. Recently, we had somebody presenting on a call who sounded as if she were speaking from inside a rain barrel—a *full* rain barrel. Her slides were lovely, but we still have a few questions about her proposal.

It's a good idea to mandate practice sessions for new hires, who may be unfamiliar with your company's conference tools. This will give them an opportunity to run faux meetings, saving you and your remote teams much trial and tribulation. People will still stumble, but much less frequently, and their learning curve will be steeper. This

Meeting
Netiquette
Training

expectation should be especially stressed for staffers expected to regularly make presentations. They should do at least one dry run, if not two, and master the basics of hosting a virtual call, including locating files, sharing their screen, adding new attendees, and so on. And of course they should repeat this whenever new features

are released or your firm switches to a new online meeting platform or collaborative tool.

Presenting online is about much more than sharing screens. Staffers should also be trained in creating short, crisp, and organized presentations and in encouraging interaction. They should also know that it's OK to make mistakes. We're all human. When things go wrong, they shouldn't dwell on it but should keep their chin up and keep moving. Finally, it's a good idea to test your teams, not just the new hires and presenters, on tech competency to ensure that everyone understands best practices for virtual tools. We advise firms to set up a special online space hosted by staffers who have mastered your company's main platforms. These more experienced staff members can answer tech questions from new hires and everybody else. We have found no better way to ensure that tech speed bumps are minimized.

We also recommend seeking ways to make meetings fun. In 2020, Virtira hosted a two-day virtual conference at which we asked people to present on a topic that was important to them. Some presented on their work, while others presented on pet projects, including their pets. During the year-end holiday season, we like to find ways to generate one-hundred-dollar donations to a team member's favorite charity on Virtira's behalf. In 2021, it was a talent show in which everybody had two to three minutes to showcase their skills. The event was not without its cringeworthy moments, as people did their darnedest to get that one hundred dollars, but in the end it was a ton of fun. Best of all, we all got to know each other better—which will pay dividends down the line.

The Power of the Agenda

Your meeting invitations should always include a detailed agenda listing the subjects and issues to be discussed and the staffers expected to address each topic. This provides a clear structure to the call and gives any workers who might have valuable input enough time to prepare their thoughts. The host should always work from an agenda to ensure coverage of all key points and keep kiss-of-death moments of silence at bay.

A meeting without an agenda is sort of like an airplane without a runway. You might be able to get the thing off the ground, but are you going to be able to bring it in successfully? Embedding agendas within the invite so that everyone gets in the habit of reviewing them is a smart practice. Even a brief agenda communicates to all participants the purpose of the call and the topics to be covered, helping everybody mentally prepare. Additionally, some invitees, having gone over the agenda and found nothing of great relevance to their work, might not join the meeting, leaving you with fewer attendees to wrangle. And this is something you might want to add to your invite—giving those who are not key participants the option to decline. You might also give attendees the ability to add agenda topics, particularly if it is a series of meetings.

The Perfect Host

Most of your employees are likely to host an online meeting at some point, so it's a good idea to train everybody in meeting etiquette. Here are our best practices when it comes to organizing, hosting, and attending virtual meetings:

Schedule in advance: When it comes to scheduling meetings, preparation and timely notice are key to productivity and success. Some meetings will of course be called at the last minute to address some urgent issue. But in all other cases, attendees should be given more than enough time to prepare. At Virtira, we send out invites at least a few days, if not an entire week, before the call.

Share meeting link: It's best to include the meeting link in the invitation. If you forget, or your preferred platform doesn't allow it, send it out to all attendees the day before the call at the latest.

Set ground rules: Premeeting communications should also include meeting ground rules such as "Don't interrupt; instead, use the chat tool." Take the time to write up the rules, and include them in every invitation so that everybody is aware of what is and is not acceptable.

If it's a series of meetings, you could encourage buy-in by making establishing the ground rules part of the first call. Make it fun, maybe with an online collaboration board like Miro.

Recurring invites: If you expect your meeting to regularly recur, maybe weekly or monthly, there's no need to send out new invitations each time. Set up a recurring invite notification, and include a multiuse meeting link with your original invitation.[203] Just be sure to fill out the new agenda before the invites go out.

Autoreminders: Yes, they can be annoying, but the fact is that people are busy, distracted by other work, friends, family, or the big game. Be sure to set autoreminders for at least a day before the meeting so that someone who needs to prepare something doesn't find out about it fifteen minutes before. You want everybody fully prepared and ready to go when meeting time arrives.

Take good minutes: Whether or not the meeting is recorded, a designated notetaker should take minutes during the call and then write up a meeting report detailing key points, commitments, and deadlines, as well as next steps.

Designate an alternate host: God forbid that you get sick or face an outage or unexpected emergency, but these things do happen, and sometimes at the last minute. It's important that the meeting goes on as planned and productivity continues uninterrupted. So when you send out invites, be sure to name an alternate host who will take over the call if needed.

Meeting literature: Whenever possible, collect all presentations, reports, and documents to be discussed in the meeting, and share

---

203 Most major platforms (Webex, Teams, Google, Zoom) offer this capability.

them prior to the call. In your invitation, you could also remind attendees to review these. Be sure to send them out again just before the call; otherwise, you'll have presenters twiddling their thumbs as participants search for key files.

Check tech in advance: All workers, remote and in the office, should check tech well before the meeting starts. That way, if there is a problem, there's time to resolve it. In meeting invites and particularly in reminders, the host should remind participants to check their tech. New hires in particular will want to avoid embarrassing themselves with an accidental muting. Not a good first impression!

Log in early: A virtual meeting host should always log in early, be the first to arrive, and welcome all attendees. We advise logging in five minutes early, giving you enough time to test your tech and get set up before attendees start logging in. Arrive late, and you've already lost some of your audience's trust and attention.

Test and test again: Before pressing the launch button for the meeting or logging in, ensure that your sound is working properly. Test the microphone and, if it's a videoconference, the camera as well. Don't assume, like the cat lawyer did, that critical tech will work because it worked before.

Limit small talk: A few minutes of small talk before a call moves forward is perfectly reasonable. But if leadership is in attendance, skip the premeeting chitchat, and get to the point: "Hello, I hope everyone's doing well. Thanks for joining. Let's start with …" And off you go.

Master the mute: Do you like being distracted by coughing, typing, and barking dogs? Neither does anyone else, which is why meeting hosts should urge all attendees, in their invites, to stay on mute when not speaking. In case any attendees are unsure how to mute or unmute on this or that meeting platform, advise them to ask for help.

Slide syncing: When sharing a presenter's slides with the meeting, be sure to stay in sync with the presentation; otherwise, you could end up with a presenter talking about the latest sales numbers while everybody's staring at an ad for dog food. Patience is often a good approach, as it is 100 percent acceptable for the presenter to say, "Next slide, please."

Stop when you're done: When you block out an hour for a call, your agenda should target a meeting length of fifty minutes (for a half-hour call, aim for twenty-five minutes, etc.). For starters, one or two previously unknown issues are sure to emerge during the call, necessitating further discussion and extending the meeting a few more minutes. Additionally, many attendees, not to mention the host, are likely to have back-to-back meetings scheduled and will appreciate having a few minutes between calls to stretch, grab a coffee, or take a bathroom break.[204] For those without another meeting scheduled, you've just given them more time to do their work. Either way, it's a thoughtful gesture likely to boost morale and productivity.

Discourage Stragglers

Some years ago, Cynthia worked for a senior vice president who blocked access to meetings one minute after the scheduled meeting time. Any invitees who failed to log in by then were unable to attend,

---

204   Remember that back in the days when we had back-to-back meetings in an office, we were at least able to get up and walk to the next meeting room, giving our mind and body a bit of a break. Setting aside those brave folks with standing desks, today's remote workers often go hours on end without stretching their legs.

and the call went ahead without them. For the vice president, being sixty seconds late meant that you didn't value his time or the time of other attendees. He tolerated no excuses for arriving late and kept a list of all who failed to turn up on time, which was a real black mark. A draconian approach, to be sure, but it worked. The share of late arrivals went from about 30 percent at the start to zero just a few weeks later.

We don't necessarily recommend this approach, but we do agree that time is an invaluable commodity and that waiting for late arrivals is unacceptable. Such pauses cost the organization time, money, and productivity. Over a yearlong period, a few minutes lost waiting on each call add up to a significant expense. There's also the frustration of those forced to wait, which could curb their willingness to offer insight when the meeting finally does move forward. Suddenly, your company has lost out on important ideas. Finally, when people are consistently late, others tend to perceive it as rude and disrespectful. So perhaps take a cue from that vice president and block meeting access until stragglers get the message. If you are in an organization with frequent back-to-back meetings, consider starting them five minutes after the hour and ending them five minutes before the end of the hour to give people a chance to catch their breath and still arrive on time to the next call.

We advise managers to clearly lay out in their invites that the meeting will start on time, as planned, and to urge all attendees to be ready for the meeting five minutes early. Managers and meeting hosts who still struggle with stragglers should put in place a deadline for logging in, perhaps two to three minutes after the call's scheduled start time. If attendees continue to turn up late, they'll soon learn their lesson by being forced to sit out.

The Power of Icebreakers

We've found virtual "icebreakers" to be an excellent way to build engagement, warm up a virtual audience, and energize the discussions that follow. Usually just five minutes long, these camera-optional exercises can serve to break up an intense workday and help everyone get to know each other. They have been our top choice for engagement exercises since Shane introduced them a few years ago, when they were an immediate hit with the team. Rather than evening socializing events that tend to add hours to an already packed week, these are quick activities we incorporate into meetings a few times a week.

Again, a few minutes of chitchat prior to the start of a meeting is fine, even welcome. But icebreakers offer something more, encouraging people to let down their guard, speak more freely, and have a few laughs. This in turn leads to stronger bonds and better working relationships. See some of our favorites in the accompanying box or a more extensive list on our website.

ICEBREAKER EXAMPLES:

Name Positivity:
- Rearrange the letters of your name.
- Add or replace one letter.
- Create the most positive word you can.

Phone Poetry:
- Start a text message on your phone with the word "work."
- Choose from the phone's suggestions for the next ten words.
- Share your poetry.

Rock, Paper, Scissors Tournament:
- Agree on the rules, and divide attendees into pairs.
- Each pair plays a round, with the winner taking two of three.
- Each winner faces off against another winner.
- Continue until you have a tournament winner.

PRO TIP: FUTURE PROOF YOUR MEETING MINUTES

In the near future, designated minute takers will be obsolete, as autotranscription tools will be fast, free, and completely reliable. Most meeting platforms already offer autotranscription as a basic feature, and there are also third-party plug-ins you can use. Generally, these tools are not yet ready for prime time, but they're likely to get there soon. In the coming year or two, we expect to greatly reduce our administrative overhead with AI and online tools that perform a number of jobs like this.

To build best practices and take advantage of these tools now, it's a good idea to get your hosts in the habit of issuing instructions such as "Action item: Mike will buy drinks for the beach party," "Decision: We're having a beach party," or "Risk: The state has issued a hurricane warning." This makes it easier to later pull key elements out of the meeting, as you can easily search the transcript for "Action," "Decision," and "Risk." This also helps the software put minutes together easily and quickly instead of wading through ten pages of transcribed notes.

It's likely to be a few years before these tools catch up to human capabilities, but they can already make a huge difference, especially for multilanguage meetings. If you know how to use them properly, it can be a lot like kicking back and giving instructions to Alexa.

CHAPTER 10

Achieving Remote Accountability

On good teams, coaches hold players accountable. On great teams, players hold players accountable.

— JOE DUMARS

What, exactly, is accountability? In the simplest terms, it's about delivering on one's promises. For a firefighter, that means getting to the fire as quickly as possible and doing everything within his power to limit the damage to structures and lives. For a politician, it means living up to commitments made on the campaign trail once in office. For workers, it's about achieving this or that objective by the deadline.

Accountability is also about taking ownership and what we do when we fall short. To be accountable, the firefighter who gets to the fire too late must review his route and preparation, nail down the precise reasons for his delay, and institute changes to avoid them in the future. The accountable politician (if only!) would acknowledge his failure and lay out why he failed and how he will improve. Likewise, when your workers fail to meet deadlines and commitments—and they inevitably will because we're all human—to be accountable, they must review their performance, find the errors and glitches, and take action to eliminate them. And it's crucial that their accountable bosses do the same.

Accountability might seem like low-hanging fruit for optimizing organizational performance, but getting there can be complicated. Accountability means committing and completing, but it's also about acknowledging and improving. And even within these elements, there are smaller accountability building blocks, such as time awareness, dedication, engagement, and simple ability.

All of this is critical to optimal performance, yet today's working world is experiencing an accountability crisis of monumental proportions. A 2016 study of more than forty thousand workers delivered disturbingly problematic results.[205] For starters, eight of ten said that they got feedback only when they failed or never at all. Even more than that, 85 percent weren't even sure what their organization hoped to achieve. And 93 percent were unable to align their work or take accountability for desired results. Finally, when it came to holding others accountable, 82 percent said that they either tried and failed or avoided it altogether.

This is bad enough in an office environment, but for individuals connecting remotely, it could be catastrophic. This chapter outlines how best to address this problem in today's more complex working world. We'll assume that you know what you and your teams hope to

---

205 "Landmark Workplace Study Reveals Crisis of Accountability," Culture Partners, accessed June 12, 2022, https://culture.io/landmark-workplace-study-reveals-crisis-of-accountabil-ity/. Note that this study was carried out by Culture Partners, formerly Partners in Leadership, a consulting firm that trains organizations in leadership and that stands to gain from a working world that lacks accountability.

achieve. We will instead lay out the basics of accountability that every employee and manager should know—much the same information we constantly reinforce to our new hires. This chapter is all about getting it done and making sure that others do the same.

The Age of Distraction

Long before the pandemic, our work taught us that ensuring accountability over a distance is a major challenge. The office environment almost organically demands accountability. "If I don't do this right," the relatively new hire might think to himself, "I'll probably be replaced by that new intern." This sort of thinking trickles down from the CEO (who toils in fear of the board) all the way to mail room staff.

Improving accountability is foundational to the office concept: we gather in a single space in part because proximity drives us to compete and deliver. With remote work, this has all been erased.

> **Accountability means committing and completing, but it's also about acknowledging and improving.**

If I cannot see my competition or how my boss is pulling his hair out because of anxiety about my work, I'm less motivated to meet deadlines and deliver results.

Those old-school managers who worry about staffers goofing off when not at their desks likely had cause if they applied in-office management methods. In 2012, three of four workers polled by Siemens found remote team members likely to be distracted during virtual meetings, while more than a third (34 percent) thought that remote workers were loafing or not doing their share of the work.[206] In a 2021 study by Hubstaff, three of the top four challenges faced by managers of remote work were linked to accountability: 41 percent said that it was hard for remote workers to stay motivated without teammate interaction, 36 percent said that remote work made it more difficult to know what people were working on, and 34 percent said that it was more difficult to check in on remote workers.[207] In addition, one of four managers cited a lack of accountability as one of the biggest hurdles to successful remote work.

The pandemic-driven increase in remote work has moved the goalposts: achieving accountability was already a tough slog, and it just got more difficult. Many managers and staffers are suddenly collaborating over a distance with little understanding of how to ensure efficiency and productivity. Social media and various other apps and doodads—remember when Wordle was suddenly ubiquitous?—are constantly vying for our attention.

Hybrid work models mean that half the time, remote workers and managers may be unsure where team members are or how best to get in touch with them, as highlighted by the Hubstaff study. As our work routines have changed, we need new strategies to make sure that everyone actually gets stuff done. Using accountability practices that worked in the office to manage a distributed workforce is like trying to jam a 110-volt US plug into a 220-volt European outlet. As any traveler knows, it simply does not fit. What do we need instead? We

---

206   Siemens Enterprise Communications, "Siemens Enterprise Communications Survey Highlights Untapped Potential of Teams," Cision, October 24, 2012, https://www.prnewswire.com/news-releases/siemens-enterprise-communications-survey-highlights-untapped-potential-of-teams-175576081.html.

207   "2021 Remote Project Management Report," Hubstaff, accessed June 12, 2022, https://hubstaff.com/tasks/state-of-remote-project-management.

need training and reinforcement on accountability across all levels to prevent workflows and projects from grinding down to a snail's pace.

The Sound of Silence

One of Amazon founder Jeff Bezos's less well-known workplace innovations is silence.[208] Years ago, he banned PowerPoint presentations at all meetings. Meetings at Amazon instead begin with a period of silence, during which attendees are expected to read a report or memo and take notes before jointly discussing its content. Bezos likely didn't institute this approach because of his disdain for PowerPoint (could you blame him?) but to ensure accountability. Because so many managers and executives previously acted as if they had read the report and bluffed their way through the call, he saw this as the best way to make sure that all attendees were familiar with the material. Other tech firms, including Twitter and Square, have since instituted similar approaches to meetings, and an increasing number of consultants urge managers and meeting hosts to avoid presentations, mainly because their lack of interactivity leaves attendees feeling uninvolved.[209]

Many managers believe that when their teams are engaged and connected, they will be accountable. They therefore spend a great deal of time improving engagement and connection in the hope of improving results. Such efforts are not entirely misplaced, as social science research does show a connection between accountability and

---

208 Taylor Locke, "Jeff Bezos: This Is the 'Smartest Thing We Ever Did' at Amazon," Make It, October 14, 2019, https://www.cnbc.com/2019/10/14/jeff-bezos-this-is-the-smartest-thing-we-ever-did-at-amazon.html.

209 "7 Reasons Why You Should Stop Using PowerPoint," Speech, accessed June 12, 2022, https://speech.me/reasons-you-should-stop-using-powerpoint/.

engagement.[210] However, such studies also find that the link tends to go in the other direction: a culture of accountability boosts employee engagement. This dovetails with our experience, which is that when it comes to remote work, accountability is the start of the journey.

As in the office, it takes only one team member slacking off to bring a project to a screeching halt. With remote work, however, the added hurdle is that it's almost always impossible to tell in advance which of your workers might be dragging their feet. In the office, you can see that Edward is rarely at his desk or keeps calling in sick or taking three-hour lunches. With remote workers, the warning signs are much more difficult to discern. That's why, in the past few years, managers have desperately tried myriad ways to boost accountability with constant check-ins, tracking hours and mouse clicks, more on-camera meetings, and regular team-engagement exercises. They've mostly failed.

Our approach to accountability begins with the expectation that everybody will be distracted and nobody will be accountable or even know what they need to do. From there, a strategy takes shape. We ensure that there's a record of what everyone is being held accountable for—all targets, deadlines, and commitments—and a reinforcement structure must be in place to be sure that they follow through. The main objective is to enable everyone to cut through the distractions of remote work, to quickly and clearly convey the importance of deadlines and commitments, and to ensure that everyone knows how to meet them.

The Power of Meeting Minutes

In the previous chapter, we advised you to assign someone to take meeting notes, or minutes. Well, they come in most handy when it

---

210   Catherine Park, "Accountability in the Workplace and How It Ties into Employee Engage-
        ment," Hppy, accessed June 12, 2022, https://gethppy.com/employee-engagement/
        accountability-workplace-ties-employee-engagement.

comes to accountability. More often than not, it is during meetings that teams and departments assign tasks—Julie will get feedback from the new clients, Sam commits to researching caterers and choosing one for the big event, and Tony agrees to complete our latest prototype next month. With a well-developed meeting accountability process, all of these assignments end up in the meeting report, which is saved in an easily accessible folder in an online drive and is available to all.

At Virtira, we train everyone to take notes during meetings and whip up minutes after the call has ended. What's important is that everyone in a meeting knows that everything that's said in that meeting, every task and deadline commitment, will be held to account. With this, an appreciation of the seriousness of their commitments is woven into their meeting DNA. Results depend on decisions made during meetings; if the latter are lost, the former will be as well. Most workers find taking meeting notes as exciting as white-washing a fence. But it's in meetings that many of the verbal agreements and decisions that determine productivity and performance are made, and creating a record of these is a key component of achieving accountability over a distance.

> *Our approach to accountability begins with the expectation that everybody will be distracted and nobody will be accountable or even know what they need to do.*

In the absence of a meeting recording, without good notes there's no way to prove who agreed to what. Capturing all of the key takeaways—such as targets and deadlines set, commitments made, actions planned—makes it easy to follow up. Just choose your notetakers wisely, or you could end up with notes like this one from a court clerk in old Cairo: "Then they said a lot of things that would take too long to explain."[211] Good luck explaining that one to the boss.

Having someone designated to capture key items frees other attendees from having to worry about making note of any important assignments or decisions. Of course, minutes shouldn't be a rambling narrative of every comment made during the call; they should always be concise and to the point. See our website for a template.

Meeting
Minutes Template

Shortly after the meeting, send the minutes out to all invitees, including those unable to attend. You might also append a note urging attendees to share the minutes with any others who might be interested in the information. The minutes should clearly communicate who will be held accountable for what. This might seem obvious, but it's especially common in a remote context for leaders not to specifically identify who is responsible for outcomes.

Time and time again, we hear of meetings where a team member points out a glaring shortcoming—several partially redundant internal instructional guides could be edited and combined into one, or the system for filing report reviews has several unnecessary steps—and everybody on hand agrees that it's a real issue that should be urgently addressed. Yet when the next meeting rolls around, it turns out that nothing's been done because the task was left unassigned. Everybody had assumed that the staffer who pointed out the issue would take care of it, while the staffer herself figured that it would be addressed by the person responsible for that area of operations. Such assumptions erode productivity: ambiguity, uncertainty's fraternal twin, is also the enemy of progress.

---

211   Princeton Geniza Lab (@GenizaLab), "Next time you're the designated note taker for a Zoom meeting, a handy phrase from an 11th-century Jewish court clerk in Old Cairo: 'Then they said a lot of things that would take too long to explain,'" Twitter, January 1, 2022, 1:29 p.m., https://twitter.com/GenizaLab/status/1477361390490816512.

A detailed plan of action that identifies the responsible parties and sets firm deadlines and targets must be nailed down. Commitments must be secured for completion dates and who is responsible for which tasks. When assignments are not linked to deadlines, time frames are left open to interpretation and, not surprisingly, team members will have varying perceptions of how to prioritize.

Setting a timetable for everyone helps them plan and organize their work and creates a sense of urgency, ensuring that tasks won't be set aside or simply ignored. A deadline is vital to helping employees deliver results. If leaders fail to establish clear deadlines, they should not be surprised when tasks are not completed on time. More importantly, when deadlines are firmly and publicly set, everybody is aware when somebody has failed to deliver, which is often enough pressure to drive workers to deliver.

Multiplatform Reminders

At the heart of remote accountability is a commitment to no assumptions or ambiguity. Everybody should know what they have to do, and everybody should be aware of what others are doing to encourage a broader culture of accountability. The reality is that most employees will be aware of their commitments and deadlines. But the best way to keep workflows and projects on track is to expect that this is not the case.

For years, we've used a series of tools, starting with Excel and moving to Smartsheet, to track actions and display status. On larger cross-functional initiatives and with clients, we may need to use a project management tool. At the individual level, Cynthia uses good old pen and paper and a daily to-do list, while Shane uses Smartsheet. Others send themselves emails or calendar reminders. Regardless of how individuals keep track of their actions, we have overlay systems that report progress daily. Most importantly, we have humans who follow up on progress across all levels.

Online systems with autoreminders enable us not only to see progress on any project with one click but also to generate dashboards for the entire team so that everybody knows who's ahead of the game and who's falling behind. Online systems also enable users to submit thoughts and ideas before a management call, giving attendees time to adapt, prepare, and cover the relevant issue in detail during the meeting.

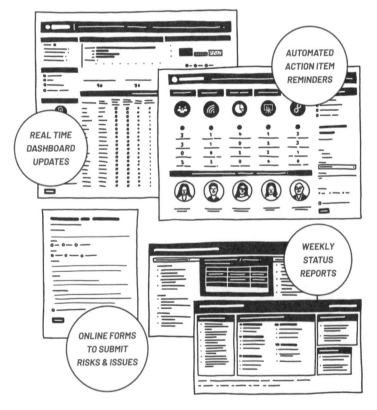

Dashboards help keep things on track.

These images highlight a few of the online dashboards we use to keep ourselves and our clients on track. Encouraging staffers and particularly new hires to post to these dashboards helps promote tech competence and provides broader exposure to your firm's communications and operational practices. These dashboards can be programmed to automatically update cross-departmental data, keeping crucial bits of information such as financial reports and human resources announcements up to date and accessible to all.

The Human Element Is Key

Everyone on our team knows or quickly learns that achieving accountability requires proactive involvement. At Virtira, we teach that managers and team leaders cannot simply communicate expectations and a deadline and leave it to autoreminders to ensure that everything will be done on time and to their satisfaction. This is particularly true with remote work, when bosses are unable to stroll over and check on a staffer's progress. The solution is regular check-ins and reminders, sometimes via a dedicated staffer.

Dashboards and workflow charts should be updated with the latest status so that when the team meets, everybody knows how projects are proceeding and who's holding things up. All levels expect that if they commit to something, someone will regularly check their progress on that deliverable. And even if the staffer doing the checking is five levels below the executive being held accountable, the latter knows to be responsive and respectful.

Yet many organizations face accountability challenges from the top down and bottom up. Leaders are often hesitant to regularly check in out of fear of being labeled a micromanager or being seen as distrustful. Such concerns are outweighed by the fact that checking in reinforces the importance of the task and provides team members with an opportunity to seek additional information or request assistance if needed.

Checking in also increases the likelihood of a task being completed on time, which means that it's also a productivity issue. By training all new hires that this is an expectation and grounding this behavior throughout the organization, it becomes embedded in the culture.

In addition, by establishing regular, mutually agreed-upon checkpoints, leaders can avoid negative perceptions, assess team members' progress, and offer feedback and coaching as needed. Rather than waiting until the completion date to assess progress—at which point it will be too late to adjust—leaders can identify challenges early and offer guidance to ensure completion.

At the same time, many lower-level staffers avoid holding their superiors to account because they fear being put in the doghouse and not receiving that long-expected raise or promotion or, even worse, getting fired. But even leaders sometimes need reminders and prodding. In fact, in many organizations, it's the leaders who most appreciate reminders and check-ins. This is because they have so many plates in the air that they fear that this or that task may be lost in the shuffle.

It's therefore essential to establish a policy that nobody is above the law: any staffer, from the CEO on down, who fails to deliver on commitments will be held to account. We establish early in training that there is organization-wide agreement on universal accountability. We make clear that nobody will be allowed to slack off because of their pay grade. In our organization, if a vice president has said that she will do something, it is perfectly reasonable for a junior manager and an intern to check in on the vice president's progress. Without this embedded in the culture, you simply will not be able to make progress because key individuals will not be held to account. Accountability has long been one of the more prominent concerns of our working world, and it's even greater today with the sharp increase in remote work. These strategies can help your organization achieve it.

PRO TIP: SAY NO TO FIRE DRILLS

At Virtira, the term "fire drill" means a last-minute request from a client or a manager to change course. Fire drills are usually a result of poor planning and tend to devastate productivity.

Last-minute, out-of-the-blue emergencies that necessitate dropping everything do sometimes happen and do require a shift in priorities and a significant response. But these are, in our experience, very rare. And these are actual fires, not "fire drills."

A typical fire drill would be a Friday-afternoon message from a manager to a staffer: "Hey, can you have this in my inbox Monday morning?" Suddenly, the staffer who received this message has the not-so-subtle directive that the work is expected over the weekend to get it done.

Over the years, we've also noticed that it's rare for those who actually make such requests to even assess whether the recipient followed through. The task or target is often

less urgent than originally presented, and the manager's real objective was simply to flex their authority and make that task a priority.

In remote, this type of management behavior, if not checked, will lead to burnout. In this scenario, even if the staffer has no special plans that weekend, time off needs to be respected. That manager needs to either request that staffer's time in advance or refrain from sending that message and causing a five-alarm fire drill.

As a result, one of our core values, which we reinforce during onboarding training and mentoring, is "say no to fire drills." We want everyone to know that surprise last-minute requests, especially those that lead to unnecessary overtime or weekend work, are unacceptable.

Most importantly, we empower our employees to say no to unreasonable eleventh-hour demands from clients and senior management and escalate if these occur on a regular basis.

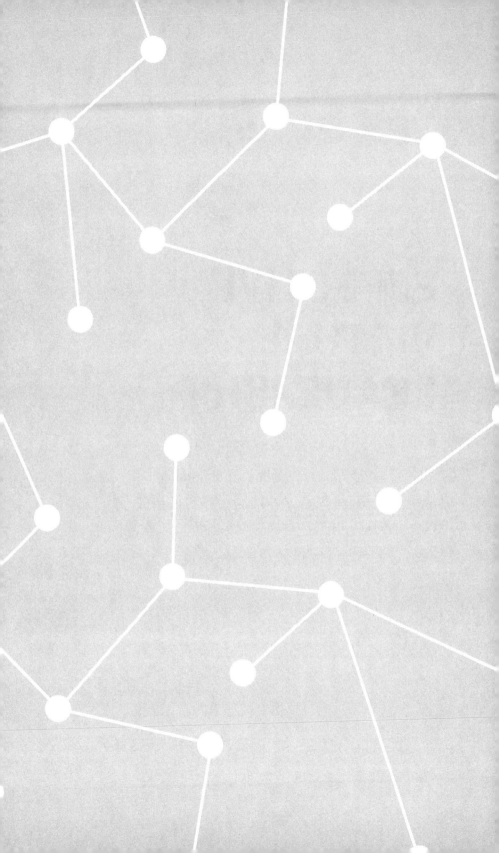

EFFECTIVE VIRTUAL LEADERSHIP

The secret to success is good leadership, and good leadership is all about making the lives of your team members or workers better.

—TONY DUNGY, SUPER BOWL–WINNING
HALL OF FAME NFL COACH

When COVID-19 first began to rear its ugly head, Robert Bowness, a manager at BC Pension Corporation, knew that his team would be nervous about coming into the office and risking infection. So he decided to take the decision out of their hands and do something pretty amazing (and maybe a bit crazy). One morning, Bowness and a couple of workers strolled into company headquarters, visited each of his team members' workstations, and grabbed their ergonomic chairs and computers. They then drove to the homes of each of the team members, placed the chairs and computers in their driveways or building entrances, and texted the team member from the delivery van. When team members came out to see what was happening, Bowness smiled and waved and then drove to the next team member's home. Oh, and before dropping off the chairs and computers, Bowness and his helpers wiped them all down with isopropyl alcohol.

To be clear, we're not urging business leaders to start carting furniture all over town. That was an extraordinary moment that inspired an extraordinary gesture. But Bowness understood that his actions would demonstrate great empathy for his employees and their needs, strengthening their connection to him and the firm. He was betting that this would motivate them to continue to give 110 percent, despite their world suddenly being turned upside down by a raging pandemic. Our point here is that the more you are able to demonstrate concern for your people, particularly amid crises and over a distance, the more engaged they are likely to be, increasing efficiency and productivity.

You've built a fantastic remote and hybrid team that's begun to dive into their work. The crucial question now is, Are you ready to lead them? Leading an in-office team is child's play compared with leading one that stretches across time zones, mindsets, workdays, and settings. It requires significantly more discipline to ensure that everybody arrives on time to team meetings and one-on-ones, which will need to happen with greater frequency to keep everybody on the same page. Of course, as discussed early in the book, it's crucial that you avoid micromanaging, as staffers who feel that their boss is always looking over their shoulder tend to be less-than-stellar performers. You'll also need to find meaningful ways to demonstrate empathy remotely and inspire your team to new levels of efficiency and productivity.

What are your objectives as a leader of a remote team? As with an in-office team, it all begins with purpose, or helping the team to understand the importance of their work, and alignment, getting everyone on the same page. Establishing ownership through key metrics is crucial, as is creating engagement via an inspiring and positive culture. Finally, at the peak of the pyramid is the ultimate objective: instilling the type of passion that makes team members excited to tackle projects, learn new skills, and create their own goals.

Part IV will climb through these steps one by one right after the next chapter, in which we share some broad strokes about being an effective virtual leader.

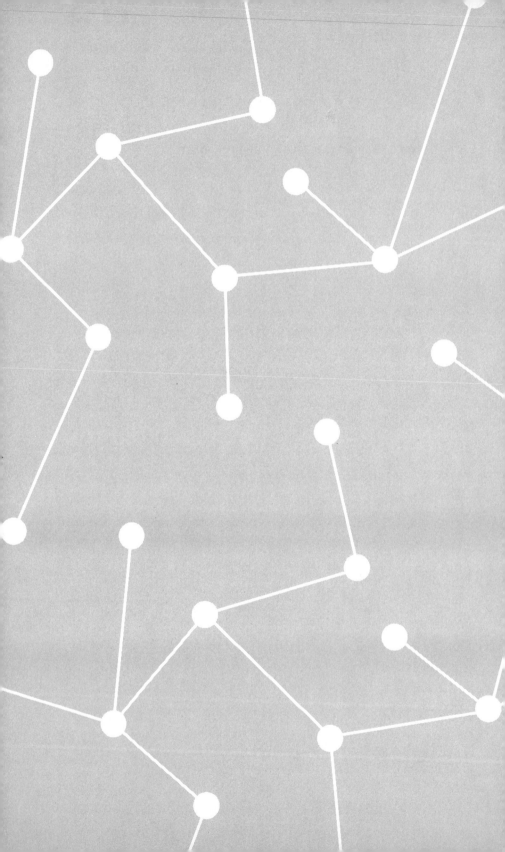

CHAPTER 11

Optimizing Remote Leadership

*Great things in business are never done by one
person. They're done by a team of people.*

—*STEVE JOBS*

I n the days before the pandemic, millions of people around the
world saw the 2019 Marvel blockbuster *Avengers: Endgame*,
but very few, we'd bet, noticed how accurately it highlighted
the pitfalls of managing remotely. For what seemed like weeks, poor,
beleaguered Black Widow tried to keep the team on track, Hawkeye
battled a crime syndicate in Tokyo, Captain Marvel zipped off to who
knows where, Iron Man did his stay-at-home-dad thing, and Captain
America assumed that they'd all hung up their superhero capes. It's
hard to imagine a remote team communicating less effectively, which
is why in the first half of the movie they get almost nothing done.

The Avengers' main problem may have been that they had no
clear leader. Effective remote teamwork requires a high level of coor-

dination, and as the department manager or project manager, you bear this responsibility. If you have little remote management experience, you, like your workers, will need some training. This is no slight against you or your abilities; overseeing remote teams is a skill set most managers lack simply because it's so different from traditional office management. Luckily, most remote management challenges aren't as severe as those Black Widow faced, although they often feel that way.

This chapter lays out best practices managers can use to get their team of Avengers on the same page and embracing the same culture. And keep in mind that when we discuss teams in this chapter, we are referring to teams working within a single department such as marketing or accounting, rather than a cross-functional team working across several departments, which is addressed later in the book. Intradepartmental remote teams may be less complex than cross-functional units, but that doesn't mean that they don't require some wrangling to get them to function effectively, particularly over an extended period of time.

The primary challenge of managing remote teams is obvious: without regular in-person interactions, you as the team lead need to find ways to overcome that hurdle and keep the team connected. The ancillary challenges created by this physical separation are significant. Because you're not speaking directly or daily to your charges, feedback is often perceived differently and can be more easily misinterpreted. For instance, a chat message sent by a manager you haven't seen in person in months is much more likely to come across as cold and critical than the same message sent by a manager you just chatted with an hour ago in the break room. After all, emojis can go only so far.

These communication risks aren't limited to managers. Miscommunication among team members can cause even more complications. What's more, even if you do have regular virtual meetings, and we recommend you do, the risk of misinterpretation is still high. Perhaps most critically, since you no longer have the casual conversations with team members that you'd enjoy if you ran into them in the hallway, the personal rapport that strengthens bonds and understanding is greatly reduced.

But it's not all doom and gloom. Remote work also offers some advantages. Supervising remote workers forces you to structure communications and accountability in a way that might spur quicker progress than if everyone were in the same office. Plus, the nature of remote work forces employees to work more independently. Basically, it's sink or swim: a team member either will or will not be able to perform well toiling away on their virtual island. Those who are able to handle it will make your job easier because you will be able to rely on them.

Approaches to Managing Remotely

Remote management does demand more, well, managing than in-office management. Rather than actively staying abreast of team members' latest doings, understanding what needs to be done by which date and by whom, and grasping how the team's results align with corporate values and objectives, someone managing office staff can place a sticky note on a team member's desk and leave it to that person to deal with. Such lax oversight isn't possible when managing remotely.

Some of the most important components of remote leadership, such as being consistent and proactive, keeping everyone focused, and staying agile and able to pivot when needed, do also apply in the office. But remote managers need to lean into these concerns, mainly because remote work is less social and more about the actual work.

A recent study found that in-office workers spend less time working than scrolling through social media, taking breaks, and discussing out-of-office activities with coworkers, among other non-work-related activities. On average, the nearly two thousand office workers polled worked on their actual work for a bit less than three hours per day.[212] Remote workers, on the other hand, work up to 30 percent more hours than they did in the office.[213] And because remote teams are working more hours, they're also asking more questions and making more demands on managers' time, which means that team leaders need to be more engaged and focused than ever before.

For managers overseeing remote or hybrid staff, the following should be primary objectives:

Consistency: Consistent communication with remote teams is essential. Without it, confusion rules, productivity droops, and insecurities bloom. A remote worker tasked with producing content in the annual corporate report, for example, will likely start to feel anxious if the manager she relies on for content guidance fails to provide a timeline or respond to queries about initial drafts. Communicate and follow up; wash, rinse, and repeat. Strong remote work is often simply about repeating processes that work.

Proactivity: Your remote team members are out there working on their own islands and thus need to know that they

---

212   "How Many Productive Hours in a Work Day? Just 2 Hours, 53 Minutes … ," Vouchercloud, accessed June 12, 2022, https://www.vouchercloud.com/resources/office-worker-productivity.

213   "Remote Workers Work Longer, Not More Efficiently," *Economist*, June 10, 2021, https://www.economist.com/business/2021/06/10/remote-workers-work-longer-not-more-efficiently.

can depend on their manager's guidance regarding assignments, responsibilities, protocols, deadlines, and more. Being proactive rather than passive is a crucial element of making your team feel more confident and secure. The more you allow remote workers to drift off course, the farther out to sea they'll end up. Stay ahead of the game through proactive engagement.

Focus and flexibility: Good remote management involves keeping everyone focused on the same goals, even while setting flexible deadlines. Stay on top of what each person is working on, and make corrections when necessary. This doesn't mean that you substitute surveillance for skilled management. Good remote workers can manage themselves. But you should provide support when needed. Rather than constantly telling them what to do, trust that they already know, and provide the structure that helps guide them to their deliverables.

In terms of timelines, sometimes you'll need to be flexible. Business is unpredictable, and you never know when a partner will fail to deliver or when corporate strategy or the economic reality will shift, rendering the existing deadline an impossibility. Even setting those possibilities aside, team members may be unable to meet deadlines for a variety of personal or professional reasons. When possible, it's a good idea to let remote workers suggest their own deadlines and then negotiate an agreeable compromise.

Where Virtual Management Diverges from Traditional Management

There are several areas in which virtual management diverges from traditional in-office management. Because they're out of sight, remote workers often feel like their efforts will never result in advancement within the company. This is not, in fact, unreasonable. As detailed in chapter 2, chances of advancement are considerably lower for those who work outside the office. Although it's important to note that these are historical data, recorded in the days when remote workers were much more rare, and thus this may well be changing. Either way, managers can help close this gap by working with team members to lay out a path for progression and set milestones. This helps remote employees feel more appreciated and shows them that the organization is looking out for their best interests by aligning their skills and goals with corporate objectives.[214]

Managers should also shift their managerial style from being *task based* to being *results based*. Obviously, managers will not always be there to assign every team member their next task, so remote workers should be given intermediate and longer-term targets and be able to extrapolate what they need to do to hit them. As also highlighted in chapter 2, remote worker productivity should never be about hours worked, mouse clicks, or keyboard strokes—or even tasks completed.[215] The primary metric must be results delivered or targets met by individuals and the team as a whole.

Finally, because you are far from your employees, they may start to feel helpless if they come to a roadblock or moment of uncertainty. Collecting quarterly feedback via anonymous surveys and sharing the

214 Alignment will be discussed in greater detail in chapter 12.

215 "Company or Cult?"

results with the team is a great way to minimize this risk. And it's crucial that the survey questions are specific rather than vague. At least one or two of the queries should be open ended rather than multiple choice, allowing the staffer to write their views in their own words. But it is wise to use both. Since quantifying written data is less clear cut than simple checkmarks, closed questions help provide a broad overview of your team. In addition, team surveys spur greater ownership and engagement, as does results transparency. This regular survey feedback should offer detailed guidance for reforms and improvements that, when implemented, should be linked to the feedback so that team members see that their input has value and makes an impact.

Reinforcing Company Culture

If you stacked all the books about corporate culture on top of each other, you wouldn't need Elon Musk's SpaceX to reach the moon. There's a very good reason for this: strong culture is core to company success. As detailed in chapter 6, a company is defined by its culture, the set of shared principles and assumptions that guides its behavior. As a result of these agreed-upon beliefs, certain actions, stances, and decisions are either encouraged or discouraged.

Culture doesn't equal "social"; rather, culture is the collective habits of the organization.

To build and reinforce culture, we have to remember that culture doesn't equal "social"; rather, culture is the collective habits of the organization. Moreover, company culture can differ from team culture, as teams within that company may have their own collections of habits and beliefs. This is understandable because, over time, people in constant collaboration develop their own social frameworks and sets of acceptable behaviors. This is even more true for remote teams because they're not immersed in the on-site company culture. The problematic result is that subcultures that challenge broader company culture may emerge.

Inculcating remote workers with a strong sense of company culture is, therefore, crucial. In-office workers experience the culture firsthand every minute of every day—interacting with colleagues, seeing the corporate values poster next to the watercooler—and learn it almost by osmosis. Remote workers lack this advantage, so the culture must be constantly communicated and instilled. Doing so strengthens their organizational bond, keeps them from straying from the pack, builds a sense of purpose, and creates a feeling of community.

Much of the burden for cultivating culture falls on leaders and managers, who should refer to company values on a regular basis, linking them to decisions and outcomes. People tend to associate company culture with the office setting, such as rules that dictate in-office interactions and how one should approach superiors. Remote culture tends to be looser and more fluid, a vague collection of team members' habits and practices, such as whether calls require video and how new employees are hazed, errr … onboarded. As suggested throughout this book, with remote management, communication must be more deliberate, and company culture needs to be more explicitly and frequently defined, too. Managers need to reinforce culture by keeping it front and center, regularly referring to it on shared work sites, and demonstrating it in daily communications. At Virtira, we keep key elements of company culture prominently displayed on shared drives and workflow tools.

In addition, managers should define their personal operating principles. Great things happen when everyone knows how the boss operates. Transparency helps build team trust, understanding, and belonging, which are invaluable when it comes to productivity. So be sure to encourage a culture of sharing, of trusting one's colleagues and keeping everybody informed and headed in the same direction.

Another good way to build remote culture is to transform individual success into team success. This is done by fostering a culture in which employees feel that their own achievements and the achievements of their colleagues are part of broader team success. Encourage them to share successes and praise each other, to be open to each other's ideas and respect each other's time. Everybody should feel like a star so that no one feels left out. At Virtira, we have an incentive program that rewards high-achieving teams—for instance, when they do such great work that the client extends their contract. But it can also be more personal. If you want team members to care about your mission, it's important to care about who they are and recognize their contributions. Our human resources manager, for instance, created a dedicated public channel in Webex so that people can "high-five" each other for even minor accomplishments.

We also maintain a tip fund that any manager can use to request swag or gift cards for up to $500 for top performers. The tips are financed by funds allotted to workplace social events, which are of course much less frequent in this age of remote work. Of course, you don't want to make any of your team members feel as if they have disappointed, but at the same time, it's important to recognize team members who have exceeded expectations and consistently delivered impressive work. Keep track of those who have played a key role in driving the success of your team and your company, and be sure to reward them. Keep in mind that even a ten-dollar tip has value; it's really about being recognized.

It is important to distinguish that the tip fund is private praise, while a high-five channel is public and is therefore generally used for team members to recognize other team members. Managers need to be conscious that not all team members want public praise and that some may feel envious of teammates who keep receiving honors while they receive none. Our research suggests that nine of ten remote team members are not interested in public praise from management but only from their team.

Circumstances may require reviewing and updating key components of culture statements. The early-2020 arrival of the pandemic, for instance, spurred many firms to alter their practices, particularly in regard to reinforcing their culture. As highlighted in chapter 6, top tech firm Slack remade its onboarding process, converting all printed materials into online materials and presenting cultural values in interactive sessions rather than on paper. Systems that work in traditional offices often falter when applied to virtual work. Keep your eyes open wide, and don't insist on retaining a process that's curbing productivity or connection just because you're used to it. Remote work is a new world, and being flexible is crucial to success.

Finally, a burned-out team is an unproductive team, and although working hard should be a key part of your company culture, it's important to prioritize work-life balance. To ensure accountability, it's important that managers and leaders remain vigilant for signs of fatigue and waning enthusiasm. These may mean that an employee is working too hard or needs to be more engaged. Passionate people provide great results, and allowing your remote workers to take time off or switch to more fulfilling or engaging work is likely to help their passion bloom.[216] Unless it's necessary, avoid making demands on your workers' off-hours. During work hours, check to make sure that nobody's plate is too full, and push back on managers who make unrealistic requests. A significant component of this is accountability. Giving team members the opportunity to tell you when they can have

---

216   See chapter 5 for more on burnout and wellness.

something done rather telling them when it has to be done, as detailed above, is key to curbing burnout.

The more you're there for your team—the more you have their back and fight to keep them satisfied—the more they'll be there for you. Remember, your leadership sets the tone: lead by example, and team members will follow. One of the key takeaways from Gallup's annual management survey is the "cascade effect," which shows that employee engagement is directly influenced by the level of engagement shown by their managers.[217] Creating a sense of belonging, particularly in a virtual work environment, accelerates efficiency and productivity. "Culture eats strategy for breakfast," management guru Peter Drucker said years ago, and it still holds true today.[218] Build a constructive and inclusive culture, and your team will do all it can to deliver for you.

217   Amy Adkins, "Only 35% of U.S. Managers Are Engaged in Their Jobs," Gallup, April 2, 2015, https://www.gallup.com/workplace/236552/managers-engaged-jobs.aspx.

218   Shep Hyken, "Drucker Said 'Culture Eats Strategy for Breakfast' and Enterprise Rent-a-Car Proves It," Forbes, December 5, 2015, https://www.forbes.com/sites/shephyken/2015/12/05/drucker-said-culture-eats-strategy-for-breakfast-and-enterprise-rent-a-car-proves-it/?sh=5080fcf32749.

PRO TIP: ADD YOURSELF TO YOUR CALENDAR

You expect your team to always be on time and set reminders for their regular duties, so demand the same of yourself, and create weekly reminders of all the proactive steps you need to take to keep your team engaged and on task. These could be about goal setting and timetables, regularly reinforcing quality work, and monitoring for roadblocks and emerging problem areas. While many in-office managers already make a habit of calendar reminders, remote work demands greater vigilance.

CHAPTER 12

Aligning Team and Purpose

When you're surrounded by people who share a passionate commitment around a common purpose, anything is possible.

—HOWARD SCHULTZ

Are you looking to achieve anything beyond making money? Hopefully, you and your staff have a decent answer to this question because as *Harvard Business Review* points out, "You cannot spreadsheet your way to passion."[219] Especially when it comes to remote work, communicating and reinforcing company purpose can be a great challenge, yet it's also vital to attracting and retaining the right people. Establishing and sharing purpose is the first step to creating a community committed to doing their best work for a greater goal.

---

219   Lisa Earle McLeod and Elizabeth Lotardo, "Financial Targets Don't Motivate Employees," *Harvard Business Review*, February 26, 2021, https://hbr.org/2021/02/financial-targets-dont-motivate-employees.

For remote organizations, establishing purpose is not vastly different than it is in the office. Remote employees, however, need a more direct strategy when it comes to messages about purpose. In an office, as you might guess, employees' sense of purpose is enhanced by the proximity of so many colleagues and superiors, as well as by frequent in-person collaborations with fellow team members. Consequently, workers are able to get by with less focus on purpose and more reliance on their interactions with colleagues, which consistently reinforce culture. This all disappears with remote work, so managers of remote teams need to understand and regularly and clearly communicate purpose to their teams. Once you have instilled a strong sense of purpose, your team will put more of themselves into their jobs.

The story of how a small midwestern energy firm found its purpose shows just how true this is. Gerry Anderson never believed in the power of organizational purpose, so when he became president of Detroit-based DTE Energy, he sought other ways to motivate his thousands of employees—incentives, training, stronger oversight. Then the Great Recession hit in 2008, and his employees seemed even less engaged than usual. That's when Joe Robles, CEO of USAA, the leading financial services firm for the US military, invited Anderson to visit a USAA call center. There Anderson saw enthusiastic, fully engaged staffers going the extra mile for their clients. He learned about USAA's immersive four-day orientation of videos and instruction that ends with the new employee vowing to provide extraordinary service to those who have given the same to their country.[220]

Back in Detroit, Anderson made a video showing DTE's office workers, corporate leaders, truck drivers, and plant operators talking

---

220   Robert E. Quinn and Anjan V. Thakor, "Creating a Purpose-Driven Organization," *Harvard Business Review*, July–August 2018, https://hbr.org/2018/07/creating-a-purpose-driven-organization.

about their work before the company's customers—factory workers, teachers, doctors—described the impact DTE's services had on the local economy and community. The first group of employees to see the video gave it a standing ovation. When union members viewed it, some were moved to tears. Never before had their work been framed as a meaningful contribution to the greater good. The video brought to life DTE's new statement of purpose: "We serve with our energy, the lifeblood of communities and the engine of progress."[221]

Crucially, DTE's leaders embraced the purpose and wove it into the company's training programs, highlighting it at corporate events and meetings and incorporating it into culture-building activities. This example does not involve a primarily remote or hybrid team, but the lessons apply nonetheless. DTE staffers saw the purpose as authentic, and everything changed. Engagement scores spiked. DTE won a Gallup Great Workplace Award. Then another and another—five in a row, in fact. Best of all, from late 2008 to early 2022, DTE's stock price quadrupled.[222] Once Anderson shifted his focus to finding a purpose and hit on a strong one, his employees began to deeply engage and take pride in their work.

Managers of remote teams need to understand and regularly and clearly communicate purpose to their teams.

KPMG, one of the big four accounting firms, also experienced a purpose-driven transformation. After years of being led by executives who ran the firm like accountants—cautiously, deliberately, and with a foundation in numbers—the company did its research, discovered the impact it had had on global events, and nailed down the purpose

221   Ibid.

222   "DTE Energy Company," Yahoo! Finance, accessed June 12, 2022, https://finance.yahoo.com/quote/DTE/.

of helping clients "inspire confidence and empower change."[223] Once the purpose had gone company-wide, employee engagement scores hit record levels. One telling element of the KPMG story is the immediacy of the connection between purpose and engagement. Of the employees whose leaders regularly discussed purpose, nearly nineteen of twenty said that KMPG was a great place to work and that they were proud to work there. Of those working for leaders who did not discuss purpose, only about two of three agreed with those statements. Thus, merely discussing purpose with your employees, your team, can increase engagement and workplace pride by more than 40 percent.[224] That's a stunning leap that underscores the power of purpose, which applies even more to remote work.

More examples include Whole Foods, whose purpose "is to nourish people and the planet." The word "nourish" captures why Whole Foods is in the grocery business, while "the planet" refers to its core value of sustainability to protect the earth. In a simple phrase, Whole Foods captures what it does and why it's important. That's the kind of mission that can spur engagement and lead to passion. In 2016, Tesla changed its purpose statement from "To accelerate the world's transition to sustainable transport" to "To accelerate the world's transition to sustainable energy." Tesla's use of the verb "accelerate" is a clever allusion to its speedy electric vehicles, but it's that closing phrase that captures the company's "why." The shift from "transport" to "energy" underscores Tesla's ambitions beyond cars, developing batteries and other renewable energy storage products and solutions. Translation? Buy a Tesla, support the planet.

---

223   Bruce N. Pfau, "How an Accounting Firm Convinced Its Employees They Could Change the World," *Harvard Business Review*, October 6, 2015, https://hbr.org/2015/10/how-an-accounting-firm-convinced-its-employees-they-could-change-the-world.

224   Ibid. From 66 to 94 percent at KPMG.

Managers should strive to be a conduit of purpose for their team, and they can do so by involving the team in the creation of a purpose statement. To start with, each team member picks three words or phrases to describe their team. These words and phrases are then shared and discussed before the team votes for the top three. Once the final wording has been nailed down, incorporate your purpose statement into monthly team meetings, email footers, and presentation templates. Reference it during conversations with team members to reinforce the importance of their work.

Finding people who subscribe to your company's purpose starts with recruitment. Thus, it's important to include your purpose statement in job postings and ask candidates how they align with your company's purpose during interviews. Establishing a strong purpose and an ongoing strategy to reinforce it throughout the organization can be time consuming, and there may be a desire to get on to more important matters while working on its creation. But underestimating the value of a strong, shared purpose is risky business.

The Power of Core Values in Remote Teams

When the entire staff is operating in lockstep with company values, it creates a shared understanding in terms of direction and purpose. Most companies maintain a list of core values and principles. But consistently promoting those values among your remote teams is another matter, as is truly bringing those values to life in your day-to-day work. With today's tech tools, there are a myriad of relatively easy ways to share your firm's core values virtually. Using a tool like Confluence or SharePoint, for instance, you could establish a team front page that clearly displays values and purpose and is seen by all team members as they log in every day. You could also use screen savers, desktop backgrounds, and prepresentation slides at all-hands meetings to deliver the same messages. You don't want to be constantly clubbing them over the head with culture, as if you're in some dystopic regime, but the more remote workers are exposed to company values, the more they'll internalize them.

As the story of DTE shows, a great way to communicate core values within remote teams is to tell compelling stories that humanize your company and bring its goods and services to life. Employees should also be encouraged to share accounts of how their work fulfills the company's purpose.

Meanwhile, management should constantly be challenging itself to identify and improve how values are demonstrated in the organization. Employees should be able to see how they represent a living, breathing part of how the company does business. At Virtira, we value work-life balance and the freedom of remote work, and we embed these principles in everything we do. This includes the skills we look for in new hires, involving employees in setting goals, and the way we write emails. Consequently, our employees are on board with our goals, approach, values, and purpose right from the start.

Another essential way to create purpose is to communicate to each employee how their daily tasks relate to broader company goals. Each staffer's duties and responsibilities can be aligned with short-term objectives and targets, as well as with the company's longer-term goals and that employee's personal career goals.[225]

Getting everyone on the same page is a widely shared team goal, but it's much easier said than done in most companies. Barely four of ten US employees (41 percent) strongly agree that they know what their organization stands for, while little more than one of five (22 percent) feel that their company leaders have a clear organizational

---

225   This is discussed in detail in chapter 15.

direction in mind.[226] These stats, from research giant Gallup, underscore the difficulty of aligning an organization in a traditional office setting. Imagine, then, how much greater the challenge is when it comes to remote workers.

22% of employees believe their company leaders have a clear organizational direction in mind.

41% of employees strongly agree that they know what their organization stands for.

Do your employees know where you are headed and what you stand for?

Few workers left on their own are able to mentally fit their role and daily tasks into the bigger picture of a company's purpose and objectives. It is therefore incumbent on managers to find ways to regularly align remote staffers' responsibilities, role, and workload with the strategic direction of the company. If you're able to connect individual assignments and projects to departmental priorities, which in turn support company annual strategies, long-term goals, and purpose, you help create an environment in which every team member understands how everything they do drives your organization forward.

---

226   Vibhas Ratanjee, "Leaders: Bring Your Strategy Back into Focus," Gallup, October 26, 2021, https://www.gallup.com/workplace/354944/leaders-bring-strategy-back-focus.aspx.

Getting to this level of alignment is challenging. It's crucial to include team members in the process. We've found that department retrospectives are a powerful way to give team members opportunities to contribute to the annual strategic planning process and the direction of their department.

The Remote Annual Planning Process

Assuming that your organization has a long-term strategic plan, which is typically prepared by senior executives and approved by the CEO, the challenge is to ensure that each remote employee understands and embraces how their role and contribution fits into the whole. Ideally, everyone, whether office based or remote, should understand how they contribute to the overall purpose of the organization and how each deliverable brings that purpose closer to reality. While the

Remote Planning

scope of the planning process is too broad to do justice to in a few pages, Virtira has created a course on how to go about it.

If the purpose statement guides the overall direction of a company, the annual plan provides employees with a road map to achieving purpose-aligned goals. Once created, the annual plan drives the show for that year, creating momentum with clear demarcations of progress. By April, the team should deliver this product, for instance—and by June, we should hit that benchmark. This helps motivate employees, who see a path to fulfilling a purpose that they believe is worthwhile and commit all the more keenly. They're able to monitor their own progress and will, as a result, experience a deeper connection to teammates, colleagues, and leadership.

A good annual strategic plan reflects the current state of the business and the marketplace and communicates priorities that align your team for the year ahead. It's more than a list of major projects. It's a set of directions that guides the day-to-day decisions of everyone in the organization. A strategic priority to increase productivity might encourage a team member to automate a workflow without being asked to do so. A strategic priority to gain more business in a new region could spur business developers to go after opportunities in their contact lists without the oversight of a sales director.

Failing to regularly examine your status and direction can leave an organization rudderless, adrift. "Check yourself before you wreck yourself," a well-known refrain by the rapper Ice Cube, is also excellent management advice. Companies need to regularly check themselves— kick the tires, test the brakes, check the oil—to avoid driving into trouble. If employees don't see the point of their work, where it's all headed, they tend to lose focus and drift in other directions, making deals with the wrong clients or developing poor products. The result is increased turnover, decreased profits, and stagnation. A strong strategic plan keeps purpose front and center, not just in the abstract but up close and personal.

How much more motivated will employees be if they know their part in bringing the company's purpose and strategic plan into fruition? Bill Quirke, a top communications advisor and managing director of the consultancy firm Synopsis, says that when employees understand their role within the firm, more than nine of ten (91 percent) will work toward its success. When they're unsure of their role, fewer than one in four (23 percent) do so.[227] Those are game-changing numbers.

Consequently, when you communicate the company's strategic plan, it's crucial that you provide context, explaining that objective

---

227 Art Johnson, "How to Get Employees to Align with the Company's Mission," Business Journals, June 3, 2014, https://www.bizjournals.com/bizjournals/how-to/growth-strate-gies/2014/06/how-to-get-employees-to-align-with-company-mission.html.

A leads to goal B, as well as how these objectives jointly move the firm toward its purpose. When you make requests of a team or team member, it's always wise to briefly explain the "why" as well as the "what" so that they understand the purpose behind the task. This is especially important with remote workers. Most are off on their own and relatively siloed and thus may be missing out on key bits of information that help connect the dots. Help them make those connections by taking the time to explain. Instead of "Please send me the documents from Friday's meeting," say, "Please send the documents; we need them for x, y, and z."

Achieving strong strategic planning with a remote workforce requires a particularly nuanced approach, in part because you want to ensure that immediate tasks and goals will continue to align with your purpose over an extended period. For most companies, the vast majority of annual strategic planning occurs within the strategy conversation itself. But when work is done remotely, conducting an effective and valuable planning session can still be a challenge.

We have nailed down eight key steps to creating a powerful remote strategic planning session:

1. **Plan ahead:** All research, information gathering, and other preparatory work needs to be done in advance, giving invitees time to review and digest. In addition, invitations to the meeting should be sent out long in advance, at least three weeks to a month.

2. **Don't rush:** Unlike in an office, where everybody is in the same room for a single purpose, some virtual attendees will continue to go about their day before, after, and even during the session. Some may at times be distracted by other urgent work and unable to share their views. As a result, you will most likely need to spread the meeting out over several days.

3. **Be prescriptive:** Many companies set up an off-site gathering to do yearly planning, and because everybody's already there, in close physical proximity, the schedule can be more fluid. But with remote planning sessions, you need to regularly remind everyone what's happening when, where you are in the process, and what's next. This should be done several times a day. At the same time, you will probably need to give people a series of guidelines for how they will contribute and remain involved in the session. You'll also need to follow up to make sure that they're on board. That's right—there will be some hand-holding.

4. **Embrace online tools:** Many attendees won't read your handouts, so you'll need a collaborative tool that can be easily updated and shared synchronously. We've found Miro to be a cut above other whiteboarding options, as it allows participants to collaboratively create, edit, and move notes and drawing segments. Feel free to check out our blog, where we compare the various tools, and "Miroverse," which offers sample templates.

Miroverse

5. **Have a strong facilitator:** Remote strategic planning demands assertive facilitation because the meetings are so long that it's easier for participants to disengage. Your facilitator needs to be able to keep track of everyone's talk time and maintain a balance, interject when participants speak disproportionately, and encourage quiet attendees to contribute.

6. **Be sure to recap:** Because the session will take place over several days, you'll need to review progress along the way, include time to briefly recap the previous day's events, remind

attendees where discussions ended, and let them know what's coming next.

7. **Take breaks:** Again, because the meetings will be long, it's crucial to schedule breaks every hour or two. This will help prevent fatigue and planning burnout and give attendees time to process and discuss on their own, as well as attend to any urgent work.

8. **Assign ownership:** As soon as the planning meetings are done, people go back to their regularly scheduled work. Someone needs to take ownership in following up with people on all of the decisions that were made. The strategic plan needs to be documented and then executed.

The Department Retrospective

Prior to the start of annual planning, we run each department through a retrospective to find out what's working and what's not. This gives people the chance to express their views and ideas, which are then filtered up to management. We run a quarterly net promoter score survey that asks, "On a scale of zero to ten, how likely are you to refer your company to others as a good place to work?" Additional space is provided for a written response, and the entire survey is anonymous, which minimizes self-censorship. These are important inputs for finding and addressing problem areas at all levels.

A retrospective is a facilitated, collaborative meeting in which a core group reviews and rehashes the most recent work period (anywhere from a quarter to an entire year). The group also documents lessons learned so as to apply them in the weeks and months to come. Retrospectives are an invaluable tool for collecting and sharing feedback, and they should be conducted prior to annual planning to provide guidance for the leadership team on areas for improvement and guidance for department heads on departmental goals. It's a good idea to run a retrospective for each team or department in your organization. We generally use a cloud-based interactive platform like Miro to manage and organize our retrospectives.

In some cases, the manager may lack the necessary influence to pass their team's feedback up the chain, so the retrospective helps define their departmental priorities with company objectives in mind. The following steps lay out the retrospective process:

1. Schedule a ninety-minute call for your department.
2. Let people know ahead of time that they will be answering questions such as the following: What have we been doing well/poorly? How might we change? What might we start or stop doing? What should we continue to do? What are your most common challenges, hurdles, or roadblocks?
3. Teams should spend the first ten to fifteen minutes jotting down answers to these questions.
4. For the remaining time, a facilitator, preferably from outside the department to eliminate bias, goes through each team member's responses and discusses them with the group.

The key differentiator between a retrospective and a regular group discussion is the gathering of feedback from participants before the discussion begins. Writing the answers down gives all participants an equal voice and helps ensure that even the softest-spoken member shares their ideas.

Record the meeting to allow for future review. Additional steps to take include setting up the entire team with access to your collaboration tool in advance and urging the team to consider topics of discussion beforehand. Following the retrospective meeting, take your time capturing the results and summarizing key findings before sharing them with the team and company leaders.

For large teams, it's better to break into smaller groups of eight to ten people and do a retrospective for each. This gives each member adequate time to relay their views and ultimately delivers more comprehensive feedback. You might also limit the number of discussion topics—for example, allowing no more than four per person—or set a time limit for each topic. Not only does this keep that one productive individual from monopolizing the time, but also it encourages people to focus more on their top three answers to each question rather than hurriedly jotting down the longest possible list. Another option for large teams is to ask participants to submit their topics beforehand and then go through them and eliminate duplication. But be careful not to censor any input; negative views are sometimes the most crucial to company success.

Remote
Retrospectives

Once you've conducted your retrospective, you'll be better prepared to conduct your annual strategic planning session. Visit our website for further guidelines.

PRO TIP: REINFORCE YOUR CORE VALUES

Instilling and reinforcing culture in remote workers often takes some creativity. Here are a few options:

- Start your weekly leadership meeting by asking whether anyone has any recent examples of living the core values. If they do, recognize these employees via the tip fund. At Virtira, we like to say, "Here's coffee on us for impressing the client."
- Relate stories of people living the purpose and core values in your weekly newsletter.
- On performance evaluations, ask for examples of living the core values.

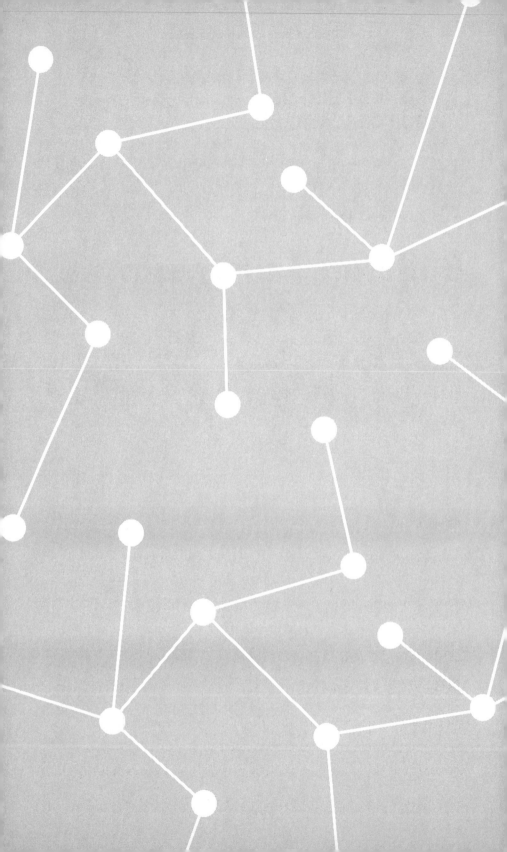

CHAPTER 13

Building Ownership

Leadership is about stepping up when it's the appropriate time and then making sure everyone knows that we're all on the same page.

—ROBERT KRAFT

Understanding purpose and creating a strategic plan to align your remote workers helps employees build ownership in their work. But how can managers create and measure ownership? To start the ball rolling, leaders need to foster a sense of autonomy, delegate authority, and identify and embrace meaningful metrics.

Encourage Autonomy and Delegate Authority

Your team members shouldn't feel like cogs in a machine. Rather, they should have an appreciation of their roles, not only within the company but also in terms of achieving something meaningful, developing their skills, and furthering their career. Each of their achievements should advance these goals. To get there, managers should work with each team member to identify at least one developmental or career-building goal, such as gaining programming expertise or significant marketing experience.

When you inform team members of their responsibilities within the company, you could begin to delegate authority by highlighting areas in which they could be proactive. For instance, you might tell John, the new marketing associate, that the tech team is often sluggish about informing marketing of new developments, so it would be great if he could open a regular channel of communication. Assuming that he runs with it—creates calendar reminders and keeps the techies on their toes—suddenly, John's responsible for keeping IT and marketing aligned.

Note the soft touch. The manager did not tell John exactly what he had to do to be reliably informed by the IT team but rather gave John the autonomy to determine the best approach. When delegating authority, a bit of guidance is crucial, but it's important to avoid being prescriptive. For instance, if John's manager had told him, "Create calendar reminders to email the tech team lead every two weeks requesting an update. Let me know about any new tech developments," John wouldn't have gained any authority. He'd just be doing another mind-numbing task for the boss. The better route is to explain the issue to the employee—tech leaves us out of the loop—and let him get to work. If he's not finding his own path, you haven't really delegated.

Another way of delegating authority is to bring team members in on the decision-making process. When appropriate, handing over some decision-making influence can be beneficial, such as when approving a new project that will require widespread commitment to succeed. Initiate the process by presenting your point of view, making clear that you're open to other perspectives. Delegating decisions fosters ownership because it boosts autonomy and underscores your confidence in their abilities. And when you do delegate, endeavor to do it publicly so that the transfer of authority is seen and acknowledged. There will be no questioning Sheila's oversight of the new sales team, for instance, after you've sent out an email about it to the entire department, cc'ing all top executives. At the same time, ensure Sheila's accountability by setting achievable targets.

Be willing to encourage discussion and even disagreement during the decision-making process. As long as the tone remains positive and collegial, some disagreement is healthy and, in the end, leads to a more informed decision. Making autocratic decisions on policies that affect everyone is a good way to hurt morale, so it's best to save those for minor decisions and emergency situations, when there's no time to poll the team. The more inclusive the decision-making, the better it is for the team and the department. Although democratic decision-making can be time consuming and complicated, the end result—a more satisfied, engaged, and empowered staff—makes it all worthwhile.

> **Delegating decisions fosters ownership because it boosts autonomy and underscores your confidence in their abilities.**

In an office, a manager can make decisions on the fly while engaging with the employee for unrelated reasons, even sociably. Remotely, oversight must be front of mind all the time: "Who is responsible? Who is accountable? Who needs to be consulted and informed?" The manager needs to think about all the key players related to every decision, and this must become second nature.[228]

---

228   For more on this, see chapter 17 and the RACI.

Collaborative and delegated decision-making not only builds the team's sense of ownership but also builds decision-making muscle. As a result, it's likely to lead to future decisions that are more comprehensively considered and inclusive. The whole team benefits if every team member shoulders some responsibility. If your team includes a member with zero responsibility and that employee is not a recent hire, you might want to brush up on your delegation skills. That said, as manager, be prepared to shoulder full responsibility for poor decisions and share the credit for good decisions. If you take all the credit for good decisions but blame others for mistakes, you will quickly erode your team's sense of ownership for anything beyond their immediate job responsibilities, as well as their trust in your leadership.

Once you've established ownership and delegated responsibility, it's time to move on to the third step of creating ownership, measuring performance. This is especially true of remote teams because when it comes to working remotely, measuring ownership doesn't involve counting the number of hours worked, mouse clicks, or butts in seats.

Establish Meaningful Metrics

Valuable metrics are crucial to gauging the extent to which you and your team have advanced your key performance indicators (KPIs), which should be aligned with your company's purpose. The most useful and meaningful metrics measure not only quantity but also quality and impact. To determine which metrics will be most meaningful for you, identify which of your firm's KPIs are most applicable to your team, in terms of alignment with team members' roles and the team's progression toward strategic goals.

This will likely involve asking key questions about your team and its vision. When determining the KPIs, look at team members' daily tasks and how their work aligns with broader company goals. How might their daily workload be brought into closer alignment with team goals and the company's overall strategic direction? A manager establishing metrics for a content writer, for example, might focus on the number of blog posts completed. But if boosting engagement is the KPI, then a more meaningful metric would be increasing the number of views for each blog post, the number of conversions generated, or social media shares. Valuable metrics for a team tasked with raising $30,000 for a charity event might include contacting one hundred potential sponsors by the end of the month. A meaningful metric for a product launch might be delivering final advertising content to all national media two months prior to launch.

Be sure to establish team targets and goals first, before establishing metrics for individual members. And when you do get to the latter, bringing team members in on the process of identifying and developing meaningful metrics significantly improves buy-in. Employees who participate in the process of determining which of their duties are most meaningful and which spur greater collaboration and achievement better understand their manager's expectations and how they relate to achieving team and company goals.

Identifying meaningful metrics is merely the first step. To embrace and leverage these metrics, you and your team will need to set deadlines and regularly monitor progress. Depending on the timeline, you could schedule weekly or biweekly progress updates that could be done in a ten-minute call. Alongside this, each team member should also submit regular status reports and perform monthly metric check-ins, in addition to quarterly reviews. With all this coverage, no laggards will be left behind.

Managers should prioritize and encourage ongoing conversations about metrics and repeatedly emphasize the link between meeting expectations and achieving specific goals. It's also a good idea to periodically review the relevance of performance metrics. In fact, consistently evaluating whether metrics remain meaningful to broader goals is as important as assessing progress made. Do your best to avoid "vanity metrics," which tend to make people feel good but have no real value. For example, it's great to have thousands of daily visitors to your website, but does it really matter if none of them buy your goods or click on "Contact us"?

You might also consider making these discussions about metrics publicly accessible in a shared online dashboard and allowing the entire team to contribute. Team members working on other tasks might be able to shed new light on why one team member's work is more important than had been previously thought or suggest a novel, time-saving approach improving productivity. This platform could also enable team members to document task completion, which could lead to healthy competition as team members are able to see, in real time, the performance of their colleagues.

This will enable you to keep a close eye on results and keep remote workers from neglecting to report roadblocks. Perhaps because they prefer to always give a positive spin, some workers like to report that a project is on track even when it's not. This can happen with in-office workers as well, but it's much more common with remote work, which offers less oversight. Laggard workers might believe deep down that they'll be able to iron out the issues in time to meet a deadline, or they may simply be unable to acknowledge that they're in too deep. Either way, with a public dashboard, there will be no hiding their lack of progress, which means that problems will receive more prompt attention. A good approach is to emphasize early on that such transparency is in the best interests of manager, employee, and company. At the same time, you could apply some pressure by regularly asking your team questions such as the following:

- What *specific* progress did you make this week?
- How do you feel about the progress you're making?
- What hurdles are you encountering or anticipating, and how do you plan to overcome them?
- What do you hope to achieve next week, and what support do you need?

Because this line of questioning is focused on achieving established goals, no team members should be upset or feel caught out. Establish a regular one-on-one with your team member to regularly check in on their progress. We will dive deeper into one-on-ones in chapter 16. Keeping everybody in line and achieving optimal productivity is your job, so don't be afraid to press ahead and get satisfying answers. Even so, be reasonable and flexible. Goals will sometimes change, perhaps because of a shift in strategy or a downturn in the market. Nothing can be done about this. You'll simply need to accept it and adjust metrics accordingly, making sure that the team remains aligned with KPIs and delivers the right outcomes. To put it simply, getting there matters a great deal more than the path taken.

Establishing clear expectations and setting clear goals is crucial for managers. From there, constantly gauging performance via meaningful metrics gives you greater control, fosters a sense of ownership among team members, and creates trust through transparency, thus furthering engagement.

PRO TIP: AVOID VANITY METRICS

A vanity or cosmetic metric is a number that makes you feel good or is interesting but offers no real value in helping you understand progress. The number of "hits" on a website is a vanity metric, for example, as it doesn't tell you whether you're attracting the right type of visitors or what they're doing when they land on your home page. The number of hours logged is another commonly measured KPI. Unless there is a specific relationship between hours logged and revenue, and there rarely is, you are missing the big picture.

When selecting a metric, ask yourself what decisions you will make when this metric changes. Are you able to control the results of the metric by changing one of the inputs? Or how does this impact the bottom line or measure success?

Establishing targets for your metrics is another surefire way of weeding out vanity metrics that will ultimately lead you down a blurry path.

CHAPTER 14

Ensuring Remote Engagement

It goes without saying that no company, small or large, can win over the long run without energized employees who believe in the mission and understand how to achieve it.

—JACK WELCH, FORMER CEO OF GE

Employee engagement is often defined as a sense of commitment and loyalty, as well as an emotional connection, to one's workplace.[229] As in any relationship, engagement results from feeling valued, heard, supported, and respected, and survey after survey has shown that companies that build an environment that encourages such forms of appreciation see greater employee engagement and increased productivity. At consulting giant Deloitte, for example, 83 percent of

---

229   Anjan Pathak, "How to Engage Remote Employees in 5 Simple Steps," *Forbes,* December 27, 2021, https://www.forbes.com/sites/allbusiness/2021/12/27/how-to-engage-remote-employees-in-5-simple-steps/?sh=742ac2456af6.

executives and 84 percent of employees rank engaged and motivated employees as the top contributing factor to a company's success.[230]

Building Trust

Trust is a crucial element of employee engagement, particularly when it comes to remote work. Telecommuters are working on their own islands, without an office or boss in sight. If you want to keep them engaged, remote team members need to trust each other and their managers. So the question is, How do you build trust? Real trust doesn't happen overnight. It must be built over time, in a cumulative process that involves collective effort and embraces several key practices.

Transparency is the practice of honest and open communication, and it's a key step to building team trust. Transparency is of course a two-way street, requiring commitment from managers and employees, and it should take a central role in company culture. Ensuring transparency should be established as a company-wide policy and made clear during the hiring process—in the hiring of employees who share this value and in the clear communication of expectations. From there, transparency should be regularly stressed as part of daily interactions—especially when it comes to remote employees.

Transparency can be challenging, and there will likely be times when it cannot be fully embraced, as when dealing with strategically crucial information, perhaps in response to a key competitor. In such times, it's important to explain the situation to employees who have not been made privy to the information, detailing how it's to their and the company's benefit and when the information will be made publicly available. But in general, the more you and your employees

---

230 "About Us," Deloitte, accessed October 20, 2020, https://www2.deloitte.com/us/en/pages/about-deloitte/articles/about-deloitte.html.

are able to communicate honestly and openly, the more that trust and respect will develop.

Helpful examples of transparency from a manager include admitting that you don't know the answer to an emerging problem, acknowledging a mistake, explaining your or the company's reasoning behind a recent decision, requesting advice on improving your decision-making process or honest feedback on the effectiveness of a process you implemented, relaying bad news personally rather than in an email, and being honest in crisis situations—for example, highlighting your level of anxiety in the early days of the pandemic. All of these point toward openness and vulnerability, which help build and strengthen emotional connections and understanding.

Following through on commitments is a key building block for growing trust. A manager who vows to give a bonus to any team member who reaches a certain metric but then fails to deliver when that metric is met, for instance, will quickly lose the trust and commitment of his team. Before you commit to something, be certain that you will be able to fulfill that commitment. Once you commit, take the steps you need to take to follow through. Unforeseen circumstances that might prevent you from following through do sometimes arise, and in such cases, this should be explained to the team, with apologies. They need to know that you are disappointed in yourself for failing to deliver as promised—that you, the manager, do not accept failure to deliver on a commitment. You can also go even further—explain the problem to your team and ask for input and advice on a possible solution. Your failure to follow through could end up being a team-building collaboration that encourages trust and engagement. (Just don't make a habit of it!)

As noted in chapter 10, as with other aspects of remote engagement, remote employees need to be held accountable to their commitments, which should include a vow to embrace remote working best practices: to work hard, even while far from the office; to stay in regular contact with the team; to be accessible during work hours; to embrace corporate culture; and to be responsible for their home-based workstation. Team members who publicly make commitments along these lines increase overall trust and engagement.[231]

Consistent and equitable information sharing also contributes to a broader environment of trust. If you tell your marketing lead one thing and then tell your sales lead something contradictory, employees might soon start to question everything you say (as advised in chapter 8, assume that all communications will eventually be made public). Sometimes, information-sharing errors are accidental, such as when you inadvertently omit a key detail from a report or forget to include a key colleague on an email. In such cases, apologize, let the relevant employee know the nature of your mistake, and correct it as soon as possible. Generally speaking, though, the best way to build trust is to maintain your messaging regardless of who you're speaking to and to share as much information as possible with the entire team.

Accessibility is another key element of trust. Keeping your virtual door open during office hours and welcoming off-hours emails and questions of any kind shows your respect for and interest in your team's concerns and wishes. You could also make your calendar public so that people can see when you're free and book a quick call. Being accessible also means maintaining an accurate status on work chat platforms like Slack or Teams rather than displaying the green dot when you're away from your desk. In addition, being open to quick

---

231   Ken Gossnell, "Commitments Good Employees Make while Working Remotely," *Forbes*, July 17, 2020, https://www.forbes.com/sites/forbescoachescouncil/2020/07/17/commitments-good-employees-make-while-working-remotely/?sh=26100aaf3c51.

calls when an issue can't be resolved through text helps your team members feel that you've always got their back.

Collaborative decision-making essentially puts team members on the same level as managers, and few things better encourage employee trust than a horizontal organizational structure. As discussed in the previous chapter, whenever appropriate and potentially beneficial, bring teams or team members into the decision-making process. It's hard to overstate the extent to which an employee's sense of connection increases when she feels that she's able to communicate with her boss as an equal. Not only being heard and listened to but also seeing firsthand how her views helped shape and influence the final decision—that's priceless. You might also extend this even further and build new processes with your team. That way, they have a stake in laying out achievable goals and implementing them effectively.

Solicit regular feedback on your performance, team goals, relevant systems and processes, tech use and communications, the company's strategic direction, and more. Send out monthly or biweekly requests for team views, insights, and concerns. Embrace and publicly implement any strong recommendations—and consider whether they might be worth developing into team, department, or company goals. Again, the more people see that their ideas and concerns have real value, the more comfortable they become speaking up and the more engaged and committed they are to their work.

Regularly recognizing remote team members for their achievements is a key contributor to trust and engagement. Remote workers often feel unseen and underappreciated. A late 2020 poll of two thousand US workers found that more than two of three (68 percent) of those working from home felt unmotivated to work "since everything they do seems to go unnoticed."[232]

One good way to keep them engaged is to frequently let them know that their hard work is appreciated. There are many forms this could take. It could be a monetary bonus of anywhere from ten dollars to thousands of dollars or a small gift. It could be highlighting their impressive achievements on a public dashboard for all the team to see and comment on. It's also a good idea to use emoticons in such recognitions. Most social media and messaging platforms have enabled a variety of emoticon responses in each post. In work settings, people have come to expect likes and smiley faces and view them as a measure of acknowledgment. The flip side is that sharing a bit of great news and getting no emoticon reactions, especially from a boss, can be really disheartening.[233] Recognizing the work of remote workers could be as simple as clicking that smiley face emoticon or sending them a quick message like "Thank you for your great work."

While recognition should be doled out publicly, reprimands should not; it's never appropriate to call someone out publicly.[234] A public relations director for the consulting firm Gartner recommends that team leaders identify the specific type of recognition each employee most craves and provide that whenever suitable. "If the need for achievement prevails, recognize their good work by engaging them

---

232   Bryan Robinson, "New Research Says Remote Workers Want More from their Employers or Else," *Forbes*, November 16, 2020, https://www.forbes.com/sites/bryanrobinson/2020/11/16/new-research-says-remote-workers-want-more-appreciation-from-their-leaders-or-else/?sh=701cccbd5fa2.

233   Keep in mind that emoticons can also be a double-edged sword. Some news requires a proper written reaction, and sending a thumbs-up can feel inadequate for the occasion. This is the new version of "reading the room." Managers must pay attention to the significance or seriousness of the news shared and react appropriately.

234   Barasha Medhi, "12 Amazing Virtual Employee Recognition Ideas," Vantage Circle, June 16, 2021, https://blog.vantagecircle.com/virtual-employee-recognition-ideas/.

in challenging projects," Laurence Goasduff wrote for *Forbes*. "If the need for status prevails, involve the person in a prestigious project."[235]

Coaching

Engagement happens on the individual as well as on the team level. That's why it's crucial to leverage coaching to help every member stay positive and head in the right direction. This can be done anytime you feel the need for a slight course correction or just to offer congratulations.

We're not going to dig too deeply into coaching here, as there are many fine books dedicated to the subject. We would, however, like to make a few salient points about the differences between in-person and remote coaching and how coaching enhances engagement.

Effective coaching requires managers to make a personal connection with individual team members, as without a real bond, any attempts at coaching are likely to fall on deaf ears. And despite considerable advances in technology, coaching is still best done in person. This means that it's more difficult when it comes to remote workers, something that managers should keep in mind. Even so, a manager can be an effective coach to a remote worker with face-to-face meetings every six months and monthly calls to check in on progress and concerns. The goal should be to use each face-to-face meeting to generate enough engagement and commitment until the next in-person meeting, while intermittent check-ins let them know that you're available and always there to support them.

What should these monthly chats entail? It often helps to have a simple checklist of questions to go through each time. How are you

---

235   Laurence Goasduff, "The Leader Checklist to Foster Trust on Remote Teams," Gartner, July 30, 2020, https://www.gartner.com/smarterwithgartner/ the-leader-checklist-to-foster-trust-on-remote-teams.

progressing on goals A and B? Have any new concerns emerged? Have you altered your personal goals and priorities in any way? How might I help right now? The team member's answers to these questions will likely provide opportunities for the coach to share some guidance and insight. You might also deliver some constructive feedback, rather than expecting that they wait six months between performance reviews.

When it comes to feedback, however, proceed with caution. Feedback provided remotely requires greater tact and a keener sense of timing. As previously mentioned, feedback should be delivered via email or message only if it has previously been shared in person or over a call. Always call first to share feedback, and follow up in writing afterward. But know that the follow-up is also critical, as people often forget things that aren't written down or may misinterpret something you said over the phone, especially if they're working remotely and may have been trying to meet a deadline or keep their children at bay during your feedback call. Similarly, be sensitive to the employee's feelings, as well as willing to listen to their response, when you deliver feedback.

For one thing, it's often not the best approach to ask someone to stay online for a quick chat just as a meeting is ending. This tends to make the employee feel apprehensive about being singled out. Employees generally know that managers offer praise in public and reserve private chats for less positive feedback. Even if such concerns are misplaced, it's better to avoid that extra anxiety for your team members, which hinders trust and engagement. Messaging an employee to offer feedback while they are presenting should also be avoided at all costs. Doing so will likely fluster the presenter, potentially throwing them off track.

Finally, remember that positive feedback is important, but it's even more effective in promoting employee engagement when it's combined with constructive feedback. Telling an employee that they're doing a "great job" is all well and good. But telling them why their work has been great and how it embodies a core value not only makes that employee feel better but also gives them a greater understanding of how their work is viewed and appreciated. This reinforces precisely what you want them to continue doing, improving their commitment to the most important elements of their job.

Positive feedback is important, but it's even more effective in promoting employee engagement when it's combined with constructive feedback.

Last but by no means least, we want to reiterate the importance of asking for permission to provide feedback. People need to be ready for it, and if you don't ask, you might trigger a fight-or-flight response. Avoiding dumping on people who may already be feeling down is not only the right thing to do but also good for the team. Just a simple query via chat message to make sure that the employee is in the right mental and emotional state for feedback goes a long way toward showing that you care, again building trust and engagement.

Remote Coaching Best Practices

Like remote work, remote coaching relies on a certain degree of employee autonomy. So remote coaching is less about the coach identifying what employees need to work on and more about encouraging them to identify areas for improvement and helping them work through challenges and dilemmas. Leading employees toward their own discoveries requires being a careful observer and crafting probing questions about their work. Asking an employee why he made an error and what he might do differently the next time, for instance, could spur him to more thoroughly weigh his actions, question his approach, and establish a more thoughtful process.

Whether remote or in person, coaches should resist the urge to jump in with the right answer. Most managers know (or at least they think they know) how to do what their team members are doing and have answers to every situation. But beware—prematurely providing direction to a team member shifts the responsibility of the task back onto you, the manager. As with poor delegation of authority, suddenly it's become something they have been told to do rather than something they resolved on their own.

Yet even the most self-reflective employees come upon blind spots. If they're really stuck and a few pointed questions fail to lead them to a solution, offer your help. If they accept, provide some advice on how to solve the problem, in the hope that they're able to work through it on their own. If not, go ahead and walk them through it. Sometimes people need a little push in the right direction.

Consider a Virtira manager who's responsible for coming up with quarterly goals for her department. We review her suggestions and tell her which we believe will best move her department toward company objectives. She receives and weighs our guidance, but in the end, she has the freedom to choose the goals she believes are most fitting. Much the same can be done with any employee.

Particularly with remote work, it's crucial to coach in a way that doesn't intimidate employees or make them look bad in front of the team. Develop a coaching process that's as private and personal as possible. If, for instance, you schedule a coaching call a day or two after an incident, this could create added stress, as the employee will fret in the interim about what you might tell them. And while you might initiate a coaching call via text, don't use text to actually do the coaching. At minimum, use a voice call. As with feedback, providing coaching over text or email is less effective. For one thing, it's difficult to show compassion through words alone, even with liberal emoji use. For another, text and email all but eliminate the possibility of an engaging back-and-forth about this or that bit of coaching guidance.

Avoid saving all of your coaching insights for the biannual performance review, which could turn it into something the employee dreads rather than an opportunity for them to connect, seek advice, and discuss their place in the team and the firm. During even short coaching calls, focus on outcomes. Be open to the fact that you may not know the entirety of the situation. Listen, and try to understand the employee's perspective. Be sure to outline next steps, and then follow up to make sure that progress is made.

Mix it up. Coaching calls should not always be about correction or adjustment. They should be used to give positive feedback. Let your people know when they did a great job so that they know they're valued. Give shout-outs in team meetings as well. You could even block off a few minutes in every meeting to praise a top performer. It's not the same as personal coaching, but it is good leadership.

Last, be open minded. Coaching gives two people the opportunity to come up with a new solution to a problem or a new way to attack a challenge. You can learn from your employees as well.

PRO TIP: MAKE MEETING OUTSIDE WORK OPTIONAL

Remember that engagement can also be encouraged outside work hours through social activities. But be wary of emulating in-office activities in the virtual work environment. It's safe to assume that some team members may not be interested in associating with colleagues outside work. Even when team members respect and trust each other, they may not share common interests beyond work. So break free of that mentality, and don't assume that everybody will be all in on social events.

Some communications experts suggest encouraging nonwork engagement by creating a voluntary online forum where remote workers can create profiles highlighting their interests and hobbies.[236] Staffers with a passion for riding horses, surfing, or Dungeons & Dragons, for example, could connect on such a forum and build personal relationships that later play into their work. Even if these connections never make a direct impact on work, they represent an engaged and connected workforce—a positive result in itself.

One of the cardinal rules of remote work is that it increases autonomy and values the quality, not the quantity, of communication. So requiring employee participation in events outside working hours, especially if those events are unrelated to work, must be avoided.[237]

---

236   Ibid.

237   Unless we're talking about a team-building gathering, such as a weekend-long retreat.

CHAPTER 15

The Fire of Passion

Nothing great in the world has ever been accomplished without passion.

—GEORG WILHELM FRIEDRICH HEGEL

Passion is a profound sense of connection to one's work that inspires consistent peak performance. Once you've brought a team member to this level, they will be self-motivated and always looking for every edge to improve their skills and boost their productivity. Some may be so passionate that they don't view their job as work at all—which is precisely the sort of commitment that drives great change and growth. Sounds too good to be true? It almost is. Deloitte found that just one of eight US workers (12 percent) feel real passion toward their job.[238]

Before we dig in, clarification is needed. It's crucial to avoid confusing passion with ambition. Both may inspire employees to work extra hours and be performance oriented, but the motivations

---

238   John Hagel III et al. "Passion at Work: Cultivating Worker Passion as a Cornerstone of Talent Development," Deloitte, October 7, 2014, https://www2.deloitte.com/us/en/insights/topics/talent/worker-passion-employee-behavior.html.

of ambitious workers tend to be self-oriented. They seek rewards, recognition, promotions, and power. They're generally more focused on personal success than on doing the best possible job or delivering optimal results. They are also less likely to challenge the status quo, as they tend to be more pragmatic when it comes to their careers.[239]

Passionate employees, on the other hand, are motivated by the work itself and driven by the company's purpose. They tend to be more willing to think outside the box and thus are more innovative and are often willing to take on risky projects. Because they believe in the value of their work, passionate workers tend to be more centered and confident. Ambitious workers are often insecure and looking over their shoulder at who might overtake them. Passionate workers are more willing to collaborate with others to hit on valuable solutions and have a desire to significantly influence the field rather than simply move up the corporate ladder.

Passion is the ultimate engagement. A passionate team member will take on more and deliver more than the average worker. They've found their groove, their zen, their happy place, and they are far more productive than the average worker because of it. Even when they're unable to help you, they'll find someone who can. Passion, therefore, serves organizations and employees better than ambition.

The Power of Mentorship

To help an employee succeed in their role, one of the most important things a manager can do is to find a mentor from another part of the organization. Mentors offer access to diverse perspectives and experience beyond the limits of the manager. For someone working remotely, however, a mentorship offers introductions and the potential to create

---

239   Ibid.

relationships that would otherwise be unavailable to them. This leads to new career opportunities and helps socialize the employee's achievements more broadly. Managers should also encourage their employees to mentor. As they say, "To teach is to learn twice." Mentoring encourages people to review what they believe in while reinforcing their passion for the job.

Use One-on-One Meetings to Instill Passion

Instilling passion in remote team members is best done via individual, one-on-one meetings.[240] In remote work settings, these tête-à-têtes are a way for employee and manager to connect on progress, career, and growth and for managers to do some coaching. Building personal relationships is key because it is close personal bonds that tend to spur emotions like passion. No two people have the same wants and needs, which means that trying to instill passion in workers through grand all-hands speeches is a fool's game. The smart approach is to take the time to understand what drives each team member to commit to their work and leverage that to begin discussions that tap into their passion. This can be done only with a direct personal connection, and your leadership can make the difference.

"Leaders' one-to-one performance management and coaching interactions with their team," *Harvard Business Review* asserts in an article on virtual teams, "are a fundamental part of making any team work."[241] If remote workers don't feel connected to their managers and don't feel understood by their leaders, they are unlikely to feel

---

240 "One-on-One Meetings: A Comprehensive Guide for Managers and Employees," Hypercontext, accessed June 12, 2022, https://hypercontext.com/one-on-one-meeting-guide. One-on-one meetings have a variety of names, including check-ins, 121s, 1:1s, and one-to-ones.

241 Michael D. Watkins, "Making Virtual Teams Work: Ten Basic Principles," *Harvard Business Review*, June 27, 2013, https://hbr.org/2013/06/making-virtual-teams-work-ten.

engaged in their work. This could lead to burnout and alienation from the team, the company, and its purpose. For these employees, passion is not in the cards.

It's incredibly important during one-on-ones to ask your staffers what they care about in terms of job-related goals, career goals, and even personal goals. Be prepared to respond to their answers with some personal tidbits of your own. Sharing and engagement, remember, go both ways. At the same time, when they share their personal goals and interests, find ways to link them to their work. This way, they might feel closer to achieving their objectives. Also ask whether they're happy in their work and whether they have any ideas about handling their tasks differently. Find out how they feel about their role within the company. If those feelings are negative, acknowledge them, jot them down, and look for ways to address them. One helpful step is to allow team members to work on projects they find appealing, even if those projects are not within their area of expertise. The team member will feel heard and empowered and might develop a new skill set.

Notes, especially on a shared collaborative platform, prevent misunderstandings and signal that you take their concerns seriously. Use a cloud-based tool to set up a private collaborative journal for each of your one-on-ones, as typically, to keep the tone conversational, you won't want to record them.

We have a basic set agenda for one-on-one chats that most managers vary. Usually, there is a brief introduction asking them how their day or week is going. If they have just returned from a break, ask them about their vacation. Just some pleasantries to break the ice. Next is five to fifteen minutes reviewing their weekly report. We ask our team members to write a brief weekly report detailing "headlines from the past week," "next week's milestones," and "risks" to be shared across the team. This not only gives the employee an opportunity to think through their week before talking to you but also shows them that their report has a purpose. Far too many reports are written and ignored. This hopefully spurs discussion on a given hurdle or achievement. It could also turn into a conversation about an interaction with another team member. The manager takes notes in the journal throughout.

The remainder of the time is spent working through any items in the collaborative journal—alternating between topics for the manager and the team member. If we run late because of an important discussion, we ask them whether they want to reschedule or continue talking. It's important to get permission to extend the chat. Remember, this is their meeting, not yours. You're there to listen and ask questions. Do your best to never skip or miss these—they are likely your most important meetings each week.

PRO TIP: BE PREPARED FOR THE ONE-ON-ONE

Avoid asking random open-ended questions to fill time. This does little to benefit you or your employee. If you don't have a plan to deal with the answer, don't ask the question.

Take some time at the start of each week to think about what you want to achieve in your one-on-ones. Consider setting up a monthly cycle:

- Week One: Check in on their personal goals.
- Week Two: Dive deep into a project, asking probing questions on how and why.
- Week Three: Review their relationships with other team members.
- Week Four: Discuss their nonwork lives—hobbies, family, interests.
- On the occasional fifth week, ask for feedback on your performance.

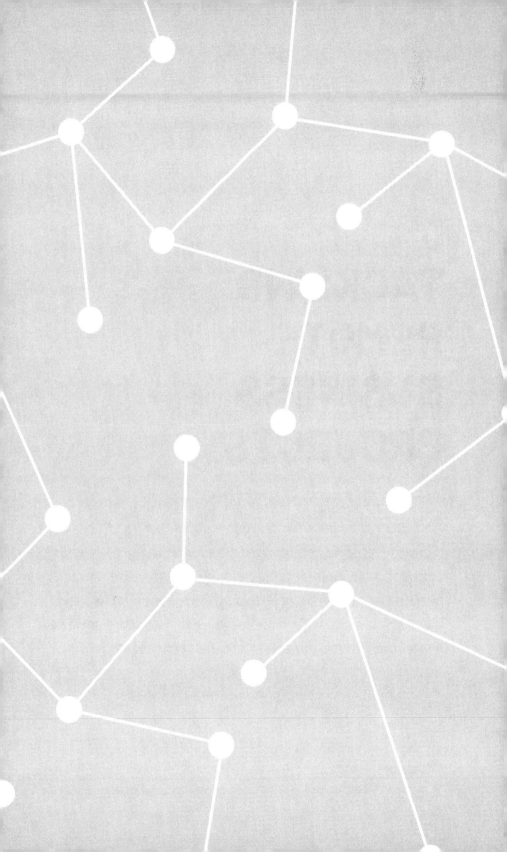

PART V

TACKLING REMOTE BUSINESS PROJECTS

All military services have long ago learned that the officer who has given an order goes out and sees for himself whether it has been carried out. At the least he sends one of his own aides— he never relies on what he is told by the subordinate to whom the order was given. Not that he distrusts the subordinate; he has learned from experience to distrust communications.

— PETER F. DRUCKER

n recent years, the corporate world has been "projectized." A product pivot, a strategic shift, layoffs, new additions, or new sponsors seem to emerge every few weeks as part of constant churn and change, spurring projects that seek to keep the business ahead of the game. Firms might reorganize as often as once a year with big layoffs, dozens of hires, and new management.

When project management first emerged in the 1950s, it was mainly applied to construction, engineering, and defense projects. Within a few decades, the concept had migrated to the broader business world, largely because its practices and guidelines tended to boost efficiency and results for nearly any group of people working side by side. Lately, managers the world over have been doing their darnedest to apply traditional management tools to remote projects, only to discover that it's like trying to jam a square peg into a round hole. They've plugged in PMP, Six Sigma, Agile, Scrum, and more, with limited success.

We're certified in all of these, and although they work great for colocated teams, each faces serious hurdles when it comes to virtual work. Today's business projects and budgets are smaller, most projects lack a dedicated project manager, teams can be spread across the world, and organizational shifts mean that the team can change in an instant. To top it off, the emergence of ad hoc cross-functional project teams has added another set of challenges. Now, instead of the IT development team sprinting to complete the latest software update, a client-facing project might require a team that includes staffers from finance, marketing, and sales working alongside two specialized external contractors.

Back in 2015, before the spike in remote work made things even more complicated, *Harvard Business Review* reported that nearly 75 percent of cross-functional teams were dysfunctional.[242] Thanks in part to the rise of remote work, the situation has not improved in the interim. In this section, we address that crisis head on, laying out key steps and best practices to ensure optimal efficiency and productivity for complex teams, even if they're spread across the globe.

Left: A 1960s project meeting. Right: A 1990s project meeting.

Today's project meeting.

---

242   Behnam Tabrizi, "75% of Cross-Functional Teams Are Dysfunctional," *Harvard Business Review*, June 23, 2015, https://hbr.org/2015/06/75-of-cross-functional-teams-are-dysfunctional.

CHAPTER 16

A Better Way to Manage Remote Projects

Projects don't fail at the end, they fail at the beginning.

—GALVIN HALSE

I n vehicular lingo, "RPM" refers to revolutions per minute, or how many times over a sixty-second period a car engine's crankshaft makes a full rotation. RPMs increase as you press on the accelerator, and so does power—up to a point. Most cars operate at peak performance well below the highest achievable RPM count. This is why a car's tachometer, which measures RPMs, has a red area to the far right—because going past the red line undermines your engine's power and can even damage it.

Over the years, we've evolved our own RPM framework, and although it addresses remote project management, we like to view it as a way to rev your company's virtual engines. Our framework combines lessons learned from decades of remote experience with elements of Agile, traditional project management, and change management. Developed specifically for remote business, Virtira's RPM guides projects from start to finish while emphasizing direct communication and executive buy-in and engagement. This framework also aims to ensure that regardless of what's being developed, all of the key figures, from clients to executives to crucial contractors, are fully on board at the earliest possible stage.

What Is RPM, and Why Is It Useful?

Before the arrival of COVID-19, just 6 percent of US office employees, a.k.a. "white-collar workers," worked exclusively from home. By May 2020, the share had leapt more than tenfold, to nearly two of three workers (65 percent).[243] In the wake of the pandemic, more and more companies are shouldering the complex burden of virtual projects run by cross-functional teams. To clarify, we're referring here to projects that involve key members in various locations (San Francisco, Toronto, London, and Hong Kong, for instance) working for a variety of different departments (marketing, IT, accounting) and even for a number of different entities (your firm, the client, a third-party contractor, and a government official). Just a handful of years ago, projects that involved such a diverse and distant team were uncommon for all but the biggest firms.

RPM helps remote collaborative projects adapt to dynamic, fast-paced environments. Today's projects might involve lawsuits, mergers, sales drives, product launches, and a dozen other types of initiatives unimaginable to the forefathers of project management.

---

243 Emma Goldberg, "A Two-Year, 50-Million-Person Experiment in Changing How We Work," *New York Times*, March 10, 2022, https://www.nytimes.com/2022/03/10/business/remote-work-office-life.html.

Often, the project objective is as much about satisfying a CEO's whim as any corporate objective. Maybe the boss wants project completion to coincide with a public stock report or hopes to make a splash announcement at an upcoming sales meeting.

Traditionalists will tell you that most projects fail because the project managers bite off more than they can chew and grossly underestimate the time and financial requirements. This is unfair to project managers. Our decades of experience have taught us that the most frequent cause of failure in business projects is an executive setting an unachievable target. The deadline your new vice president has set for project completion is rarely based on any discussions with IT or marketing but rather is based on the simple fact that she will meet with the board the next day and hopes to highlight significant progress. It happens all the time, and it places enormous—and unnecessary—stress on the organization.

Here's one of our favorite anecdotes. A gas company and a telecom firm grew up together over a period of one hundred years. After their monopolies were crushed in the 1990s, new executives came in to deal with the changed marketplace. At a cocktail party, the CEO of a top competitor to the telecom company strolled up to the new CEO of the gas company and declared, "We can cut your telecommunications costs 30 percent." He probably meant to say that his firm could save the gas company 30 percent on long-distance costs, but the gas CEO heard 30 percent across the board for all telecommunications services. Envisioning a huge win, the next morning he called his IT chief and told him to put the firm's entire telecommunica-

> *Our decades of experience have taught us that the most frequent cause of failure in business projects is an executive setting an unachievable target.*

tions infrastructure up for bid—everything from the high-speed lines between buildings to the phone systems and satellite-linked sensors on all the gas lines.

"I can save you thirty percent!"

The IT chief called Cynthia, told her the story, and said that she needed to manage a request for proposal process that absolutely, he advised, should not end up changing the gas firm's vendors. So here we have a project in which its originator sought to cut his telecom costs, at any cost, while the project lead or sponsor, the IT director, understood the nightmare-level risk in swapping out active gas sensors and the millions it would cost to accommodate a new supplier and thus had another objective in mind.[244] The project took eighteen months, and the incumbent telecom company emerged with the highest bid. A "goodwill discount" of 25 percent, however, enabled the company to sneak in with the lowest adjusted price, so Cynthia ended up handing over to the winning bidder a telecom business it had run for decades. And the telecom firm that started the whole thing? It never made a bid.

---

244 We term the person who came up with the project the "project originator" and the person who hands us the project the "project sponsor."

In another case, the head office routinely made planning decisions for the remote satellite office, selecting delivery dates and scope that served its agenda without consulting the people who would actually do the work. Just before a big holiday, the executive team decided that three projects had to be ready ahead of schedule. Each project had its share of challenges, and Shane was the lucky bloke tasked with getting all three delivered on time. Seeing the massive workload that lay ahead, he called for a one-time special effort by the entire office to stay the weekend and get caught up. After oceans of overtime, several scope changes, a ton of quality concessions, and the emergence of a few heroes, all three projects made it across the finish line. But they were shadows of the original visions and caused issues for their customers and users for years to come—all because of an out-of-touch leadership team interested in its own agenda rather than the capabilities of its team.

With today's remote cross-functional projects, project managers rarely have the authority to call on an entire team to stay the weekend because few, if any, of the team members report to the project manager. They work for various departments and report to different managers who may also be in different locations or even work for different companies. Team members are likely working on other projects while also trying to keep up with the responsibilities of their position. Your manager may have just placed you on the team because their manager placed them on it. Sometimes ending up on a team is like losing a game of musical chairs: you just happened to be the one left standing. Like Shane, team leads and project managers are often there only to minimize failure and sometimes to serve as scapegoats—and rarely is any team member brave enough to stand up and point out the glaring problems. Also, while anybody can still reach out to human resources or shoot a message to their superior, many of the informal back channels available in an office are unavailable remotely.[245]

Most business projects come with fixed beginning and end dates that have next to nothing to do with actual work timelines and available resources. Executives, much like politicians, are often not very concerned about feasibility. A typical project might start with a high-level executive's simple objective, such as "I want this new software completed by the fifteenth." The expectation, then, is that everyone in the organization will fall in line to meet this demand.

But the first possible stumbling block is misinterpretation. Perhaps the executive only wants to be able to announce the new software on the fifteenth, not start shipping it to clients. Or the IT team could take the executive's statement as setting a target date for them to complete their work, when in reality he expects the new tech to have also gone through marketing and legal by his deadline. If the initial statement is never clarified and the precise objective remains vague, it's more than likely that different teams will progress with different objectives in mind. It's even more likely for remote teams, who'll only be hearing about the vague target third- or fourthhand.

Meanwhile, the project probably lacks fully dedicated human resources—even the team lead is wrestling with several other projects at the same time. For most businesses, a dedicated project manager is assigned for only the most crucial projects. The vast majority of remote projects, therefore, will be overseen by a team lead who may have several emergencies vying for her attention. Even in the best of times, projects add work to an already busy normal work schedule, which means that team calls are often about wrangling highly distracted attendees. Managing them can be like herding cats, which means

---

245   See chapter 10, where we detail the need for universal accountability.

that you need to build virtual structure and control and engagement tactics to keep things on track.

Building a Better Mousetrap

Given this environment, we endeavored to find ways to keep projects on track while keeping everyone engaged and largely stress-free. We needed a way to manage projects that would work with the reality of the corporate environment and the challenges of remote work. Our objective was to seamlessly blend cross-functional teams with a straightforward approach geared to team members without project management credentials. Our first step was to adapt traditional project disciplines for today's fast-changing and distracted remote reality. We replaced the inches-thick binders with a nimble approach geared toward short attention spans—one that would communicate key bits of information in the clearest and most succinct way possible. This is the guts of what our approach offers and a key differentiator compared with traditional methods.

First, we needed to change our definition of project success. When handed a lemon of a project, like Shane was in the example above, a savvy manager will be on the lookout for small, achievable wins that suggest a modicum of project success. This requires taking the time to nail down precisely what the originator of the project needs and endeavoring to see it from their perspective. Suddenly, what the vice president said he wanted is not at all what he's actually looking for or would even be willing to accept. And this should be the starting point. At the outset, the team lead needs to ask herself a series of questions to determine the outcomes the sponsor will consider a success. From there, she can map out how realistic the initiative is and begin to reenvision outputs and outcomes. We have developed an RPM Quickstart sheet that provides a comprehensive overview of this critical planning stage, which forms the foundation for the entire project.

The emphasis should be on creating a positive outcome for the project sponsor because they will in turn need to report their success back to the originating executive. Furthermore, because a project in midstream could lose funding, team members, or a key supporter, it's important to follow Agile principles and produce discrete wins along the way. Creating regular short-term successes builds a sense of progress and

RPM Quicksheet

achievement and gives team leads positive results to point to in the event that the project fails to meet its primary objective. As much as possible, we think about potential breakout initiatives, rolling out partial solutions to smaller user groups, and other ways to divide larger projects into smaller, achievable pieces.

We also engage key stakeholders, including sponsors, executives, tertiary managers, client partners, the government, contractors, and end users, earlier as part of a more proactive communications strategy.[246] Traditional project management tends to assume that team members are going to accept change and that managers and executives will enforce it. This rarely happens in the real world, where people tend to be resistant if they can get away with it.

When looking out for potential risks, pay special attention to team members who are lacking enthusiasm or are unable to make decisions. In one project we oversaw, a key team member never

---

246   The widely used business term "stakeholders" is defined in a variety of ways, but we see it as encompassing everybody involved in a project—from the instigator, client, and sponsor to the supervising executives, project manager, team members, and third-party contractors—as well as any possible end users and external partners, which might even include government representatives. Other departments, such as marketing and finance, can also be stakeholders. Often overlooked when launching a new piece of software are the needs of new hires, who need to learn how to use the new tools when they are onboarded. The larger the project, the broader the impact and the longer the list of stakeholders.

responded to emails or showed up for meetings. He was an absolute ghost. Why? It turned out that he was looking for a new job. Not only that, but his manager was looking for a new job as well! We ended up working around him for weeks, delaying the project until his replacement had been brought on board. Fortunately for us, this was an obvious slacker. In many cases, however, the problem is more subtle; for example, a team member who is responsive and enthusiastic keeps making errors or doesn't understand the ultimate objective. That's why vigilance is crucial.

In 2014, leading consulting firm Deloitte examined thousands of completed business projects and found a strong correlation between project complexity and outcomes. It's no surprise that more complex projects do fail more often. Deloitte's surprising finding was that it's not the complexity itself that creates failure—it's not having the right people and controls in place. And this is precisely why we developed our robust approach to complex, cross-functional remote projects.

Planning Anchored on Communications

We developed RPM to help people who aren't project managers successfully manage remote initiatives. Whether we're coaching the project lead, facilitating team meetings, or managing the project, the first thing we implement is the communication platform necessary to ensure that everyone knows the objectives and next steps and who is responsible for what. RPM is a simple, proven way to communicate and execute project management in dynamic, distributed work environments. We created RPM to be project methodology neutral. Whether you embrace PMI, PRINCE2, Agile, or some other project methodology, RPM adapts to teams working over distances. It's also platform neutral and thus is effective on Excel, Smartsheet, Basecamp, Asana, Notion, or whichever tool you and your team prefer.

RPM aims to create a cohesive network of internal and external resources with information channels that seamlessly highlight risks, scope changes, and personnel issues and provide early warning signs of the need for course correction. When a course correction is necessary, RPM forms a virtual SWAT team that moves in and tackles the problem head on, ideally transforming large, unruly projects into smaller, more efficient, and manageable parts.[247]

> **RPM is anchored in planning and communications and is fulfilled through execution and control.**

RPM is anchored in planning and communications and is fulfilled through execution and control. With remote projects, the early planning phase is often rushed in an effort to get the team working as soon as possible. Many plans only vaguely define targets, or they fail to lay out a chain of command or highlight the roles and responsibilities of all key players. It's crucial to project success that managers spend the time to get this phase right. As Benjamin Franklin once said, "By failing to prepare, you are preparing to fail."

Your preparatory work should build in a process through which significant risks are properly escalated and contingency plans are added for uncertainty. This might be something like "If our growing supply chain issues keep us from getting this product into stores on deadline, the team will pivot to working with logistics and supply chain management to overcome any hurdles."

---

247   Diving into the full scope of RPM could fill an entire book, so instead we'll take you through the thinking behind it. There are more detailed guides and case studies on our website, including a Project Quickstart guide that gives a complete list of questions critical for remote project planning. This is not yet another textbook on project management but a framework for doing it effectively over a distance.

Meanwhile, check and recheck to make sure that your information is accurate. Be journalistic in your approach. A classic reporter's dictum is "If your mother says she loves you, check it out." The point is that a good reporter should never assume but rather should confirm all the facts. A project planner must be similarly doubtful, and it's important to rope in team members to regularly review your draft and provide feedback. You could also send early drafts to the sponsor, executives, and other key figures to help build buy-in and review your work. This can be as simple as presenting a few slides at a brief one-on-one meeting, which encourages the cross-pollination of ideas and will put your thinking to the test.

A few years ago, a client asked us to streamline an in-process project that sought to take advantage of a billion-dollar market opportunity. The client was developing a new digital mail system in conjunction with a national courier service in another country. This model would serve as proof of concept for global expansion of the service. The account rep working on the deal had set aside all of his other work to focus on this, and we were hired to make sure that the twenty to thirty staffers focused on the project delivered what was needed. After two months of intense work, the project was ready to roll out. Then someone expressed fears that there might be cross-border data restrictions, as the mail service would be fulfilled on US-based servers, while the servers providing the courier service would be in another country. A quick check with regulators proved this to be the case: our plan for cross-border mail and data would violate existing regulations.

Since setting up the infrastructure in the destination country and each subsequent partner country would have been prohibitive, the project, after all that, was scrapped. The company wasted millions of dollars, and the account rep made no sales that year, fell from overachiever to underperformer, and ended up leaving the company—all because someone didn't ask the right questions at project inception.

Why This Project Now?

If you were to ask someone to tell you about the project they were working on, they would likely tell you the main deliverables. "We're building a sustainable bicycle," they might say, rather than "We're transforming personal travel." People tend to focus on the output of their project rather than on the outcomes. However, when you tell someone about the new building you're developing, often the follow-up question is "Why?" The two need one another; you can't have a "what" without the "why" and vice versa. To understand a project, people need to be able to understand the final product and how it fits into the world around it.

> "What is it, and why are we doing it?" should be your first two questions when assigned a project.

"What is it, and why are we doing it?" should be your first two questions when assigned a project. Take it a step further, and ask why you are doing this project now. The addition of the "now" will help you understand how the project fits in with the priorities of the rest of the business. Shane has personally worked on projects where it wasn't clear from the start that the project had to be delivered ahead of the holiday season or that the due date had been aligned with a planned marketing blitz—yet the project had to be up and running two weeks before the blitz!

Unfortunately, many business projects are handed down through levels of bureaucracy, and you may not have the privilege of hearing about them from the instigator. As projects funnel through the organization, from vice president to director to manager and, finally, to you, key details are often lost—even including the project's initial context. To compound the issue, each layer will often add some wiggle room to ensure that they can weather late deliveries and scope changes. By asking why the project is being done now, we start to peel away all the layers of the onion.

Another anecdote helps illustrate this point. A few years ago, one of our clients called us in a panic over a large initiative that appeared almost out of the blue. He had been seconded onto a global team to shift the client's sales force from a legacy system to one of the leading customer relationship management systems. The global sales leader wanted to announce it at the sales meeting in September. They were told to start putting plans together pronto. Although it was October, we knew that this was a minimum two-year effort. For a sales force of thirteen thousand reps spread across the world, aside from the IT challenges of getting very old internal systems to talk to the new system, there were considerations about multiple training sessions for the reps, their manager, and everyone up the ladder to adapt to the new system.

In this organization, it was rare to question leadership, but the system cost of more than $100 million and the certainty of failure seemed likely to tank the global sales leader's career and negatively affect everyone on the team. We flew into Chicago for an emergency meeting and decided that someone needed to take this back up the channels with a proposal that the project objective be an announcement rather than an implementation. We presented it to the executive administrator, and she understood immediately what the stakes were and agreed to relay the message—because if we were fired, her job was at risk too. A week later, she called and gave us the green light.

We spent the next ten months putting together a stunning sound-and-light show to promote this new solution, with the sales leader at center stage. It turns out that all the leader wanted was to announce the shift, and he was pleased that we were going to be producing a strong narrative to support it. The person who had been given the initial instructions had misinterpreted the "ask," and by the time it reached our client, seven levels down, it had turned into a full-fledged systems implementation. We were able to produce a success at the initial stage and help our client plan the implementation and adoption of the system properly by simply asking, "Why are we really doing this now, and what does success look like?"

What Does Success (Really) Look Like?

People love this question but almost always fail to answer it correctly. This question is really "How will we know that the project is having the impact we want it to have?" But people tend to view project completion as success. This may be technically accurate. But if the project had set out to ship a new video game by a certain date, should we view that project as a success if the game is released on the target date but goes on to sell only three copies, losing the company millions? That's setting the bar rather low.

It's important to consider impact, and it's crucial to nail down precisely what the sponsor is aiming for or expecting. Keep in mind that this may well be something other than what she has requested. If your interpretation of success is vague or inaccurate, your project might succeed at the wrong thing. But if you get this right, you've taken the first step toward making your sponsor successful, which will in turn make you and your project team successful. Being clear about objectives at the start empowers everybody executing and overseeing the work.

> *If your interpretation of success is vague or inaccurate, your project might succeed at the wrong thing.*

To understand how to answer this question, you need to first identify all key figures. Once you've gotten your list, ask these stakeholders to describe what project success will look like to them. Next, ask them how their working life might change after this project is delivered. Look for quantifiable ways to measure the outcomes. Doing so often reveals additional requirements to achieve success. For example, if your project aims to reduce customer wait times, you need to capture wait times prior to starting so that you have a data point to compare against when you're done. You may need to add a survey to your project to gather qualitative feedback before and after delivery. As we'll see below, these measurements can also be used at interim milestones to prove that you are on the right track.

This will increase confidence among your stakeholders and teams that progress is being made and that the project continues to be a good investment. Identifying proper success criteria is frequently overlooked and rushed. People often want to get on with things and don't want to wait to break ground. You can combat this by adding the gathering of success metrics and criteria to your project plan even if it is only qualitative.

Here's an example of a success the originator may not have envisioned. A number of years ago, while visiting his European headquarters, the CEO of a multinational, let's call it "TLE," dropped in on an intensive four-day sales training course in Germany. He was so impressed that he announced that he wanted every TLE account rep to receive the training. The small training firm was ecstatic—from four twenty-person training sessions in Germany, they now had the prospect of training six thousand reps across the world, which at $1,000 per person would equate to $6 million in new revenue, not to mention an incalculable boost to their reputation. TLE sales operations formed a team from the five global regions to respond to this mandate, and the US training eventually found its way to the overloaded manager in the United States, who turned to Virtira.

Europe had the budget for it, but US TLE already had its own dedicated sales training facility and had not planned for this expense, which would cost more than $4 million, including training and travel costs and the cost of taking reps out of the field for a week. How to fulfill the CEO's request? We convinced the vendor to run four in-person sessions at the US facility with forty reps apiece, with the rest of the sessions done virtually. The last hurdle was dragging the remaining reps through four days of online training, so we persuaded the vendor to give us their materials. We reduced their presentation to the essentials and sharply reduced the role-playing. We eventually boiled it down to a four-hour course, had the vendor approve it, and, thanks to a robust communications campaign up and down the sales organization, achieved 100 percent attendance. By the time this was all completed, the CEO had likely forgotten about it. Still, we delivered the US sales leadership a "win," as they could show that all the reps had completed the course.

What Are the Key Project Milestones?

Once you have a firm grasp of success and a clear picture of acceptable deliverables, work backward to set interim milestones that inch you closer to your ultimate goal. Short-term milestones allow you to demonstrate forward movement. They also help you learn, reduce risk, and reevaluate the project, and most importantly, they allow the project sponsor to claim small victories. For example, if your project aims to globally roll out an enterprise software platform, set an interim milestone to roll out a portion of the software locally. This enables the sponsor to point toward progress and gives you the opportunity to measure deployment time and test for bugs and other problems.

To help set milestones, hold a brainstorming call or two with a core project planning team, and seek input from other team members. Develop a realistic plan with a time frame that fits your project, identifying milestones and decision points along the way. For remote projects, project plans need to be easy to understand, designed for all team members as well as executives and non–project managers. Your first communication about the plan should be as simple as a timeline with a small amount of detail about expected deliverables at each milestone. As much as possible, express information visually so that the concepts are easily grasped and organized.

By identifying interim milestones, you make your project nearly invulnerable to last-minute changes from above. As stated at the outset of this chapter, remote business targets can change in an instant because of changing budgets, shifting priorities, internal reshuffles, new hires and fires, and more. There is nothing more discouraging than putting together a detailed project plan and getting approval from all stakeholders, just to be forced to redo the entire thing at the eleventh hour. Setting milestones provides some insurance, as they can prove the validity of the ultimate objectives and show that your team is progressing toward success.

Generally, you want to keep a schedule of major milestones and a detailed plan of no longer than ninety days. Every month, extend the plan another thirty days, and adjust the long-term plan as needed. With the deliverable of each milestone, bake in time to review with your team and sponsors, and adjust as needed. Again, this is an opportunity to confirm that your project is on track and to enable vice presidents to highlight progress.

Much of this may be subject to change as project pace and complexity demand, but in most cases one quarter is enough time to execute the meat of a project and deliver results.

What Are the Hidden Costs?

In remote work, the primary cost is worker hours. Anyone who has spent significant time in weekly team calls for a ponderously slow project can do a rough calculation, based on the estimated salaries of attendees, of precisely how much all those meetings cost. Yet these costs are rarely considered.

At Virtira, we estimate the hourly costs for every internal project. For our clients, we highlight this whenever possible so that they know just how much they are spending and how much they might save with a few changes. It's a worthwhile endeavor either way. Particularly if you expect your project to be an uphill slog, doing a rough yet comprehensive estimate of the people costs—and adding in any additional costs, such as those for reports, presentations, and project delays—can sometimes sway the sponsor to reduce scope, alleviating the burden on you and your team.

Let's say that your senior vice president, who makes $400,000 a year, has twenty hour-long meetings per month with ten vice presidents (each making a $200,000 salary) for three months straight as part of a charity drive. Each of the vice presidents has five staffers making $80,000 a year who work an average of five hours a week following up on tasks assigned during the calls. The project manager makes $100,000 and spends two hours organizing each call. The worker costs for these meetings thus total nearly $35,000.[248] This

---

248   Senior vice president: $1,442; meeting costs for ten vice presidents: $7,200; project
       manager: $800; staff: $25,000; total: $34,442.

excludes the opportunity costs for any important work that may have been delayed while this takes place. There will also be costs for online leaderboards detailing the funds raised by each department, marketing, and executive messaging, as well as online and off-line events to celebrate success. You might also need to increase overtime spending to keep productivity on schedule and pay consultant fees to resolve unforeseen problems.

Always keep in mind that a budget, no matter how carefully planned, is just a best guess. Expect the total to deviate from the initial estimate, and stay as flexible as possible in terms of time, quality demands, and available funding.

How Do We Communicate across a Distance?

Let us now take a moment to restate that strong communication is absolutely fundamental to remote project success. This is why a well-planned cross-functional project requires a detailed communications strategy, with all those involved in the project in near-constant contact to stay coordinated.

One area the team needs to plan for early in the project is how you're going to produce the inevitable reports and presentations that you'll need to support communications. Many years ago, we noticed a number of our projects were stalling because we had to wait for our clients' internal marketing to produce the presentations or collateral needed as part of project deliverables (e.g., custom brochures for a regional partner launch). Or we needed IT or business analytics to provide reporting

Knowledge is power; thus, sharing knowledge early and often via reliable communication tools empowers everyone.

on legacy data to provide updates to key executives, customers, or regulators. Because Marketing, IT, and Analytics are usually geared to larger corporate initiatives, not departmental ones, relying on these internal departments, even if we had planned for them, often took the project off its timeline. So we developed these capabilities in house in order to provide end-to-end project execution services. These days, if you plan for these deliverables early enough, there are a myriad of online services that can provide top-notch presentations and data reporting.

A cohesive and consistent communications strategy ensures that the team is able to recognize and solve problems early, as well as to react to any changes or surprises in time. Knowledge is power; thus, sharing knowledge early and often via reliable communication tools empowers everyone—team members, sponsors, execs, and third-party contractors.

Uniform messaging and check-ins should start as early as possible to ensure buy-in, which in turn ensures on-time delivery. Project plans should also be geared to communicating concepts over a distance. Replace wordy project documents no one is going to read with visuals like boxes and headers to make key points and capture readers' attention. Consider which parts might be more easily digested as charts or graphs, convert milestones into a timeline, and use callouts to accentuate key messages. If your project plans need to include a good deal of statistical or analytical detail that can't easily be converted into a visual form, it's often better to link to external documents rather than include such minutiae.

Unlike the siloed approach of traditional project management, with remote work it's important to ensure that everyone essential to and affected by the project is involved early and contacted often. The goal of a worthwhile communications strategy should be to cut through today's distracted corporate environment with simple and clear messaging that keeps everyone on the same page.

Who Affects or Is Affected by This Initiative: The RACI

One tool we feel compelled to emphasize is the RACI, which clarifies who is responsible for a project, who will be held accountable, who should be consulted, and who needs to be kept informed. We embrace the RACI—completing it as part of the planning process with every project—to identify early on who needs to be involved in decision-making and who will be responsible for project deliverables. At Virtira, we keep the RACI publicly available throughout the project lifetime, highlighting key items such as decisions required, important milestones, and departmental roles.

RACI charting has been used in project management for decades but has been adapted in recent years for broader use in organizational strategy and planning. In remote projects, boundaries are often blurry, and roles can be vague. Without crystal clear knowledge and delegation of all decisions and activities, teams risk responsibility confusion.

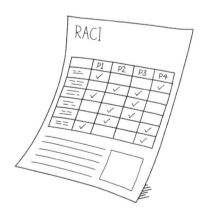

The RACI chart.

Such misunderstandings lead to errors, poor decisions, excluding people from decisions they should be involved in, no decisions, or too many decisions, and they're a major cause of dysfunction and remote project failure. RACI charting helps avoid these pitfalls by explicitly describing the actions that need to be taken, who should take them, and who should contribute to them—and alternately, who has agreed that they don't need to be involved. Shane likes to say that the RACI provides an opportunity to ask difficult questions and clarify expectations on who is needed for project success. More importantly, it clarifies publicly exactly who has to be involved in decisions.

With most business projects, every team member represents a department or an interest group expected to contribute to the outcome. Whether the objective is to get consensus on a new corporate tagline or roll out an IT update to sales, most every team member will serve as a sort of departmental ambassador, representing and expressing that department's interests and mission. Once the project is done, each department's leader should highlight her department's contribution to the project and its impact, and managers should include these details on their calls. Departments should be aware of what they've achieved.

PRO TIP: ENABLE TWENTY-FOUR SEVEN PROJECT COLLABORATION

As we've repeated throughout this book, remote work demands strong communications and collaboration, and nowhere is this more true than in cross-functional projects. Remember that most people on the team will be seconded from their normal job, so you want to make things as easy and streamlined as possible.

Here's a situation that happens all the time: your global project team has a pending deadline, and a staffer in the United Kingdom, for instance, needs a document, pronto. The problem is that the employee who created and manages that doc is fast asleep over in Singapore. The solution is to set up a collaborative space where all reports, schedules, and files can be stored, viewed, and edited by all, twenty-four seven. This allows you to quickly answer any "Where do I find ... ?" questions by sharing a link. In addition, make contact information available, along with working hours, time zones, and preferred communication methods. Allow people to book time directly into team members' calendars using an online scheduling tool. It's hard to overstate just how important centralizing such knowledge is for effective collaboration on a complex remote project.

If you have collaborative online work spaces, keep all plan documents publicly available so that everybody can view them and make suggestions and alterations before they're presented to executives and sponsors. Online dashboards that include the project overview, schedule, risks, metrics, and key team members enable sponsors and management to monitor progress without bothering the team or interrupting the flow of work. This shows respect and consideration for everybody's time and concerns, and it keeps everybody up to date and informed. Even for project managers, who can sometimes get too deep within a project to sense its momentum, a strong dashboard can help show project status and progress more clearly and identify potential gaps and pitfalls before they become problematic.

CHAPTER 17

Remote Project Execution

The only way we succeed as a group is not simply following directions but in keeping each other accountable for our actions.

— A. J. DARKHOLME

Keeping cross-functional teams accountable is the focus of a methodology we developed called Days of the Week ©, which enables greater control and better ensures project execution. Days of the Week involves a set of daily activities designed to keep remote project teams on track to deliver the best possible results with minimal stress. It organizes team members' action items to make sure that everything gets done. If something is unclear, we follow up. If something isn't getting done, we flag it and escalate.

Days of the Week was expressly developed to handle the instability of remote projects, which is why it shines a daily spotlight on action items, status reports, and risk escalation. With this approach, no team members, steps, or hurdles will be ignored or left behind. At Virtira, we employ Days of the Week at the outset of any project, as soon as the team is set. It's essential to establish the cadence of follow-up and status reporting early so that team members accept and embrace it. Once we've captured all the team deliverables in a project plan and know exactly what everyone should do, we follow it to create a weekly cadence and a regular, set schedule.

In essence, Days of the Week lays out what to do and when to do it. You and your firm can choose the approach that works best for you and adapt the methodology. But at heart, it is all about following up, early and often.

The Weekly Cadence

Here's what we do on all of our projects, whether they are internal or for clients. This is what works for us, but another cadence may work for you and your business.

📅 **Monday:**

- Send individual reminders to the people responsible for deliverables this week and next.
- Make contact, and confirm with anyone responsible for any high-risk or overdue deliverables.

📅 **Tuesday, Wednesday, Thursday:**

- Hold a team status meeting on one of these days, depending on client wishes.
- Update the project plan after the meeting has concluded.
- Prepare and send out meeting notes.

- Follow up on high-risk deliverables using an agreed-upon escalation process.

📅 **Friday:**

- Send out a summary of the status of all deliverables to the entire project team.
- Prepare and send out a weekly status report to executives.
- Update project documentation, including any changes, as needed.

This simple weekly cadence makes it easy to remember. People know what to expect on Monday, and they will learn that they will be called out publicly on Friday if they fail to deliver. As primitive as this sounds, in our experience, it is the best way to ensure that people pay attention and respond.

A great way to think of Days of the Week is to imagine that you have to design and introduce a new car. Regardless of how well designed or inventive the car is, the project will not move forward without any momentum, without something to propel it toward fruition. With no driving force, your gorgeous project will forever remain an idea, a project, rather than an actual car. If RPM is the engine that makes a project run, Days of the Week is the gas pedal that propels it forward.

For many business projects, the project team members have never reported to your project sponsor or worked together, and they often work in different departments. They might be scattered across the globe and will likely work on other projects while also doing their darnedest to fulfill the responsibilities of their regular day job. Days of the Week was built with these constraints, as well as the possibility of remote distractions, in mind, and it aims to keep the team laser focused. We teach new hires and clients not to simply assume that team members will find time to fulfill their responsibilities. Rather, everyone learns that people need reminders to ensure that everything is done on time and up to par.

Sponsors and management will expect regular status reports. What you include on your reports and how they are delivered depend on the personal preferences of the executives involved. Ask them early about what sort of information they would like to receive regularly and how. It's worth knowing whether your vice president will read your report on Saturday morning on their cell phone instead of at their desk Monday morning. Take the additional step of asking them why they need a report and what value they hope to get out of it. It's not uncommon for a director to have to generate a report for their superior as well. Reduce the time they'll need to repackage your report by understanding what they plan to do with the information.

Status reports could be anything from a Smartsheet dashboard update or a Google Sheet to a detailed email or virtual presentation. Whatever it is, it's crucial that the process is standardized so that every week, at the same time, the higher-ups receive their status report in the same format and platform. Don't overload them with information and platform shifts. Just highlight key steps and examples of progress, and call out potential risks and roadblocks so that management is ready if escalation is required later.

Establish an Escalation Strategy

Because objectives and trajectories change so quickly nowadays, Days of the Week includes a robust escalation strategy, which means coaching the team to be comfortable sharing issues upward.

Let's say that Julie, the business development lead communicating with the client to ensure the utility of the new software your project is developing, learns that she may need to leave the project soon to care for her ailing mother. She holds off on telling the project lead because she's uncertain about whether she will need to leave— after all, she can't predict her mother's future health. The worst-case scenario, of course, is that Julie's mother takes a turn for the worse at a crucial moment in the project, and Julie is forced to quickly walk away. The result is likely to be an extended delay as the team looks for a replacement who also knows the client.

For the project to stay on track, Julie needs to be comfortable letting the project lead know about the situation with her mother as soon as it emerges. This will give the team time to prepare for a possible change in advance. We like to post online dashboard updates of risks and roadblocks, as we have found that public exposure increases the pressure on the key figures, making it more of a priority and leading to greater accountability. Risks and roadblocks can range in level of concern from nearly nothing to absolutely massive, and they can also quickly escalate from one to the other. These escalations might involve the following:

- Computer failures, internet connectivity, blocked access
- Lack of IT knowledge or ability regarding software, apps, and/ or other tech tools
- Team member or management departures
- Sponsor redefining success or target
- New government restrictions or regulations

If a roadblock forces a change to project scope, this should be immediately communicated to the sponsor to discuss the redeployment of resources or a shift in objectives. This underscores why scheduling relatively easily achievable "wins" throughout the course of the project is so valuable. For lesser risks and roadblocks, each team member should be prepared to make their own decisions with regard to how and when to escalate. If it's another team member who's being a laggard and slowing progress (again), this can be escalated to the project lead, who is ultimately responsible for keeping the team on track.

Keep in mind, however, that escalating in this way is a delicate business; you're essentially going behind someone's back to tattle on them, and they're unlikely to be terribly pleased about it. So first, be absolutely 100 percent positive that it's that team member who is holding up progress. Second, consider all other avenues before escalating to the project manager because you might well be losing an ally, even as you help put the project back on track. Maybe you could talk to the laggard directly and explain how he is falling short and how the issue might be overcome. Or maybe you and the laggard have a colleague friend in common, and you could explain the situation to the friend, who could then speak to the laggard. Or you might be able to word your next status report in a way that subtly points the project lead in the direction of the laggard, without mentioning him or her by name or role. That might be your best option. If all these options either fail or are unavailable, however, then it's time to escalate.

The exception is if the laggard team member is your superior. Not your boss, of course, but a manager or executive a few steps above you on the totem pole. Do you really want to call out someone who in a snap could have you fired or dispatched to corporate Siberia? Unless you have strong executive support above the rank of the laggard, it's wise to mull your options and investigate other avenues before escalating the failures of a superior. The sad reality is that such a decision can ultimately be career limiting, even if it is in the best interests of the project and overall productivity. All that often goes out the window when pride and ego have been hurt.

Here's an example of an escalation gone sideways. The new vice president needed a win, a signature accomplishment to cap off a stellar CV. In this case, he hoped to develop a new reporting function within Salesforce.com that would enable sales leaders to easily identify new business opportunities. Sounds like a worthwhile goal. The team consisted of fifteen representatives from IT, training, operations, partners, and customer satisfaction departments, all senior-level managers, all working sixty-hour weeks because of their involvement in other business-critical projects. Each week, the team would meet for an hour and discuss the project before everyone presented a status report, which was usually much the same as the previous week.[249] Mostly, the vice president would excitedly relate all the benefits this deliverable would have for the company, would encourage everyone to be excited, and almost as an aside would ask about the status in terms of progress. Each week, IT would say that they were at capacity and could not add resources to the project, while operations would make clear that there had been no approval for the budget. The vice president would shrug all this off: "Well, hopefully things will change by next week."

After five weeks of this, one of the leads from Europe suggested, "If there's no budget and no people to do the work, I'm wondering if we should put this project on hold." Basically, why are we wasting our time on this? Everyone held their breath as the vice president weighed his options. He reluctantly concurred; we all breathed a sigh of relief, and all upcoming meetings were canceled. The vice president called the boss of the European lead who had piped up and asked that he be fired. Word got around, and when the vice president's project later resurfaced, those assigned to the team did their best to work on other things during the calls, hoping that it would all be over soon.

---

249 With an average compensation package of $150,000, these calls were costing more than $1,000 per hour (average of seventy-eight dollars per hour times fifteen).

Check In for Course Corrections

Be sure to check in on how your team is doing and how their individual work and collaborations are going, not just how the project is progressing. The software development industry has long known the benefit of reviewing team functionality and making course corrections as needed. Software teams commonly hold biweekly retrospectives to work on collaborations and productivity. This, of course, assumes a dedicated team that benefits from fine-tuning. In a complex business project, with people split all over the globe and dedicated to other responsibilities and projects, it's often unreasonable to get together every two weeks for an afternoon of "Stop, Start, and Continue."

Furthermore, Jim from London is much less likely to be open about his concerns with Fran from Toronto when they both know that there's a strong likelihood they will never work together again after this project. Yet there are still benefits to be had from fine-tuning your project team. Better to know sooner rather than later, for instance, that a simple workflow adjustment will reduce the time it takes for your outsourced graphic design to return from Brazil.

If you have a core group of team members on your project, run the occasional retrospective. As described in chapter 12, retrospectives are ideal for remote project teams and provide an excellent forum for a diverse group of people to provide feedback and work through issues. Keep the frequency of retrospectives to once every three months, and align them with the delivery of major milestones. Focus the retrospective on how the team is performing, and avoid getting into feedback on what the project is delivering and why. This is crucial, as a retrospective can easily be sidetracked by unnecessary griping or legitimate issues that would better be delivered via back channels and escalated as needed.

If your team is more diverse, or time zones make a group call impractical, use an anonymous survey to gather feedback. Include qualitative and quantitative questions on your survey, multiple-choice questions, and open-ended queries such as "What one thing would you change to improve project communications?" Keep a portion of your questions standard for every survey to be able to see improvement over time. Finally, using the same survey across multiple projects will help you identify team issues early on.

PRO TIP: CELEBRATE SMALL WINS

In one European survey, eight of ten respondents reported that the review and evaluation of their completed projects had been inadequate.[250] Project management folks like to say that about 60 percent of projects fail. But without thorough evaluation and review—a comparison of forecasted outcomes, benefits, and losses—it's all but impossible to gauge the level of success or failure. The project might be completed, sure, but how do we know that it has been a success?

Keep your scope front and center so that everyone uses the same yardstick. Every time you deliver a milestone, allow for a little celebration. Particularly when there are challenges along the way—the project takes longer or is more expensive than expected, or the outcomes are disappointing—it's crucial to recognize the team's hard work and accomplish-

---

250   John Ward, Elizabeth Daniel, and Joe Peppard, "Building Better Business Cases for IT Investments," *MIS Quarterly Executive* 7, no. 1 (March 2008): 3, https://aisel.aisnet.org/misqe/vol7/iss1/3/.

ments. In fact, an integral part of remote project success is ongoing evaluations—not just at the project's close but at regular intervals throughout.

The more challenging and difficult the project, the more frequently you should gauge progress. After these evaluations, reward the team for staying ahead of schedule and delivering, if warranted. Regular evaluation helps prove and celebrate successes while continually reinforcing and documenting the project's value. In essence, midproject evaluations take the typical process of the project's close and build it into the project itself, incorporating the inevitable shifting of goalposts. It's an opportunity to do a sanity check on whether the project still makes sense in light of market shifts, corporate pivots, and funding issues.

By gauging progress every few months, you create a history of project success that boosts morale and offers something for sponsors and executives. What's more, the data might help you advocate for more funding or show diminishing returns.

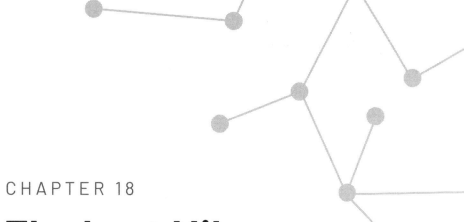

CHAPTER 18

The Last Mile in Remote Sales

All endeavour calls for the ability to tramp the last mile,
shape the last plan, endure the last hours toil.

—HENRY DAVID THOREAU

Thus far, we have covered just about everything you need to do to improve remote performance: finding, hiring, and onboarding remote workers; building effective communications systems; improving team performance; achieving project success; and more. We have, however, yet to touch on perhaps the most important element of your business: doing actual business.

Whether it's goods or services, a lemonade stand, or a billion-dollar deal for intellectual property, somebody somewhere has been pitching something to someone almost since the start of recorded history. For eons, humans have been piling their wares onto caravans and beasts of burden and traveling great distances to find customers and make deals. Some two millennia ago, traders traveled four thousand miles along the Silk Road to sell spices, textiles, and much more, connecting cultures and peoples and laying the foundations of early globalization. Sales has more experience overcoming great distances than any other line of work. In 2017, nearly three of four sales deals (72 percent) occurred outside the office, at golf courses, restaurants, hotel bars, and the like.[251] Although these deals likely included an in-person handshake, it's a stunning figure that underscores the extent to which salespeople are comfortable outside the office.

When asked which hurdles sales professionals most often face, Jill Konrath, leading sales strategist and author of several best-selling sales books, pointed to the constant struggle with increasingly complex sales processes and decisions, the demand from buyers to know more, and the need to embrace and incorporate new technologies. This chapter will not review the more than one thousand sales tools available today and make recommendations, and it will also not offer advice on creating meaningful market reports or on the best sales training courses. We will instead focus on solving a problem that the vast majority of sales methodologies completely ignore: the logistical issues of going the last mile from a verbal "yes" to a signed sales agreement.[252]

The Last Mile: From "Yes" to Closed

A B2B deal might involve anything from a fleet of cars modified for a specific purchaser to a conferencing solution sold to and implemented within the branch offices of a multinational corporation. In

---

251   Harshit Jain, "What Is Field Sales and Why Is It Important?," LeadSquared, updated October 25, 2021, https://www.leadsquared.com/what-is-field-sales/.

252   Business to business (B2B) sales tend to be larger and more complex and are conducted over greater distances than your average consumer sale, so these will be our main focus.

most cases, these deals will require product and service customization, special pricing and financing, and custom contracts across multiple companies and government agencies. As a result, it is increasingly rare that all the staffers providing these functions will work in the same office. These deals almost always involve remote teams, often across multiple departments, organizations, and even continents.[253] Yet despite all this vast complexity, nailing down that final piece of a customer's contract—custom solutions, financing, advanced partnerships—often falls on somebody with minimal administrative and management training, the sales representative.

The last mile in sales.

This may be because taking that last step and closing the deal is a process left out of nearly all major sales productivity initiatives, which tend to focus on skills that help sales reps convince prospective buyers of the value of a particular solution. There's no arguing that

---

253 "Complex Sales," Wikipedia, accessed June 12, 2022, https://en.wikipedia.org/wiki/ Complex_sales.

the established tools, training, and incentives contribute to sales force productivity, but they represent only 90 percent of the deal. The other 10 percent is finalizing the transaction. It may be only a small slice, but that last 10 percent is everything because if it's left incomplete, the entire sale can fall apart.

To solve the "last mile" challenge, reports often call for sales reps to be trained on project methods to boost efficiency or for long-term project management tools to be applied to sales pursuits. This misses the point. Making a sales rep wear dual hats—keeping the customer engaged while clarifying and reinforcing the accountability of all stakeholders—is likely to bog your salespeople down and stop a deal in its tracks. Most reps have been endlessly trained on moving a customer through the sales stages, and they possess a great deal of drive, discipline, accountability, communication skills, time management, and collaborative abilities. But even the most process-savvy sales professionals might find themselves wholly—and somewhat uncomfortably—immersed in administrative tasks in an effort to finalize a client's initial green light. A surer route to sales completion would have the sales rep focusing on the relationship with the customer while a trained professional aligns resources among the company, partner, and customer and manages all the steps needed to close the deal.

The Overburdened Sales Rep

Freeing up highly paid and valuable sales team members to focus on what they do best is smart business. Most companies do this well— up to the customer saying "yes." This, sadly, is not far enough. The reason sales productivity initiatives often fail to lead to more deals is that there is often inadequate focus on helping sales representatives complete the process. Even if the buyer has signed a letter of intent, somebody still needs to pull together the pricing and financing and the legal and technical inputs, as well as organize all those involved. In some instances, as many as forty people might be needed to put the final contract together. The client may agree to a solution, but if that sale fails to close within the fiscal year, the sales rep is in danger of losing their commission and possibly being demoted. The company, meanwhile, loses all that revenue—and potentially a key client.

Sales organizations operate in a fast-paced environment. Staying ahead of competitors and maximizing opportunities require shortening sales cycles by reducing friction and delays. Shorter sales cycles maximize revenue while motivating sales reps and improving productivity. The reality is that today's sales reps spend most of their working hours on activities other than making actual sales, which erodes their sales, their understanding of customers, and ultimately their ability to close deals. The solution lies in making sales professionals more efficient by identifying time-wasting nonselling activities and off-loading them.

Let's assume that as vice president of sales, you've been given aggressive sales targets by a new CEO. You know that if you don't hit these new targets, you're not going to get that long-desired promotion and may even be out of a job. Just about every consultant will tell you that the best way to increase sales revenue is to either increase sales staffing or improve sales productivity. Industry studies support this fairly consistently. But for this company, increasing sales head count is not an option because the new CEO has put hiring on hold, so your best option is to increase sales team productivity. You suspect that your reps are pretty close to the industry standard and spend about a

Freeing up highly paid and valuable sales team members to focus on what they do best is smart business.

third of their time selling—so there's lots of room for improvement. The problem, however, is the expense. Most sales productivity studies point to training, incentives, coverage model changes, and customer relationship management (CRM) investments as the best fixes. But the price tag for all of this usually comes to about $20,000 per sales rep—which is often a bridge too far.

Still, you fight for funding, get it, and implement the programs. Your sales reps and management become well trained in your product and service offerings, while your sales team and partners use your CRM expertly, know exactly what's in the pipeline, and have no issues overcoming competition and pricing obstacles. Your marketing department gives your reps all the collateral they need to sell, from custom proposals to customer needs research to access to extensive databases for background information.

Yet not only do sales fail to spike, but also somehow the competition gains ground, and as a result, some of your best sales talent departs. How could this be happening? The reason, especially for complex sales, is that this approach focuses on getting to "yes," forgetting that finalizing the deal takes a great deal more work. The real productivity losses come from the burden of administrative details that bury enterprise sales representatives during the last stages of the sales process.

The key issue is that sales reps are often not working on sales but on administrative tasks and aligning their work with other departments. A 2011 McKinsey study found that the sales reps of a logistics firm spent about 35 percent of their time selling because they were "consumed by nonsales activities such as billing system updates, fire-fighting, and internal communications."[254] So for nearly two-thirds of their day, these sales reps were unable to work on sales, and this is much more the rule than the exception. A 2013 study by Pace Productivity turned up an even lower figure, finding that salespeople spend just 22 percent of their work time—barely more than one of five hours!—actually selling.[255]

Understanding how all of this affects salespeople—the primary link between your firm and clients—is crucial to boosting sales and sales productivity. Imagine that you have a top-performing sales rep who has reliably proven that he knows how to get his client to "yes." But then to close the deal, he often ends up chasing after key figures for weeks on end, taking him away from bringing in new business. What began as a relationship and persuasion process has turned into an administrative nightmare for a sales rep with a vastly different skill set and role within the company.

Sales administrators typically become involved *after* the sale has been signed on the dotted line, which is also when all the logistics of organizing the sales support staff and multiple departments shift into fulfillment mode. But we have seen countless examples of a major sales "yes" lurching too slowly toward the close, and in the end the deal implodes because key decision makers move to other positions.

When executives see sales stalling, their response is often to install new tools and boost training, which just adds another layer to fight through before achieving closing. The problem isn't getting the customer to shake hands on a deal; it's getting the customer to sign the contract.

---

254 Olivia Nottebohm, Tom Stephenson, and Jennifer Wickland, "Freeing up the Sales Force for Selling," *McKinsey Quarterly*, July 1, 2011, https://www.mckinsey.com/business-functions/marketing-and-sales/our-insights/freeing-up-the-sales-force-for-selling.

255 Mikita Mikado, "5 Things Your Sales Team Wastes Too Much Time On," National Association of Sales Professionals, accessed June 12, 2022, https://www.nasp.com/blog/5-things-your-sales-team-wastes-too-much-time-on/.

This is because for most firms, the standard operating procedure is that several departments need to provide input, which then needs to be approved by higher-ups. Inevitably, somebody somewhere along the line is unresponsive, and the process comes to a screeching halt. Team members are busy and miss a deadline. There are more negotiations in response to a market shift. A new partner needs to be integrated, and a new addendum to the deal requires authorization. A few months pass, and the client is suddenly poached by a competitor offering faster closing. Oops.

To simplify, you might ask what exactly needs to happen to complete these administrative tasks and put this sale to bed. This is the guiding light of our approach, which off-loads this last mile to someone trained in cross-functional team accountability. Many of our clients have asked us to train their sales administrators to shoulder this burden, which sounds like a logical solution. But we've discovered that many of the people needed to complete these tasks—to sign off on an implementation or approve the latest changes—are either external or several levels above the administrator, which can be intimidating. For one client, we actually trained fifty administrators to take care of these tasks. But in the end, this approach failed because helping to close sales had never been part of their job description. In follow-up interviews, the administrators said that they had been uncomfortable attempting to convince superiors who far outranked them to take the required steps.

The Sales Support Consultant

We hit upon a smarter approach, which is to name a talented administrator as a senior "sales support consultant" or "SSC"—a floating resource within the organization, empowered to unburden internal sales reps in the last stages of complex sales pursuits. Most senior administrators have outstanding logistics skills—and if they are trained in remote accountability and assigned this crucial role, they will likely be more willing to harness the people and deliverables needed to bring sales to a close.

Our experience on hundreds of sales pursuits has taught us, beyond any doubt, tthat devoting a few SSC hours a week to help complete a major sale results in more sales closed, faster close rates, reduced attrition, and more satisfied clients—not to mention sharply increased revenue.

The impact of the presence of a capable human being dedicated to assisting with the final sales stage is transformational. Depending on the complexity of the sales involved, one SSC can typically work on as many as eight closings simultaneously.[256] And because many of the scarce technical people needed to close deals are often the same sale to sale, having a central contact point sharply increases efficiency.

By off-loading the many activities that drag down account reps' productivity, you can spread your most valuable salespeople across more customers. This means that account reps can focus on key relationships to push sales toward completion instead of being bogged down in endless red tape and details. Deals close faster, and customers enjoy a more cohesive process. Let someone else track and follow up on action items and provide concise, clear reporting on status and risks on a daily basis. After the sale closes, depending on the strength of your sales support functions, the SSC might stay on board to assist deal fulfillment for a month or two.

We had one regional sales manager who called us so that we could assist one of his reps who had gotten agreement on a massive deal. The customer, one of the world's largest companies, had agreed to purchase a

---

256   We've seen situations where the initiatives are so large that there have been five full-time SSCs needed for one account.

videoconferencing solution for fifty of its offices worldwide. To prepare the contract for signature, each country's partner needed to be engaged, all the technical aspects needed to be priced, and leasing and training plans needed to be approved for each country. Even though the account representative had a team of five working on the account, everyone was soon overwhelmed by the size of the deal. Romania, for example, hosted a customer office, but there was no partner to deal with. Another country had cabling requirements that involved an iffy power grid. With the help of one SSC working ten hours a week, the team was able to plow through the massive list of details and sign the contract. After contract signature, the SSC even continued to assist the team on difficult fulfillment areas—such as getting the system installed in Romania without a country partner in place.

Sales teams, and particularly sales pursuit teams, tend to be close-knit groups, and understandably so. They work together daily, sharing information and ideas and striving toward a common—and crucial—goal for the large organization. They see their work as important and unimpeachable and establish strong bonds. It's understandable that they might be reluctant to allow an outside person to finalize their deal or listen to and report on their strategy sessions and sales status calls. It's a bit like the resentment local police officers tend to feel, in cop movies, when the FBI agent shows up to take over the case and, once it's solved, take all the credit.

Your sales reps might fear being micromanaged or imagine changes to their quota. Or they might fear that the SSC will replace them. The sales rep is already up to his eyeballs in work, and the last thing he and his team need is to spend precious hours explaining what needs to be done to a new arrival. Maintaining the status quo seems the simpler, less fraught path. Thus, bringing an outsider into this somewhat hostile environment to oversee the closure of a deeply complex sale is basically begging for disaster.

Much better, then, to start with sales that have a relatively simple route to closing, with most major aspects under control, and use these closed deals to create a sort of advertisement for your last mile program. There's nothing like seeing SSC-driven sales results to encourage buy-in from other teams.

Account managers usually agree with the logic that the final stages of a major sales pursuit should be similar to any other sales-enablement initiative. Still, getting them to hand over management of a major sales pursuit requires careful negotiation and a concerted effort on the part of the sales leader and the SSC. It is important that the sales rep hears from other sales reps who have benefited from SSC assistance. It is also important to establish ground rules and reassure sales team members that what they say in the meetings will be confidential. Emphasize that the SSC's role is merely to help close the deal, not claim credit for the sale or change the way the sales teams do their jobs.

Almost without fail, bogging down top sales performers with time-consuming nonsales tasks leaves them exhausted, dispirited, and stressed, undermining crucial customer relationships and leaving many sales short of the finish line. Providing committed expertise to help these complex deals close faster, on the other hand, boosts morale and profits and reduces attrition.

PRO TIP: THINK VERTICALLY

It's not uncommon for companies to have several sales reps looking after clients in related industries. And while each rep's customers are unique, businesses in closely related industries generally have similar needs and require access to the same busy, in-demand resources to move the sale forward.

In this situation, a wise approach is to consolidate and introduce a team dashboard to share ideas and solutions within that industry category. We've seen vertical-focused teams in which each member operates in a silo when it comes to booking meetings with specialized resources. We've also seen firms bring in an industry leader to help on a large initiative in one city and then fly that leader to another city to work with another rep, only for a third rep to bring him back to the first city. By working with the account team to share best practices and coordinate people who add expertise to the sales process, the entire account team can accelerate each individual sales effort.